# Only One Hill!

## A History of the
## Mount Washington Road Race

### Dave Dunham

ISBN 978-0-7414-3159-2

Published by:

1094 New Dehaven Street, Suite 100
West Conshohocken, PA 19428-2713
Info@buybooksontheweb.com
www.buybooksontheweb.com
Toll-free  (877) BUY BOOK
Local Phone (610) 941-9999
Fax  (610) 941-9959

*Printed in the United States of America*

*Published May 2006*

# Table of Contents

<u>**Introduction:**</u>

I stood on the starting line of the Mt Washington road race already drenched in sweat.  It was 1994 and it would reach nearly ninety degrees that day.  It was already in the eighties and word from the summit was that it would be in the sixties when we reached the top and there would be no cooling breeze today.  I thought to myself "why am I doing this" and "why are the other 900 people behind me doing this".  A bunch of years have passed but my answer remains unchanged, and it is probably the answer many of the other 900 would give.  I really enjoy the unique challenge of racing to the top.  There are many races out there, and even many Mountain races, but Mt Washington is where it all started for me.  My heart belongs to <u>**the**</u> Mountain.  I ended up winning the race in 1994 through a mix of patient early running, others not running smart, and a fair amount of luck.  I also started thinking about compiling the complete results of the race. What started as that thought grew, and this book is the result.

I spent an unknown number of hours combing through old magazines and newspapers to get any results I could, and then pounded away at the keyboard to enter the more than 22,000 individual results.  I interviewed numerous well-known and not so well known Mt Washington runners.  If nothing else, I had a great time learning more about the race I love.

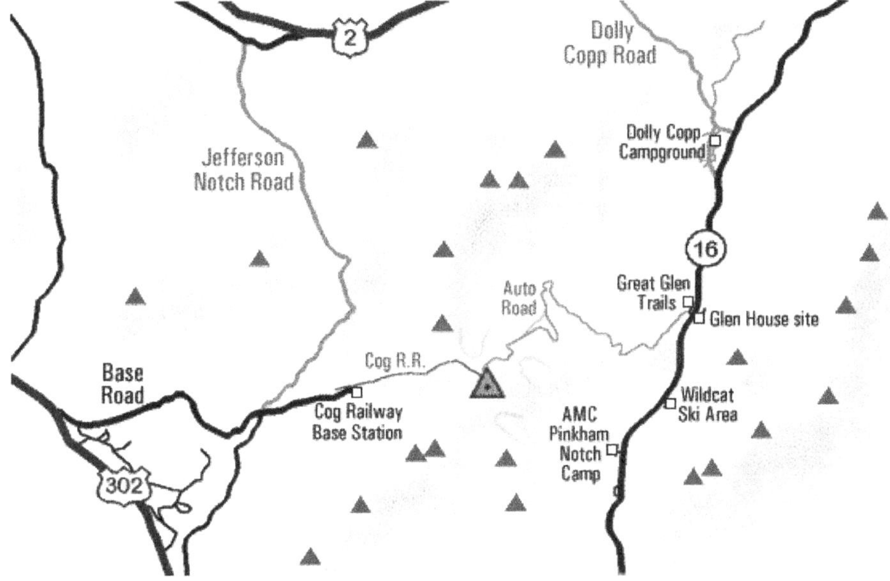


**Mt Washington Highway map**

Mount Washington is the highest peak in the Northeast United States, rising 6,288'.  The mountain can be reach via Route 16 in New Hampshire.  As of this writing *Into the Mountains* notes that "About one third of the people who climb Mt Washington do so on foot, out of a total of approximately 250,000 summit visitors per summer".

**The Summit circa 1900**

*Into the Mountains* also notes "the first white person to climb Mt Washington is generally believed to be an Englishman named Darby Field" in 1642.   The Crawford Path, which Ethan Allen Crawford and his father cut in 1819, was the first trail up Mt Washington.  Tourism on Mt Washington took a huge step forward when in 1851 the Atlantic & St Lawrence Railroad connected Gorham with Portland, ME.  The following year a stone summit house was built and in 1853 the "Tip-Top House" was erected. Since 1932 there has been a permanent weather station on the summit.   The summit has had many different buildings on top over the years.

**Tip Top House circa 1895**

The Mt Washington Auto Road (which at the time was called the "Carriage Road) was built over the course of seven years and when completed was the world's first mountain toll road.  On July 1, 1853 New Hampshire Governor David Macomber issued a charter for the Mount Washington Road Company.  Surveying the road took over a year.  Construction started in 1855, with the first four miles completed by 1857.  At that time work was halted as money to build the road had been exhausted.  The Mt Washington Summit Road Company was incorporated in 1859 and construction continued.  When the Carriage Road opened in 1861 it was the only way, other than hiking, to get to the summit.  Vacationers were taken to the top in a horse drawn mountain wagon.  *Into the Mountains* notes that "records for accomplishments on Mt Washington were intentionally set as early as 1850, when guests of the Glen House vied for who could post the fastest time walking up the carriage road."  It continues noting "About 1900, Edgar Welch of Hiram Maine, after having 'loosened up' in the Tip-Top House tavern, ran down the carriage road in about forty-five minutes."  Welch continued running down the mountain every year, at least until 1907, when he set a personal record of 45 minutes at the age of 51 years.

Some early history of the auto road includes the tale of Harlan P. Amen (1853-1913) who is credited with running up the recently completed road in 1875 in less than two hours (1:57). Amen would later become the Principal at Philips Exeter Academy and the Republican delegate to the national convention.  It is also noted that on August 16, 1904 at 10:00 AM, Dr. George S. Foster of Manchester, NH ran from the old tollhouse to the Tip-Top House in 1:42 at the age of 18.  Foster prepared for the race by running the hilly roads around Pinkham Notch while spending a month leading a boys group.  The group, called Next-to-nature, maintained a camp at the base of the auto road.  At the time of his summit run Foster's time was faster than any vehicle had ascended.   Winds that day reached gust of up to 80 miles per hour.  Foster is also credited with a record breaking 42 minute descent at some point, while he was a medical student at Tufts University.  There are indications that in 1929 a race was held that attracted three starters and one finisher.

Harlan P. Amen

Other events on the mountain include the first auto ascent by Freelan and Flora Stanley in 1899 in a steam-powered Locomobile.  On July 11-12, 1904, the first "Climb to the Clouds" was held. Auto manufacturers believed that the road was a place to demonstrate the ability of the early version of the automobile.  The race was held off and on throughout the years.  The centennial race was held July 9-12, 2004.  On March 20, 1932 a ski race was held from the summit to the Glen house, the race was won in just over 12 minutes by Edward J. Blood.  A bicycle race has been held numerous times over the years and includes a category for tandem bikes.

**The Stanley Locomobile ascending the Auto road in 1899.**

Mt Washington has some of the most severe weather in the world.  The highest wind velocity recorded anywhere in the world was recorded on the summit on April 12, 1934 when the wind gusted from the Southeast at 231 miles per hour.  Typical weather for June (when the footrace is now held) features a normal daily high of 50.3 degrees, and a normal low of 38.5 degrees.  The record temperatures for June are 72 degrees in 2003 and 8 degrees in 1945.  Normal precipitation in June is 8.3 inches and normal wind for June is 27 MPH from the West.  The peak gust recorded in June is 136 MPH.

<h1 style="text-align:center">Guide to abbreviations used in the book.</h1>

With the many different teams represented throughout this book and limited space to print the full name of each I have resorted to abbreviations.  I found that many of the abbreviations used in the results changed from year to year.  I tried to be consistent; however I have occasionally used multiple abbreviations for the same team.  I have listed them alphabetically below and listed the first year that particular abbreviation was use.

| First Used | Abbrieviation | Meaning |
| --- | --- | --- |
| 1936 | AGR | Age Group Record |
| 1936 | CR | Course Record |
| 1936 | FW | Future/Former Winner |
| 1936 | BAA | Boston Athletic Association |
| 1936 | Cntrl CT AA | Central Connecticut Athletic Association |
| 1936 | Del-Val AA | Delaware Valley Athletic Association |
| 1936 | Electric Boat | Electric Boat Track Club |
| 1936 | NETC | New England Track Club |
| 1936 | NMC | North Medford Club |
| 1936 | NY Pioneer | New York Pioneer Club |
| 1936 | NYPC | New York Pioneer Club |
| 1936 | Reipas AC | Reipas Athletic Club |
| 1936 | Spartan AC | Spartan Athletic Cub |
| 1936 | St. Anthony's | St. Anthony's Boys Club |
| 1961 | Lynn AC | Lynn Athletic Club |
| 1962 | NYAC | New York Athletic Club |
| 1966 | Central Conn. AA | Central Connecticut Athletic Association |
| 1966 | Gorham AC | Gorham Athletic Club |
| 1966 | Metro AC | Metropolitan Athletic Club |
| 1966 | Millrose AA | Millrose Athletic Association |
| 1966 | Mt Park AA | Mt Park Athletic Association |
| 1966 | Mt Royal of Canada | Mt Royal Athletic Club |
| 1966 | NYC | Unknown |
| 1966 | UNH | University of New Hampshire |
| 1966 | Viking Ski Club | Viking Ski Club |
| 1967 | Cambridge Y | Cambridge Young Mens Club of America |
| 1967 | Hartford TC | Hartford Track Club |
| 1967 | Mt Royal | Mt Royal Athletic Club |
| 1967 | Ottawa Ski | Ottawa Ski Club |
| 1967 | Waterville AC | Waterville Athletic Club |
| 1968 | Rochester TC | Rochester Track Club |
| 1968 | SAC | Shore Athletic Club |
| 1968 | Salem AC | Salem Athletic Club |
| 1968 | SJTC | South Jersey Track Club |
| 1968 | WAC | Waterville Athletic Club |
| 1970 | CSU | Cambridge Sports Union |

| First used | Abbrieviation | Meaning |
| --- | --- | --- |
| 1970 | Penn AC | Pennsylvania Athletic Club |
| 1971 | CCAA | Central Connecticut Athletic Association |
| 1971 | McGill Univ | McGill University |
| 1971 | MRFA | Mt Royal Frans Amis - Quebec |
| 1971 | No. Country AC | North Country Athletic Club |
| 1971 | Strafford Spartans | Strafford Spartans |
| 1971 | Turtletown | Turtletown Athletic Club |
| 1972 | Augusta REC | Augusta Recreation Association |
| 1972 | NCAC | North Country Athletic Club |
| 1972 | Turtletown AC | Turtletown Athletic Club |
| 1972 | UMASS | University of Massachusetts |
| 1973 | ARTC | Augusta Recreation Track Club |
| 1973 | MSTC | Mystic Side Track Club |
| 1973 | OSC | Ottawa Ski Club |
| 1973 | SSTC | Strafford Spartans Track Club |
| 1973 | TTAC | Turtletown Athletic Club |
| 1973 | VTRR | Vermont Road Runners |
| 1973 | WP | Unknown |
| 1974 | BCTC | Unknown |
| 1974 | Bethel Bananas | Bethel Bananas |
| 1974 | Buffalo TC | Buffalo Track Club |
| 1974 | Mohegan | Mohegan Striders |
| 1974 | SLAC | Sugarloaf Mountain Athletic Club |
| 1974 | Triple Cities TC | Triple Cities Track Club |
| 1974 | U of Laval | University of Laval |
| 1974 | Washington SC | Washington Sports Club |
| 1975 | BRU | Unknown |
| 1975 | CAPS | Caps |
| 1975 | GBTC | Greater Boston Track Club |
| 1975 | LRR | Larigmac Road Runners |
| 1975 | LRTC | Lakes Region Track Club |
| 1975 | LT | Unknown |
| 1975 | MAA | Millrose Athletic Association |
| 1975 | SMAC | Sugarloaf Mountain Athletic Club |
| 1975 | SS | Shenipsit Striders |
| 1976 | Cenleona RC | Cenleona Running Club |
| 1976 | Larigmac RR | Larigmac Ridge Runners |
| 1976 | Laurentian U TC | Laurentian University Track Club |
| 1976 | OTC | Oregon Track Club |
| 1976 | Plausted Harriers | Plausted Harriers |
| 1977 | ECSC | Unknown |
| 1977 | Keene State | Keene State College |
| 1977 | Lucky TC | Lucky Track Club |

| First used | Abbrieviation | Meaning |
| --- | --- | --- |
| 1977 | Seacoast | Seacoast Striders |
| 1978 | Onteora | Onteora Road Running Club |
| 1978 | SSTC | Seacoast Striders Track Club |
| 1978 | State College | Unknown |
| 1978 | Vermont RR | Vermont Road Runners |
| 1978 | YMCA | Young Men's Club of America |
| 1979 | Craftsbury | Craftsbury Ski Academy |
| 1979 | N Carolina TC | North Carolina Track Club |
| 1979 | Strafford AA | Strafford Athletic Association |
| 1979 | US Ski Team | United States Ski Team |
| 1979 | Wolfpack | Wolfpack |
| 1980 | CRC | Cambridge Running Club |
| 1980 | CTAC | Unknown |
| 1980 | DOC | Dartmouth Outing Club |
| 1980 | GRC | Unknown |
| 1980 | JWAC | Johnson and Wales Athletic Club |
| 1980 | ORC | Onteora Running Club |
| 1980 | UH | Unknown |
| 1985 | Mara Tours | Marathon Tours |
| 1985 | Willimantic | Willimantic Athletic Club |
| 1985 | WMM | White Mountain Milers |
| 1986 | GSRT | Granite State Racing Team |
| 1986 | MVS | Merrimack Valley Striders |
| 1987 | Club Neast | Club Northeast |
| 1987 | GLRR | Greater Lowell Road Runners |
| 1987 | GMAA | Green Mountain Athletic Association |
| 1987 | GNB | Greater New Bedford |
| 1987 | US Bi | United States Biathlon Team |
| 1987 | WCRC | Winners Circle Running Club |
| 1988 | CNE | Club Northeast |
| 1989 | CMeS | Central Maine Striders |
| 1990 | BRR | Berkshire Road Rats |
| 1990 | GCS | Gate City Striders |
| 1991 | BC/BS | Blue Cross / Blue Shield |
| 1991 | Berks | Berkshire Road Rats |
| 1991 | Bridgton | Bridgton Academy |
| 1991 | Liberty AC | Liberty Athletic Club |
| 1991 | Maine TC | Maine Track Club |
| 1991 | METC | Maine Track Club |
| 1991 | RICH | Rich Classic Athletic Club |
| 1991 | White Mtn | White Mountain Milers |
| 1992 | AA | Athletic Alliance |
| 1992 | BRC | Boston Running Club |

| First used | Abbrieviation | Meaning |
| --- | --- | --- |
| 1992 | CMS | Central Massachusetts Striders |
| 1992 | HTC | Hartford Track Club |
| 1992 | LAC | Liberty Athletic Club |
| 1992 | RIRR | Rhode Island Road Runners |
| 1993 | Educators | Educators |
| 1993 | MCS | Unknown |
| 1993 | Mercer | Mercer County Bucks |
| 1994 | AF | Athletes Foot |
| 1994 | OSAC | Ocean State Athletic Club |
| 1996 | GNBTC | Greater New Bedford Track Club |
| 1997 | BLO | Unknown |
| 1997 | HS | Healthsource |
| 1997 | HSK | Unknown |
| 1997 | IATC | Irish American Track Club |
| 1997 | NB | New Balance |
| 1997 | NIKE | Nike |
| 1997 | PFIZR | Pfizer |
| 1997 | WillAC | Willimantic Athletic Club |
| 1998 | HMRR | Hudson Mohawk Road Runners |
| 1998 | MR | Millrose Athletic Association |
| 1999 | AD | Addidas |
| 1999 | BBRR | Back Bay Road Runners |
| 1999 | HITK | Hitek |
| 2000 | BKVR | Battenkill Valley Runners |
| 2000 | CAA | Colonial Athletic Association |
| 2000 | CPTC | Central Park Track Club |
| 2000 | CVT | Central Vermont |
| 2000 | CVTRC | Central Vermont Running Club |
| 2000 | NYH | New York Harriers |
| 2000 | REEB | Reebok |
| 2000 | SAUC | Saucony |
| 2001 | AE | Athletics East |
| 2001 | CCAC | Cape Cod Athletic Club |
| 2001 | Hitek | Hitek |
| 2001 | Horst | Horst |
| 2001 | Millrs | Millrose Athletic Association |
| 2001 | Whirl | Whirlaway Racing Team |
| 2001 | Willow | Willow Street Athletic Club |
| 2001 | WMAC | Western Massachusetts Athletic Club |
| 2002 | GUTS | Unknown |
| 2002 | Hgel | Hammergel |
| 2003 | AR | Unknown |
| 2003 | MM&M | Moose Milers & Marathoners |

x

| First used | Abbrieviation | Meaning |
| --- | --- | --- |
| 2003 | MMM | Moose Milers & Marathoners |
| 2003 | PWBR | Powerbar |
| 2003 | TG | Team Gloucester |
| 2003 | WRT | Whirlaway Racing Team |
| 2004 | Cstal | Coastal Athletic Associaton |
| 2004 | FLRC | Finger Lakes Running Club |
| 2004 | Teva | Teva |
| 2004 | WSCR | Westchester Track Club |
| 2005 | CTVT | Central Vermont Running Club |
| 2005 | NEW | New England Trail |
| 2005 | RR | Rochester Runners |
| 2005 | SRT | Saratoga |

Runners at the 4-mile turn circa 1972

**1<sup>st</sup> Mt Washington Road Race**

August 8, 1936
Saturday 10:00 AM
9 Finishers.

The *Manchester Union Leader*, which cost three cents and had no Sunday edition, carried the headline "Steamship fired on brings English warning" as an English ship was "accidentally" fired upon by Spanish forces near Gibraltar.  Other news included the annual meeting of the New England Automobile Club of America, which was scheduled for August 10 on the summit of Mt Washington.  Representatives from the Association of Hotel Keepers of New Hampshire were on hand "intent upon showing those who direct travelers to the White Mountains… its wide variety of attractiveness."  There was also an advertisement for the Grand Finals "to select the official Miss New Hampshire" which would take place on August 8 in Bedford Grove, and would include a "Big bathing beauty parade."  The paper also had a small blurb on a mountain race.

The article stated that runners were gathered at the Madison house and would be attempting to better Dr. George Foster's 1900 record of 1:42.  Favored runners included Cecil Hill, Johnny Semple, Honore St Jean, George Durgin, and Francis Darrah who had "finished in a recent 10 mile grind".  Hill was a marathoner who finished twelfth in both the 1935 and 1936 Boston Athletic Association Marathon (later known as the Boston Marathon).  Semple was a top miler in college and an excellent steeplechaser.  Darrah was known for his mountain running abilities having recently raced at high altitude in Colorado.  The *Union Leader* told that the duo of Semple and Hill were "well known to Manchester followers of marathons.  Hill and Semple have raced in the city several times particularly in the grueling Knights of Columbus marathon."

The *Union Leader* for August 10 had a sports section headline of "Five break mark in Mountain run."  The article excitedly proclaimed, "A record of 36 years standing was shattered on the Mt Washington automobile road on Saturday when a field of nine determined marathon runners went after the mark set in 1900."  Dr. Foster sponsored the race and hoped to "make the Mt Washington Marathon an annual affair."  Appalachian Mountain Club (AMC) legend Joe Dodge set up a special short wave radio to synchronize the watches at the base and summit.

Darrah ran alone from the start, hitting the four-mile mark in 33 minutes and winning by more than 12 minutes over Honore St. Jean.  Nine runners finished including Robert Demar, brother of legendary marathoner Clarence, in just under two hours.  Fourth place finisher Oliver Pelkey was also listed as Oliver Pedkey.

Later in 1936 the state of New Hampshire incorporated the summit weather station as the Mount Washington Observatory.

1

**Results**

| Place | Name | Time | City and State | |
|---|---|---|---|---|
| 1 | Francis Darrah | 1:15:50 | Manchester, NH | Course Record |
| 2 | Honore St. Jean | 1:28:00 | Manchester, NH | |
| 3 | Paul Kanaly | 1:30:05 | Belmont, MA | |
| 4 | Oliver Pelkey | 1:36:00 | Concord, NH | |
| 5 | Cecil H. Hill | 1:37:21 | Beverly, MA | |
| 6 | Edward Duhamel | 1:50:08 | Manchester, NH | |
| 7 | David Harrow | 1:50:28 | Melrose, MA | |
| 8 | Robert Demar | 1:56:20 | Melrose, MA | |
| 9 | Henry Bridges | 2:17:00 | Summit House, NH | |

Mt Washington summit hotel circa 1900

2<sup>nd</sup> Mt Washington Road Race

August 14, 1937
Saturday 2:00 PM
27 Finishers

The banner headline in the *Union Leader* read, "Japs renew attack on Shanghai".  Also dominating the front page was a large photo of Paul Donato with the title "Winner plodding up Mt. Washington."  The event was sponsored by the "Mount Washington Run Association." and sanctioned by the New England Amateur Athletic Association.  The sponsors were quoted as hoping "that within a few years this most unique of footraces will become a classic in American sports history."  Over a thousand spectators were expected.  Race safety included the Red Cross Berlin, New Hampshire chapter at the halfway house and summit, along with water stops every mile.  In addition the Berlin boy scouts would patrol the course and the Civilian Conservation Corps (CCC) would provide assistance at halfway.  "Respirators and inhalators were available at halfway and the summit."  The list of officials included four judges, three timers, three scorers, a referee, starter and honorary starter, three clerks of the course, and three doctors as medical advisors.  The *Union Leader* described the racecourse as, "eight miles and twenty yards" and the Carriage road "constructed of gravel, presented an uneven running surface with loose gravel and small stones."

Forty-nine runners entered what turned out to be an exciting race.  The action was captured by WBZ radio, which broadcast live from the finish line from 3-3:30 PM.  Newsreel companies came to film the race, which was then shown to more than 40 million people in 30,000 theatres in the United States and Canada.  The starting command was given at 2 PM and the runners took off from the tollhouse (opposite the Glen house).  Over 600 people watched the start with Gov. Francis P Murphy sending the runners on the way (and handing out trophies afterwards).

Pre-race favorites were Francis Darrah, Paul Donato, Fred Brown and Frank Scimone of the North Medford Club (NMC). Johnny Kelley was a late scratch, but the field included many of the best runners in New England.   Darrah, the 1936 winner, moved to an early lead.  He had a lead of 1,000 feet over the chase pack at the halfway house and came through four miles in 32:15.  This put him nearly a minute faster than in 1936.   With one mile to go his lead had shrunk to 300 feet.  Stomach cramps caused him to walk.  Over 400 spectators were delivered to the finish via a special cog railway train where they saw 21-year old Paul Donato of Roxbury, Massachusetts take the victory in 1:16:24.   Donato, a 21-year-old Italian instrument maker who had only been living in the US for five years, was described by the *Union Leader* as "the chunky distance plodder."

Ten runners passed Darrah as he walked, finishing in 1:30:33, a time that would have been good enough for fourth place the previous year.   Donato would go on to place sixth at the 1939 Boston Marathon and fifth in the 1940 edition.  Both races were US Olympic trials selection races and he barely missed the team ranking fifth.  He said of Darrah at the finish "He is a swell runner and a fine sport, I'm sorry his stomach slowed him up".

3

Joseph W Plouffe, who finished in fifth place, had placed eight in the BAA marathon earlier that year. Edmund Bennet finished in twelfth place running his first race ever. He trained for three weeks prior to the race by running seven miles a day on the Daniel Webster Highway. He had to train in the dark at 10 PM as he worked as a soda clerk and couldn't run until the shop closed. Eight place finisher Johnny (Jock) Semple would go on to make his mark as not only an excellent runner, but also coach and director of the BAA and director of the Mt Washington Road Race and the Boston Marathon.

At the award ceremony, held on the summit, Dr Foster told the contestants that, "their performance was a splendid example of faith, character, and courage." Only three runners failed to finish the race. Dr John Bartlett one of the three official race physicians stated to the Union Leader "their general condition at the finish was an excellent tribute to the endurance of the group."

Other news that year included a new facility being built on the summit, which was described in Into the Mountain as constructed with "9x10 inch timber bolted...into bedrock...it was insulated with seaweed."

**Complete Results**

| Place | Name | Time | Age | City and State | |
|---|---|---|---|---|---|
| 1 | Paul Donato | 1:16:24 | 21 | Roxbury, MA | |
| 2 | Italo Angioli | 1:19:25 | | Boston, MA | |
| 3 | William Honeywell | 1:19:41 | | Madison, ME | |
| 4 | George Durgin | 1:21:06 | | Beverly, MA | |
| 5 | J W Plouffe | 1:23:34 | | Worcester, MA | |
| 6 | John Sinkonis | 1:24:21 | | Worcester, MA | |
| 7 | Louis Young | 1:24:36 | | Cambridge, MA | |
| 8 | Johnny Semple | 1:25:15 | 34 | Beverly, MA | |
| 9 | SW Bowley | 1:25:39 | | Windsor, VT | |
| 10 | Cecil R. Hill | 1:26:02 | | Beverly, MA | |
| 11 | Francis Darrah | 1:30:33 | | Manchester, NH | FW |
| 12 | Edmund Bennett | 1:31:15 | 21 | Lancaster, MA | |
| 13 | Honore St. Jean | 1:37:45 | | Manchester, NH | |
| 14 | Theodore Gunaris | 1:39:23 | | Wellesley, MA | |
| 15 | Manuel Mederius | 1:39:39 | | Arlington, MA | |
| 16 | Dana Hutchinson | 1:41:16 | | N Easton, MA | |
| 17 | Graham Brown | 1:41:20 | | Medford, MA | |
| 18 | Alfred Fredericks | 1:42:22 | | Methuen, MA | |
| 19 | Ed Durham | 1:43:04 | | Manchester, NH | |
| 20 | Robert H. Delong | 1:45:28 | | Amesbury, MA | |
| 21 | Bernie O'Hara | 1:49:50 | | Brockton, MA | |
| 22 | William Walker Sr. | 1:50:23 | | Medford, MA | |
| 23 | Edward Ladd | 1:50:53 | | Lancaster, MA | |

| 24 | Paul Martin | 1:56:00 | Medford, MA |
| 25 | John F. Garland | 1:56:42 | Portsmouth, NH |
| 26 | George Dodge | 1:56:49 | Cambridge, MA |
| 27 | Pasquale Poletta | 2:09:00 | Amesbury, MA |

Darrah (center) and Donato (right) competing at the Vertical Mile in Colorado

**3<sup>rd</sup> Mt Washington Road race**

August 13, 1938
Saturday 1:00 PM
38 Finishers


The sports headline in the Union Leader on August 13 was "Brilliant field of 57 distance runners to race up Mt Washington."  The favorites heading into the race were Francis Darrah and Paul Donato and "Such well known marathon stars as Mel Porter of Millrose AC, Andrew Zamperelli of Medford, and Johnny Semple of Beverly" according to the *Union Leader* newspaper.  Darrah and Donato both raced on July fourth on the Pikes Peak Highway in a race that climbed 5,280 feet.  According to the Pikes Peak Website "The race was won by Francis Darrah, 119 lbs, ...in a time of 2h8m 14 and '6/10s.  Jogging along as easily as at his native sea level."  Donato finished six minutes later in second place.  Donato would finish sixth the following year in the BAA Marathon, running 2:34:36.

At Mt Washington the weather was a bit harsh compared to previous years, as sunny and warm conditions greeted the contestants at the base of the Auto Road.  The temperature dropped 35 degrees during the climb and the summit had 40-60 MPH winds and was cloaked in fog and clouds.  Newsreel cameramen led the race to the summit.  The race was again broadcast live on radio.  Over one thousand spectators were expected and New Hampshire Governor Frank Murphy invited all of the New England governors to be his guest at the finish line and post-race banquet.

Darrah pulled away from Donato and a pack that included Amicangioli, Mann, Durgin, and St Jean.  He rebounded from his disappointing finish of 1937 and took the win in 1:15:27, 23 seconds under his course record.  Seventeen runners broke 1:30 as a record 38 finished.  The *Union Leader* called Donato "the stocky little Paul Donato of Roxbury."  Nicholas Shultz (age 55) and Warren Shultz (age 17) became the first father and son team to finish.  They are also the first recorded finishers in the 50+ and 00-19 age groups.  The field of 38 finishers was also a record.  It was also noted in the *Union Leader* that, "several others finished but their names were not recorded."

A victory banquet was held on the summit hosted by the Mt Washington Association along with Dr. Foster and Col. Henry Teague.  Col. Teague was the owner of the Cog Railway.  Executive councilor Virgil White presented the winner's trophy to Darrah.  A team prize was awarded for the first time with the Norfolk Young Men's Association taking the victory with 9 points.  Second place went to the United Shoe Machinery Club of Boston.  It is not clear who were the members of the teams, or how the scoring was tallied.

The third place overall finisher Italo Amicangioli may have been the same person as the 1937 second place finisher Halo Amicanquioli.  Results were handwritten and misspelling of names was a common occurrence. Amicangioli running for the BAA would place nineteenth at the 1940 BAA marathon, running a 2:51:02.

A few months later Toni Matt earned his place in history as the first person to ski down the face of the Tuckerman Ravine headwall.

## Results

| Place | Name | Time | Age | City & State |
|---|---|---|---|---|
| 1 | Francis M. Darrah | 1:15:27 | | Roxbury, MA **Course Record** |
| 2 | Paul Donato | 1:19:10 | 22 | Roxbury, MA **FW** |
| 3 | Italo Amicangioli | 1:20:17 | | Newton, MA |
| 4 | Frank Mann | 1:20:35 | | Roxbury, MA |
| 5 | George L. Durgin | 1:20:58 | | Beverly, MA |
| 6 | Ralph Holland | 1:22:21 | | Dorchester, MA |
| 7 | Clarence Bowley | 1:23:39 | | Windsor, VT |
| 8 | Armand Moring | 1:23:40 | | Jeerson, MA |
| 10 | John Semple | 1:24:45 | 35 | Beverly, MA |
| 9 | Walter H. Emery | 1:24:45 | | Lynn, MA |
| 11 | William Simons | 1:25:03 | | Needham Heights, MA |
| 12 | Howard McClarity | 1:25:22 | | Roxbury, MA |
| 13 | Roy E. Kimball | 1:26:30 | | Beverly, MA |
| 14 | Lindy Dempster | 1:26:49 | | Roxbury, MA |
| 15 | Warren H. Dupree | 1:27:25 | | Foxboro, MA |
| 16 | Joseph W. Plouffe | 1:27:48 | | Worcester, MA |
| 17 | Girard Lemieux | 1:29:33 | | Central Falls, RI |
| 18 | Roy Abare | 1:30:10 | | Worcester, MA |
| 19 | J C Welch | 1:30:24 | | Roxbury, MA |
| 20 | Walter O'Hara | 1:30:44 | | Lynn, MA |
| 21 | John Fitzgerald | 1:32:30 | | Lynn, MA |
| 22 | Richard Fortier | 1:33:14 | | Chocura, NH |
| 23 | Graham Brown | 1:33:15 | | Medford, MA |
| 24 | Raymond Wilcox | 1:34:12 | | Kingston, RI |
| 25 | Edmund D. Bennett | 1:34:22 | | Lancaster, MA |
| 26 | Warren H. Schultz | 1:35:14 | 17 | Williamsville, VT |
| 27 | Joseph Kelinerman | Not recorded | | New York, NY |
| 28 | Frank Brown | Not recorded | | Medford, MA |
| 29 | Edward A. Page | Not recorded | | Woonsocket, RI |
| 30 | Harold Ernesi | Not recorded | | Boston, MA |
| 31 | Pasquale Poletta | Not recorded | | Amesbury, MA |
| 32 | Herbert Woods | Not recorded | | Greenfield, NH |
| 33 | Lionel Paquette | Not recorded | | Haverhill, MA |
| 34 | Nicholas Schultz | Not recorded | | Williamsville, VT |
| 35 | Daniel Hoffman | Not recorded | | New York, NY |
| 36 | Walter H. Childs | Not recorded | | Springfield, MA |
| 37 | Paul Martin | Not recorded | | N Medford, MA |
| 38 | Grant Brown | Not recorded | | Medford, MA |

<h1 style="text-align:center">4<sup>th</sup> Mt Washington Road Race</h1>

August 13, 1961
Sunday 1:30 PM
79 Finishers.

The weather conditions for the revived race, returning after 23 years of dormancy, featured 60 degrees temperatures at the base and 34 degrees at the summit.  Winds just under 60 MPH blew up sand from the road and mixed with clouds and fog to make the skies very dark at the finish line.   Gusts of up to 90 miles per hour rattled the runners and finish line crew. Jock Semple took over as the race director on this 100th anniversary of the opening of the Carriage Road.  The race was co-sponsored by the Berlin Athletic Boosters and the Mt Washington Centennial Committee.

At the start Semple noted, "President Kennedy wanted men to be fit, not dead, so please quit at the halfway house if you are in tough shape."  Bagpiper Bob Cummings played before the start and sent the runners off.  All 79 finishers came in under the 2:15 time limit.  The top five all finished under the 1938 course record of Francis Darrah.

This was the first year that runners did not have to, in Semple's words, "negotiate the dozens of steps at the top."   John Kelley, who Semple called "the wing footed school teacher from Mystic CT", broke from Larry Damon, the National Amateur Athletic Union (AAU) and New England 10-mile champion, to win by one and a half minutes.  Kelley was, among his many accomplishments, the 1957 BAA marathon champion, and Damon was an Olympian on the U.S. ski team in 1956 and 1960.

Billy Squires wrote in his article Run to the Clouds, which appeared in *the Distance Running Log,* "Three weeks before …I was called on the phone by Jock Semple…about a mountain run 8 ¼ miles up a dirt road to the summit of famous Mt Washington.  I thought this was a joke at first, but soon he explained that 25 years ago they held a race and…this year wanted a renewal of the race."  Squires added, "I have always had a desire for a challenge.  In track competition there are many, but here was a real test of human fortitude."  He trained with teammates Jerry Harvey and Ken Mueller, who drove the five hours from Boston the day before.  The group camped out at the base and had a typical early 1960's athletes breakfast "oatmeal, soft boiled eggs, two orders of toast, and tea."   Squires and his teammates applied Vaseline "for protection against the cold and wind."  At the halfway point he was in sixteenth place despite trouble with a calf muscle, which caused him to walk.  Above the treeline he experienced more adversity and "walked again, putting on my sweat shirt that I had wished I had left behind me in the first mile.  It now turned out to be a welcome friend."   He was later hit by wind gusts of up to 92 MPH reporting that "a gust of wind hit us and we fell."  At the finish he "grabbed a blanket held by Bob Campbell, one of the officials and a good friend, then walked for a few minutes, after which I flopped into a car for the descent to the starting point."  Squires finished thirteenth and his training partners Mueller and Harvey finished sixth and fifteenth respectively.

At the awards ceremony Russ Foster, the son of George Foster, presented the Foster trophy as Francis Darrah looked on.  The top ten received trophies with a special Mt Washington Carriage Road Centennial medallion.  Those finishing eleventh to fifteenth place received silver medals, and all finisher enjoyed a buffet lunch.

The crowd of spectators at the race was estimated to be over 1,200.  Mike O'Hara of St Anthony's was the only recorded finisher from the 1930's to run, placing 34th in 1:30:46.  Team results were not given, however the Boston Athletic Association (BAA) placed five runners in the top six places and 13 in the top 28.  The combined time for the top five BAA runners was an excellent 6:02:47, and it would be another 16 years before a squad would run faster.  The North Medford Club (NMC) had a combined time of 7:12:59.  Later in the day a half-inch of snowfall was recorded on the summit.

**100th Anniversary sign at the entrance to the Auto Road**

Potpourri from 1961:  Yuri Gagarin became the first man in space as he circled the Globe.  US President John F. Kennedy advised "every prudent family should have a bomb shelter."  The Berlin wall was built in East Germany.  The top movie of the year was 101 Dalmatians and the top Television show was Wagon Train.  Minimum wage was $1.25, a gallon of gas was $.31, and the cost of a home was $16,500.

**All available results**

| Place | Name | Club | Time | |
|---|---|---|---|---|
| 1 | John J Kelley | BAA | 1:08:54 Course **Record** | |
| 2 | Larry Damon | BAA | 1:10:33 | |
| 3 | Duane Merchant | BAA | 1:13:02 | |
| 4 | Angus Wooten | Electric boat | 1:13:07 | **FW** |
| 5 | Al Confalone | BAA | 1:14:34 | |
| 6 | Ken Mueller | BAA | 1:15:44 | |

| 7  | Gordon McKenzie   | NYPC           | 1:16:12 |
| 8  | George Terry      | Electric boat  | 1:16:33 |
| 9  | Dick Vehlow       |                | 1:17:13 |
| 10 | Bill Smith        | BAA            | 1:18:19 |
| 11 | Erkki Kaunisto    | Reipas AC      | 1:18:30 |
| 12 | Bob Cummings      | NMC            | 1:21:11 |
| 13 | Bill Squires      | BAA            | 1:21:21 |
| 14 | Wayne Lamothe     | NMC            | 1:21:39 |
| 15 | Jerry Harvey      | BAA            | 1:22:25 |
| 16 | Bob Zollinhoffer  | BAA            | 1:24:06 |
| 17 | Stan Tiernan      | NMC            | 1:24:12 |
| 18 | Al Meehan         |                | 1:24:15 |
| 19 | George Cushmac    | NETC           | 1:25:11 |
| 20 | Raimo Ahti        | Reipas AC      | 1:25:24 |
| 21 | Don Fay           | BAA            | 1:25:36 |
| 22 | Tony Sapienza     | BAA            | 1:26:46 |
| 23 | Dick Clapp        | NY Pioneer     | 1:26:53 |
| 24 | John DiComandrea  | BAA            | 1:27:02 |
| 25 | Bob Schrader      |                | 1:27:04 |
| 26 | Ralph Eilberg     | Del-Val AA     | 1:27:47 |
| 27 | Greg Bigelow      | Cntrl CT AA    | 1:28:11 |
| 28 | Dick Packard      | BAA            | 1:28:25 |
| 29 | Bob Powers        |                | 1:28:28 |
| 30 | Bill Shrader      |                | 1:28:53 |
| 31 | Dick Moseley      |                | 1:28:56 |
| 32 | Tom Sanders       |                | 1:29:07 |
| 33 | Ron Dwyer         |                | 1:29:55 |
| 34 | Mike O'Hara       | St Anthony's   | 1:30:46 |
| 35 | Graham Parnell    | Spartan AC     | 1:31:03 |
| 36 | Bob Avery         | Spartan AC     | 1:31:19 |
| 37 | Royce Sawyer      | NMC            | 1:31:21 |
| 38 | Ed Ouellette      | Maine          | 1:32:06 |
| 39 | Sumner Sears      | Lynn AC        | 1:32:16 |
| 40 | Erik Erickson     | BAA            | 1:32:33 |
| 41 | Bill Norris       | England        | 1:33:16 |
| 42 | Sam Ouellette     | Maine          | 1:33:52 |
| 43 | Carlton Comstock  | NMC            | 1:34:36 |
| 44 | Dave Buddington   | BAA            | 1:34:51 |

### 5<sup>th</sup> Mt Washington Road Race

July 15, 1962
Sunday
84 Finishers


For the first time the race was not run in August, moving to the third Sunday in July.  John Kelley was a pre-race favorite in the field of 84 entrants.  The Amateur Athletic Union (AAU), the governing body for amateur athletics, sanctioned the race and a strong field was expected to challenge Kelley.  Fred Norris, a 40-year-old carpenter from England, was among the favorites.  He had been training with Kelley leading up to the race.  The White Mountain Recreation Association sponsored the event and Jock Semple of the BAA was again the race director.  According to Kelley's account of the race in *New England Runner* magazine Norris and Kelley "ground out a slowly winding lead on the up-and-coming Duane Merchant after trading leads with him through the first two miles."  After the halfway point Norris began to pull away. Kelley heard him "call(s) out over his shoulder, 'Does this keep on like this all the way?'"  Soon after, Norris pulled away for good in the sleet covered, fog-shrouded Summit.  Norris became the first runner to break 65 minutes, an incredible feat that would not be matched for another 15 years.  Kelley ran the second fastest time, and hence, the fastest losing time.  No team results were given as only the names of the top ten finishers was available however; the BAA had five runners finish in the top ten for a combined time of 6:07:52.  A record 84 runners finished.  Earlier in the year (according to *Not without Peril*) "six Polaris Sno-Travelers made a successful ascent of Mt Washington."  These were the earliest version of snowmobiles.

Norris's time would stand as the top for 40+ runners for almost 40 more years.  Duane Merchant lowered his time from the previous year to 1:11:17.  This time still ranks among the top times for runners under the age of 20.  Peter Burkhart of the BAA was one of the 74 finishers whose result was not listed.  He wrote to the *Hockomock Swamp Rat* stating that the weather was tough. "The hail was bal-bearing size at seven miles and ice cold.  You were frozen at an angle while running.  Dense fog?  You could see ZERO at some points."  Burkhart continued "Someone said that winner Fred Norris actually outran the storm to the top."  He also gave some insight into the camaraderie amongst the small field.  "In those days all the runners bunked together before the race at the hotel, so I managed to get an extra warm shirt after the race from Jim Welch (former USA Junior 30K champ).  As a rookie I was amazed at how all the guys pulled together as 'us against the mountain' rather than separate teams."  He also notes how strong a runner Norris was.  "Fred Norris was also the World record holder in the 1-hour run way back when.  A typical pre-race warmup for Fred was 10x440 in 70 followed by a sub 50 ten miler!"  It was also rumored that Norris would train by running behind the bus that shuttled him from the coal mine he worked in to his house.  Fred's son Ed Norris noted in a later edition of the *Hockomock Swamp Rat* that "To set the record straight, my father, Fred Norris, didn't even run hard that day because he just wanted a hill workout for up-coming races.  As a matter of fact, he ran back down when he got to the top.  His total mileage that week was an even 100. Two weeks later he won the Salem (MA) 12 in 56:58.  There is no doubt that he could have broken one hour if he wanted – snow included.  It's too bad he didn't run the Mount in his prime, when he went 22 miles, 1680 yards in 2 hours even on a soggy track in Blackburn, England wearing spiked shoes with a steel plate inside to prevent the spikes from coming through!"

The Summit buildings in 1962

All Available results

| Place | Name | Club | Time | Age | City & State | |
|-------|------|------|------|-----|--------------|---|
| 1 | Fred Norris | | 1:04:57 | 40 | Brockton, MA | CR |
| 2 | John Kelley | BAA | 1:08:28 | 31 | Groton, CT | FW |

Kelley the "younger" is met by Kelley the "elder" at the finish.

| 3 | Duane Merchant | BAA | 1:11:17 | 19 | Dennisport, MA |
| 4 | Al Confalone | BAA | 1:12:08 | | Wakefield, MA |
| 5 | George Waterhouse | | 1:15:47 | | |
| 6 | Gerry Harvey | BAA | 1:16:12 | | |
| 7 | Richard Clapp | NY Pioneer | 1:17:21 | | NY |
| 8 | Rod MacMichell | NY Pioneer | 1:18:19 | | NY |
| 9 | William Schab | NYAC | 1:19:04 | | NY |
| 10 | Richard Packard | BAA | 1:19:47 | | |

June 19<sup>th</sup> 1966
Sunday
54 Finishers

After a four year hiatus the race was back to celebrate the centennial of the Auto Road.  Leo Carroll a Harvard student from England took the victory with the second-fastest time ever (1:07:31).  Carroll's Boston Athletic Association (BAA) teammate John Kelley was 17 seconds in arrears giving Carroll the narrowest margin of victory in the six running's of the race.  Kelley was inducted into the national distance running Hall of Fame in 2002.  His accomplishments included winning the 1957 BAA Marathon and finishing second five times.  He also was the national marathon champion eight times (1956-1963) and represented the US in the Olympics in 1956 and 1960.   Third place finisher Abe Assa noted in *New England Runner,* "That was my best race ever.  I remember it was hot and I was picking people off up top.  It was a great experience."   Team scoring at the time was typically done cross-country style, with the lowest points winning.  The BAA placed five in the top eight with a combined time of 6:08:41 while the North Medford Club finished with a combined time of 7:22:37.  Nearly half the field (24 runners) represented either BAA or NMC.  Other finishers of note included Future BAA marathon winner Amby Burfoot, who placed fifth in 1:14:55 and a 20-year-old Bob Teschek who placed 34<sup>th</sup>.  Burfoot's time was the third fastest run by a finisher under the age of 20.  Teschek would go on to become the race director 20 years later.  Sixteenth place finisher Ted Corbitt was a member of the 1952 Olympic team and the American record holder for the 50 mile, 100 mile, and 24 hours on the track.  He also played a central role in developing US distance running by founding the Road Runners Club of America and establishing guidelines for measuring courses accurately.  Corbitt was known to train by running over 200 miles a week while working as a physical therapist 40 hours a week.

Potpourri from 1966:  Life expectancy in the US was 70.2 years for the population of 196 million.   A new home cost $23,000 and a first class stamp was $.05.

**Complete results**

| Place | Name | Club | Time | |
|---|---|---|---|---|
| 1 | Leo Carroll | BAA | 1:07:31 | |
| 2 | John J Kelley | BAA | 1:07:48 | **FW** |
| 3 | Abe Assa | NYC | 1:13:06 | |
| 4 | Roland Michant | MT Royal of Canada | 1:14:08 | |
| 5 | Amby Burfoot | Central Conn.  AA | 1:14:55 | |
| 6 | Art Coolidge | BAA | 1:16:36 | |
| 7 | Mike Bigelow | BAA | 1:18:08 | |
| 8 | Stu Adams | BAA | 1:18:38 | |
| 9 | Rene Chereaux | NMC | 1:18:46 | |
| 10 | Pete Burkhart | BAA | 1:19:38 | |
| 11 | Bill Murphy | BAA | 1:20:31 | |
| 12 | Dick Clapp | Millrose AA | 1:22:38 | |

| 13 | Regis Forel | MT Royal of Canada | 1:22:49 |
| 14 | Don Fay | BAA | 1:23:30 |
| 15 | Ben Chapinski | NMC | 1:23:49 |
| 16 | Ted Corbitt | NY Pioneer Club | 1:24:00 |
| 17 | Ronald Simjian | Greenwich CT | 1:24:29 |
| 18 | Robert Craigin | Mt Park AA | 1:25:05 |
| 19 | Roland Dyer | Gorham AC | 1:26:15 |
| 20 | Robert Esterbrook | UNH | 1:27:40 |
| 21 | John Valentine | | 1:28:04 |
| 22 | Bob Sullivan | BAA | 1:28:22 |
| 23 | Norman Pelletier | Metro AC | 1:29:10 |
| 24 | Robert Coolidge | Goshen NY | 1:29:27 |
| 25 | George Esterbrook | UNH | 1:29:39 |
| 26 | Gunter Vecser | Viking Ski Club | 1:30:15 |
| 27 | Harold Burke | Gorham AC | 1:30:22 |
| 28 | Brian Nann | Woodland HS ME | 1:30:56 |
| 29 | Allen Thorndike | Whitefield NH | 1:31:12 |
| 30 | William Warburton | NMC | 1:31:18 |
| 31 | Carlton Bell | Concord NH | 1:32:05 |
| 32 | Leonard Holmes | NMC | 1:32:50 |
| 33 | Sam Stallard | Viking Ski Club | 1:33:36 |
| 34 | Robert Teschek | Concord NH | 1:33:48 |
| 35 | Bob Bamberger | BAA | 1:34:15 |
| 36 | Alde Scandurre | Millrose AA | 1:35:35 |
| 37 | Sam Ouellette | NMC | 1:35:54 |
| 38 | Rick Bayko | NMC | 1:36:26 |
| 39 | Ronald Dyer | Gorham AC | 1:37:08 |
| 40 | Joe Kirby | St Anthony BC | 1:38:15 |
| 41 | Bill Ginnis | Spartan AC | 1:39:22 |
| 42 | Al Chamberlain | Newcomb NY | 1:40:48 |
| 43 | Ralph Fairbanks | NMC | 1:40:55 |
| 44 | Sigmund Podlozny | NMC | 1:41:15 |
| 45 | George Lattarulo | NMC | 1:42:18 |
| 46 | Dave Hasenfus | NMC | 1:43:15 |
| 47 | Bill Castle | NYAC | 1:43:37 |
| 48 | John Holden | | 1:49:45 |
| 49 | Bob Page | NMC | 1:53:12 |
| 50 | Raymond Maillett | | 1:55:17 |
| 51 | Gene Ketchen | Gorham AC | 2:01:05 |
| 52 | Robert O'Connell | BAA | 2:02:40 |
| 53 | Bill Marot | NMC | 2:03:02 |
| 54 | Mike Warburton | NMC | 2:10:37 |

7<sup>th</sup> Mt Washington Road Race

June 18, 1967
Sunday
44 Finishers

The seventh running of the Mt Washington Road race featured a close race with the top three separated by 1:42. Angus Wooten took the victory over Roland Cormier and Richard Clapp who were within seven seconds of each other at the summit. The Boston Athletic Association and the North Medford Club (NMC) again dominated the results with 22 of the 44 runners being members of the two teams. BAA combined for a time of 6:36:40 to NMC's 6:44:38. It would be another nine years before a team other than BAA or NMC would emerge victorious on the mountain.

Nineteen year-old Rick Bayko finished twenty-third. Bayko, a student at Boston State College with personal bests of 4:22 and 9:16 for the mile and two-mile, would later go on to finish as high as thirteenth at the Boston Marathon. He ran a 2:20:56 in 1974. Bayko was the driving force behind the *Yankee Runner* magazine which covered racing in New England in the late 1970s. Bayko noted in *the Hockomock Swamp Rat*, that his best race ever was "the 1973 New Bedford 30K run where his fast 1:34:13 defeated a young Will Rodgers."

## Complete results

| Place | Name | Club | Time | |
|---|---|---|---|---|
| 1 | Angus Wooten | | 1:12:43 | |
| 2 | Roland Cormier | Mt Park AC | 1:14:18 | **FW** |
| 3 | Richard Clapp | NMC | 1:14:25 | |
| 4 | Peter Stipe | BAA | 1:16:05 | |
| 5 | Craig Dupree | BAA | 1:17:47 | |
| 6 | Charles Dyson | Hartford TC | 1:19:02 | |
| 7 | James Daley Jr. | NMC | 1:19:34 | |
| 8 | Tom Maynard | BAA | 1:20:10 | |
| 9 | Stuart Adams | BAA | 1:20:40 | |
| 10 | Remi Charoux | NMC | 1:21:08 | |
| 11 | Richard Cordier | BAA | 1:21:58 | |
| 12 | Kenneth Klatka | | 1:22:17 | |
| 13 | George Waterhouse | NMC | 1:23:10 | |
| 14 | Mike Bigelow | BAA | 1:24:46 | |
| 15 | Don Morton | BAA | 1:25:31 | |
| 16 | Don Fay | BAA | 1:26:20 | |
| 17 | Lenny Holmes | NMC | 1:26:21 | |
| 18 | Ben Chapinski | NMC | 1:27:04 | |
| 19 | Ralph Grant | Waterville AC | 1:27:21 | |
| 20 | Roland Dyer | Waterville AC | 1:27:31 | |
| 21 | John Hurley | NMC | 1:29:07 | |
| 22 | Ron Gaff | | 1:31:03 | |

| 23 | Rick Bayko | NMC | 1:31:45 |
| 24 | John Jarek | Mt Park AC | 1:31:53 |
| 25 | Charles Scott | NMC | 1:34:23 |
| 26 | Beattie Mackenzie | Ottawa Ski | 1:34:38 |
| 27 | Sigmund Podlozny | NMC | 1:38:33 |
| 28 | Robert Page | NMC | 1:40:41 |
| 29 | Sam Stallard | Viking Ski club | 1:41:48 |
| 30 | Vin Fandetti | NMC | 1:41:56 |
| 31 | John Linscott | BAA | 1:42:24 |
| 32 | Doug Bourne | Mt Royal | 1:43:19 |
| 33 | Alton Chamberlain | NMC | 1:44:41 |
| 34 | Bill Lagueux | | 1:44:44 |
| 35 | George Leslie | NMC | 1:46:49 |
| 36 | Brian Cuerden | NMC | 1:47:13 |
| 37 | Ronald Dyer | Waterville AC | 1:47:34 |
| 38 | John Philbrick | Gorham AC | 1:51:08 |
| 39 | Bob McVeigh | BAA | 1:51:47 |
| 40 | James Daley Sr. | NMC | 1:56:32 |
| 41 | John Helpern | Cambridge Y | 2:00:40 |
| 42 | William Castle | NYAC | 2:03:46 |
| 43 | George Lattarulo | NMC | 2:04:09 |
| 44 | Stanley Sheldon | | 2:17:12 |

From left to right Rick Bayko, Larry Olsen, John J. Kelley, and John Kelley

8<sup>th</sup> Mt Washington Road Race

June 16, 1968
Sunday
69 Finishers
A large field assembled as 70 athletes from 22 states lined up for the climb.  Twenty six-year-old world-class skier Mike Gallagher from Killington Vermont was victorious in his first attempt.  Gallagher a two-time Olympic cross-country skier was closely followed by Art Coolidge.  The race was sponsored by the Auto Road and officiated by Jock Semple who was the chair of the New England Amateur Athletic Association and coach and trainer for the Boston Athletic Association.  The first two finishers ran the second and third fastest times in the races eight-year history.  Angus Wooten the 1967 champion finished seventh 20 seconds ahead of one of the pre-race favorites, Richard Clapp who ran two minutes slower than in the previous year.  The BAA and the North Medford Club (NMC) were close in the team scoring with NMC 27 points to BAA's 31.  The club's combined top five times were 6:43:33 for NMC and 6:45:41 for BAA.  NMC had a huge contingent of 23 runners finish the race.

On the same day 20,000 spectators turned out in Loudon, NH for the national motorcycle championships.


**Complete results**

| Place | Name | Club | Time | |
|---|---|---|---|---|
| 1 | Mike Gallagher | Spartan AC | 1:06:13 | |
| 2 | Art Coolidge | BAA | 1:06:39 | |
| 3 | Ken Ingles | | 1:12:34 | |
| 4 | Leo Duarte | | 1:12:38 | |
| 5 | Peter Stipe | BAA | 1:13:08 | |
| 6 | Dick Rowley | Millrose AC | 1:14:02 | |
| 7 | Angus Wooten | | 1:15:50 | FW |
| 8 | Richard Clapp | NMC | 1:16:10 | |
| 9 | Stephen Smith | NMC | 1:18:38 | |
| 10 | Russ Holt | NMC | 1:19:42 | |
| 11 | T Maynard | BAA | 1:21:15 | |
| 12 | Neil Welgandt | SJTC | 1:21:26 | |
| 13 | Ken Borches | | 1:21:54 | |
| 14 | Floyde Wilson | WAC | 1:22:17 | |
| 15 | S Adams | BAA | 1:22:20 | |
| 16 | George Waterhouse | NMC | 1:22:30 | |
| 17 | M Bigelow | BAA | 1:23:38 | |
| 18 | Ralph Grant | WAC | 1:24:59 | |
| 19 | Dick Packard | BAA | 1:25:20 | |
| 20 | Pete Sifalis | | 1:25:34 | |
| 21 | B Chipinski | NMC | 1:26:33 | |
| 22 | Larry LaCroix | NMC | 1:26:59 | |
| 23 | David Reese | | 1:27:00 | |

| Place | Name | Club | Time |
| --- | --- | --- | --- |
| 24 | Tom Derderian | NMC | 1:27:48 |
| 25 | Tommy Vannah | NMC | 1:28:12 |
| 26 | Vin Fandetti | NMC | 1:28:28 |
| 27 | Bill Ginns | SAC | 1:28:57 |
| 28 | John Wallace | BAA | 1:29:04 |
| 29 | Peter David | SAC | 1:29:40 |
| 30 | Donald Fay | BAA | 1:30:02 |
| 31 | Charlie Scott | NMC | 1:30:23 |
| 32 | Tony Sapienza | BAA | 1:30:33 |
| 33 | Winston Thommas | WAC | 1:30:50 |
| 34 | William Cracner | | 1:31:14 |
| 35 | Bill Warburton | NMC | 1:31:21 |
| 36 | Norm Pelletier | Metro AC | 1:31:38 |
| 37 | Paul Schell | NMC | 1:31:41 |
| 38 | Lloyd Slocum | | 1:32:04 |
| 39 | Bob Hersey | NMC | 1:32:22 |
| 40 | Bob Weiler | | 1:32:55 |
| 41 | Wayne Thompson | Salem AC | 1:33:40 |
| 42 | Bill McKenzie | | 1:34:14 |
| 43 | Alan Joseph | Lynn AC | 1:34:58 |
| 44 | Rick Jankowski | Lynn AC | 1:34:59 |
| 45 | Sig Podlozny | NMC | 1:38:33 |
| 46 | William Carter | Rochester TC | 1:39:14 |
| 47 | Richard Mosley | NMC | 1:39:42 |
| 48 | George Latterulo | NMC | 1:40:19 |
| 49 | Roland Dyer | WAC | 1:40:32 |
| 50 | Mike Dohrendorf | WAC | 1:41:09 |
| 51 | Ed Knowlton | Lynn AC | 1:42:49 |
| 52 | Roland Dyer Jr. | WAC | 1:43:15 |
| 53 | Mel Olkowski | | 1:43:28 |
| 54 | D Hogan | BAA | 1:45:00 |
| 55 | Joe Lennens | | 1:45:06 |
| 56 | Joe Bourne | | 1:45:08 |
| 57 | William Ingraham | Metro AC | 1:47:39 |
| 58 | Dick Crodier | BAA | 1:48:10 |
| 59 | John Proctor | | 1:48:19 |
| 60 | Dave Hasenfus | NMC | 1:48:49 |
| 61 | Sam Ouellette | NMC | 1:50:00 |
| 62 | Tom Gordon | Lynn AC | 1:53:32 |
| 63 | Bob Seaman | BAA | 1:55:25 |
| 64 | Kevin MacDonald | NMC | 1:55:53 |
| 65 | William LaCaqueux | NMC | 1:56:48 |
| 66 | Philip McGraw | NMC | 2:00:58 |

| Place | Name | Club | Time |
| --- | --- | --- | --- |
| 67 | Bob Halpin | | 2:03:59 |
| 68 | Chico Simone | NMC | 2:10:15 |
| 69 | Frank Cook | | 2:25:45 |
| 70 | Johnny Jarek | NMC | DNF |

Mike Gallagher 3 Time US Olympian

**9<sup>th</sup> Mt Washington Road Race**

June 15, 1969
Sunday
83 Finishers.

Mike Gallagher took his second straight victory on a rainy, foggy day.  Gallagher, who represented the US in three Olympics and three World Championships in cross-country skiing, took the win over teammate Leo Duarte of the Spartan Athletic Club.  Gallagher's time was only eight seconds shy of his winning time the year before.  At the time he held two of the top three times.

In the how "little things change department": An article in the *Union Leader* noted that Manager Dick Williams promised to shake up the lineup after the "Boston Red Sox were humiliated in three straight weekend losses to Oakland".

The only results available were for the top five out of a record field of 83.

Potpourri for 1969:  The US President was Richard Nixon.  The federal debt was $365 billion.  The median household income was $8,389.00 and the cost of a new home was $27,900.  A gallon of gas cost $.35 and a gallon of milk was $1.10.

| Place | Name | Club | Time | Age | City & State |
|---|---|---|---|---|---|
| 1 | Mike Gallagher | Spartan AC | 1:06:44 | 27 | VT |
| 2 | Leo Duarte | Spartan AC | | | |
| 3 | Al Meehan | | | | Stanford, CT |
| 4 | Malcolm Hunter | | | | Ottawa, CAN |
| 5 | Charlie McGuire | Spartan AC | | | |

10<sup>th</sup> Mt Washington Road race

June 14, 1970
Sunday
75 Finishers

Vermont's Mike Gallagher took an unprecedented third straight victory with a nearly two minute decision over Lou Coppens of the Pennsylvania Athletic Club.  Gallagher took the lead at the start and passed through two miles in 14:02.  He moved farther ahead and clocked 31:35 at four miles.  His final margin of victory was 54 seconds.

For the first time the BAA and NMC had another team to battle against as Cambridge Sports Union (CSU) of Massachusetts fielded a team.  The BAA came out on top with a 6:42:07 to NMC's 6:50:54 and CSU's 7:05:58.  CSU was a relative newcomer to the scene, having been formed eight years earlier by Sara Mae and Larry Berman.

Weather conditions for the race were good with 72 degrees at the base and 41 at the summit for the 78 starters.  There were 75 finishers and "many unofficial starters".  The race was managed by Jock Semple, John Canney, and Fred Brown, Sr. Trophies were given to the top ten and medals to the top 30, all finishers received a certificate.

Rick Bayko, a fixture in the New England running scene and writer of the popular *Yankee Runner Magazine*, noted, "I'd staggered to the top in my usual crappy Mount Washington performance.  Since space was limited, I thought I'd do the noble thing and give up my seat for the ride down while I jogged it.  I couldn't believe how easy it felt, and gradually I picked up the pace and was at a full run for the last four miles.  It began to get a bit uncomfortable on the drive home, and by that night it felt like I'd jammed my femur three inches up into my butt.  I couldn't walk right or sit comfortably for the next four or five days".

## Top 25 Finishers

| Place | Name | Club | Time | |
|---|---|---|---|---|
| 1 | Mike Gallagher | Spartan AC | 1:09:06 | |
| 2 | Lou Coppens | Penn AC | 1:10:00 | |
| 3 | Larry Damon | BAA | 1:11:31 | |
| 4 | Roland Cormier | NMC | 1:12:12 | FW |
| 5 | Ralph Thomas | Waterville AC | 1:13:30 | |
| 6 | Michael Canty | Spartan AC | 1:16:14 | |
| 7 | Daniel Penzer | CSU | 1:16:31 | |
| 8 | Tom Dowling | BAA | 1:16:47 | |
| 9 | Thomas Knatt | NMC | 1:16:48 | |
| 10 | Ed Ayres | | 1:17:01 | |
| 11 | Neil Weygandt | SJTC | 1:09:28 | |
| 12 | Louis Paul | CSU | 1:21:32 | |
| 13 | William McNulty | BAA | 1:22:29 | |
| 14 | Emilio Rotondi | NMC | 1:22:43 | |

| 15 | Peter Davis | Spartan AC | 1:23:44 |
| 16 | Glen Ayres | | 1:24:04 |
| 17 | Roland Dyer | Waterville AC | 1:24:22 |
| 18 | Robert Sullivan | BAA | 1:24:41 |
| 19 | William Lutz | | 1:25:32 |
| 20 | Clair Paine | Salem SC | 1:25:51 |
| 21 | George Waterhouse | NMC | 1:26:12 |
| 22 | Ken Dawson | BAA | 1:26:39 |
| 23 | Don Perkins | | 1:27:00 |
| 24 | Rick Bayko | NMC | 1:27:14 |
| 25 | John Kelso | CSU | 1:27:21 |

## 11<sup>th</sup> Mt Washington Road Race

June 13, 1971
Sunday
112 Finishers

It was 85 degrees at the base and 46 at the summit as record 129 starters and 112 finishers took to the auto road.  Mike Gallagher became the first four-time winner as he bested an excellent field.  Gallagher passed the halfway house in 31:13 and continued on to a 51 second victory over Amby Burfoot.  Burfoot, who would go on to finish 10<sup>th</sup> in the 1976 Olympic trials in 2:18, passed Malcolm Hunter in the second half of the race to finish second.  He also became only the tenth runner to finish under 1:10.

Although team results were not given, using the top five finishers combined time from each club, the NMC took first among teams with a combined time of 6:25:52 to the Turtletown's 6:59:09.  The BAA was third in 7:10:16.

## Top 25 Finishers

| Place | Name | Club | Time | |
| --- | --- | --- | --- | --- |
| 1 | Mike Gallagher | Spartan AC | 1:07:27 | |
| 2 | Amby Burfoot | CCAA | 1:08:18 | |
| 3 | Malcolm Hunter | | 1:10:32 | |
| 4 | Roland Cormier | NMC | 1:10:47 | FW |
| 5 | Al Meehan | Strafford Spartans | 1:11:21 | |
| 6 | Charles Keating | NMC | 1:12:11 | |
| 7 | Ralph Thomas | | 1:13:07 | |
| 8 | Larry Damon | BAA | 1:13:55 | |
| 9 | Neil Coville | McGill Univ. | 1:16:12 | |
| 10 | David Senechalle | St Anthony's | 1:16:26 | |
| 11 | Chet Fortier | NMC | 1:16:46 | |
| 12 | Wayne Lucas | | 1:17:07 | |
| 13 | Richard Lemay | MRFA | 1:18:41 | |
| 14 | Michael Sudlow | MRFA | 1:19:27 | |

22

| Place | Name | Club | Time |
|---|---|---|---|
| 15 | Ian Fairgrieve | | 1:19:58 |
| 16 | Richard Fahey | | 1:20:05 |
| 17 | Thomas Doyle | Lynn AC | 1:20:16 |
| 18 | Jay Sidman | CSU | 1:20:49 |
| 19 | Michael Canty | Spartan AC | 1:21:02 |
| 20 | Neil Ackley | Turtletown | 1:21:21 |
| 21 | David Ethridge | Turtletown | 1:21:26 |
| 22 | Leonard Hall | No. Country AC | 1:22:27 |
| 23 | Earl McGilvery | NMC | 1:22:47 |
| 24 | William McNulty | BAA | 1:23:14 |
| 25 | Mark Haggerty | NMC | 1:23:21 |

Len Hall of the North County AC

**12<sup>th</sup> Mt Washington Road Race**

June 18, 1972
Sunday
117 Finishers


A record 126 starters and 117 finishers completed the journey from the base where temperatures were 74 degrees, to the summit where it was 30 degrees cooler.  Tom Derderian, a sub-2:20 marathoner, led at the half.  Derderian was passed by Ralph Thomas, who had finished seventh the previous year, who then led through seven miles.  Roland Cormier, who had finished fourth in 1970, overtook Thomas and pulled away to win by 21 seconds.  This was the second closest finish in the twelve-year history of the race, trailing only Leo Carroll's 17-second margin of victory in 1966.

Charlotte Lettis, who among her many accomplishments won four New England Amateur Athletic Union Cross-Country championships, became the first official women's finisher.  Lettis, age 22, finished 84<sup>th</sup> overall, 12 minutes ahead of the only other women's finisher, Jennifer Taylor of the Cambridge Sports Union.

Team scoring was calculated cross-country style with the first three finishers scoring.  NMC beat CSU 8 points to 19 and Turtletown and BAA followed them with 29 points each.  If scored with top five times (as is currently done) NMC would have won in 6:27:33 with Turtletown moving into second with 6:37:32 followed by CSU in 6:42:16.  Fred Brown and Jock Semple directed the race.  The average time for men was 1:32:39 and for women it was 1:46:10.

Fourth place finisher Peter Crisci reminisced about the "Spartan reception we received...suffice to say the baloney sandwich and stale donuts eaten at the finish were not the only old school aspects of the race".  He recalled "running a hard 15K in Whitman MA the night before and then hitchhiked to NH to meet up with Tom Derderian, Charlotte Lettis, and Mike McCusker.  After a sleepless night in a mosquito infested tent we stumbled out to the race".

A *New England Runner's Magazine* profile of Charlotte Lettis noted she was "In a class by herself  she consistently runs six minutes per mile for road races 6 to 10 miles.  She won the women's New England XC title in 71 and regional title in 72."  In 1972 she "broke off to form her own club the Sugarloaf Mountain AC."  A UMass Junior, she trained "anywhere from 30 to 80 miles per week...on the roads and woods around Amherst."  She notes "but mostly my friends and I run in the hills."  In December 1971 she married Tom Derderian.  They became the first married couple to finish the Mt Washington road race.

Dederian's account of the race in an article titled " *To the top of New England*' includes a view of racing in the pre-running boom days.  Derderian took the lead shortly after the cannon fired and "didn't doubt that I was going to run the 8 miles to the top faster than anyone else in the field. I mean, I always beat Roland Cormier, whose back I haven't seen in years."  He continues, "I remember four years ago, running the dirt road for the first time.  George Waterhouse, weighing in at a half-century, tick-tocked past me...this is not going to happen again.  No old geezers are going past me today." He was running strong despite winning the New England AAU marathon a week ago and the Acton four mile two days ago. After five miles he ran into fog and sleet. "I'm freezing cold, so I try to run harder to warm up. I can't." As Ralph Thomas catches him "There's nothing I can do. I haven't the strength to elbow him into the gray abyss." Derderian finishes fifth and says, "My eyes can't really tell that I'm on top of New England. The mountain tells me, as I sit in the rain, wind and fog and watch gray turn to black and then into runners. A bit of each one has worn off on the mountain." This was the first mention of a cannon being used to start the runners, which is the now traditional method used to send the masses on the way.

## Top 25 Finishers

| Place | Name | Club | Time | Age |
|---|---|---|---|---|
| 1 | Roland Cormier | NMC | 1:09:16 | 31 |
| 2 | Ralph Thomas | Maine | 1:09:37 | |
| 3 | Max White | BAA | 1:10:42 | |
| 4 | Peter Crisci | NMC | 1:10:05 | |
| 5 | Tom Derderian | NMC | 1:11:53 | 22 |
| 6 | Dan Penzer | CSU | 1:12:02 | |
| 7 | Al Neegab | Stratford Spartans | 1:12:13 | |
| 8 | Neil Miner | | 1:12:15 | |
| 9 | Jay Sidman | CSU | 1:12:41 | |
| 10 | Mike McCusker | UMass | 1:14:31 | 18 |
| 11 | John Savoie | Turtletown AC | 1:14:38 | |
| 12 | Jeff Sanborn | Augusta Rec | 1:14:45 | |
| 13 | George Tuthill | CSU | 1:16:08 | |
| 14 | Chris Stockdale | | 1:16:37 | |
| 15 | Leonard Hall | NCAC | 1:16:45 | |
| 16 | John Hurley | NMC | 1:17:06 | |
| 17 | Dan Larson | Strafford Spartans | 1:17:37 | |
| 18 | Walter Chatwick | Turtletown AC | 1:17:40 | |
| 19 | Peter Hanrahan | Keene State | 1:18:13 | |
| 20 | John Connolly | BAA | 1:18:50 | |
| 21 | Ronald Stafford | NCAC | 1:19:24 | |
| 22 | Mike Sudlow | MRFA | 1:19:42 | |
| 23 | George Reed | | 1:19:47 | |
| 24 | Dave Ethridge | Turtletown | 1:19:50 | |
| 25 | Wayne Lucas | | 1:19:52 | |

## Women Finishers

| Place | Name | Club | Time | |
|---|---|---|---|---|
| 1 | Charlotte Lettis | | 1:40:08 | **Course Record** |
| 2 | Jennifer Taylor | CSU | 1:52:13 | |

13<sup>th</sup> Mt Washington Road Race

June 17, 1973
Sunday
183 Finishers

John Cederholm took first over Ralph Thomas and Raymond Currier. This marked the first time that three runners finished under 1:10. Cederholm had finished 34th in 2:26 earlier that spring at the BAA Marathon. He was a member of the BAA from 1972 and went on to become president of the BAA from 1977 - 1980. Among his many accomplishments was a victory at the National 50K championships in 1979 where he set a US record of 2:56:43. Cederholm would go on to finish 23 Mt Washington road races between 1973 and 2003 and place in the top 10 five times. He also showed incredible durability, when in the 2003 Mt Washington Road Race he ran the seventh fastest time for a 60+ runner. In the late Seventies he noted in a *New England Runner's* article, "I joined the BAA, because I wanted to be affiliated with a team. There were good runners on the team, Bill Rodgers and Ed Norris. Jock Semple from BAA and Graham Parnell head of Spartan AC began scouting me for their clubs. I was turned off by their fighting over me."

Other finishers included 1972 winner Roland Cormier who took sixth place. Long-time Mt Washington runner Keith Woodward finished fifth in his debut. Lise Demars was the women's winner, and the only recorded female finisher, in 1:51:46. NMC took the team title with a time of 6:19:26 followed by VTC in 6:31:13 and BAA with 6:49:49.

## Top 25 Finishers

| Place | Name | Club | Time | |
|-------|------|------|------|----|
| 1 | John Cederholm | | 1:08:26 | |
| 2 | Ralph Thomas | ARTC | 1:09:36 | |
| 3 | Ray Currier | TTAC | 1:09:46 | |
| 4 | Max White | BAA | 1:10:56 | |
| 5 | Keith Woodward | | 1:11:17 | FW |
| 6 | Roland Cormier | NMC | 1:11:32 | FW |
| 7 | David Quinn | VTRR | 1:11:57 | |
| 8 | Al Meehan | SSTC | 1:12:42 | |
| 9 | Ed Norris | BAA | 1:13:00 | |
| 10 | Pete Gleason | | 1:13:43 | |
| 11 | George Reed | | 1:13:48 | |
| 12 | MW Hunter | OSC | 1:13:57 | |
| 13 | Don Putnam | | 1:14:30 | |
| 14 | Don Quinn | TTAC | 1:14:36 | |
| 15 | George Tuthill | CSU | 1:14:44 | |
| 16 | Andrea Tchoukarine | | 1:15:00 | |
| 17 | Chet Fortier | NMC | 1:15:38 | |
| 18 | Dave Ethridge | | 1:16:00 | |
| 19 | Phil Ryan | BAA | 1:16:10 | |

| Place | Name | Club | Time | |
|---|---|---|---|---|
| 20 | Gary Burfoot | MSTC | 1:16:24 | |
| 21 | Tom Knatt | NMC | 1:16:49 | |
| 22 | Scott Mackenzie | WP | 1:16:54 | |
| 23 | Chuck Riley | CSU | 1:16:57 | |
| 24 | Rick Chouinard | | 1:17:07 | |
| 25 | Bill Juall | BCTC | 1:17:19 | |
| 79 | Angus Wooten | | 1:30:30 | FW |

## Women Finishers

| 164 | Lise Demars | | 1:51:51 |
|---|---|---|---|

Keith Woodward

27

<h1 align="center">14<sup>th</sup> Mt Washington Road Race</h1>

June 16, 1974
Sunday
210 Finishers

A record 228 starters almost doubled the size of the filed.  Most runners had to find their own way down from the summit, as very few cars were able to make it to the top.  A steady rain fell throughout the day and at the top dense fog and pouring rain hit the finishers.  Most cars were stopped at halfway due to the muddy unsafe condition of the road.  The weather, always a factor, featured 60 mph winds and a wind-chill of 10 degrees.  Three women were listed among the starters however the results do not clearly indicate if any finished.

Ray Currier led past 2 miles with Jim Capezzuto and 1973 winner John Cederholm tucked behind.  Gloria Ratti, one of the race timers noted, "We could not see the complexion of the race, inasmuch as we had to try to get to the top as quickly as possible and get by the stranded and abandoned cars."  Capezzuto took the lead near the halfway and held on.  He noted that he did no special training and that "the wind and muddy road conditions bothered me somewhat, but I was most disappointed of not being able to enjoy the view on my first trip to the summit."  Capezzuto, who would go on to win the 1975 New England AAU cross-country championship, took the victory by 1:30 over Tom Derderian.

Others in the field included 18-year-old Bob Hodge making his first appearance, finishing 14<sup>th</sup> in 1:15:46.  Eleventh place finisher Gaetan Breton has finished 26 times between 1973 and 2004.

Team scores were not given however; NMC and BAA waged a close battle with NMC coming out on top with a time of 6:33:01 to BAA's 6:33:30.  This was the closest team finish to date.

**Top 25 finishers**

| Place | Name | Club | Time | Age | |
|---|---|---|---|---|---|
| 1 | Jim Capezzuto | BAA | 1:07:58 | 20 | |
| 2 | Tom Derderian | SLAC | 1:09:28 | 24 | |
| 3 | Tim Smith | Mohegan | 1:09:42 | | |
| 4 | Ray Currier | | 1:11:23 | 28 | |
| 5 | Ralph Thomas | | 1:11:37 | | |
| 6 | John Cederholm | BAA | 1:12:54 | 31 | FW |
| 7 | Sam Winebaum | NMC | 1:13:24 | | |
| 8 | John Estle | NCAC | 1:13:35 | | |
| 9 | Dean Perry | Bethel Bananas | 1:14:34 | | |
| 10 | Ron Stafford | NCAC | 1:14:44 | | |
| 11 | Gaetan Breton | | 1:14:47 | 26 | |
| 12 | Richard Chauxnard | U of Laval | 1:15:02 | | |
| 13 | Bennett Beech | Washington SC | 1:15:37 | | |
| 14 | Bob Hodge | NMC | 1:15:42 | 18 | FW |
| 15 | Gary Wallace | Triple Cities TC | 1:15:46 | | |

| Place | Name | Club | Time | Age |
|-------|------|------|------|-----|
| 16 | Chet Fortier | NMC | 1:16:13 | |
| 17 | Pierre Cote | | 1:16:14 | |
| 18 | Ken Foote | | 1:16:17 | |
| 19 | John Pfeil | Buffalo TC | 1:16:58 | |
| 20 | Bradon Gothard | Buffalo TC | 1:17:05 | |
| 21 | Clifford Connor | Millrose AA | 1:18:10 | |
| 22 | John Garlepp | Millrose AA | 1:18:39 | |
| 23 | Paul Fahey | Wakefield TC | 1:18:46 | |
| 24 | Jeff White | | 1:19:26 | |
| 25 | Randy Phillips | LRTC | 1:19:29 | |

Jim Capezzuto

29

June 22, 1975
Sunday
276 Finishers

Gary Johnson of Irasburg Vermont led eight men under 70 minutes in clear conditions. Temperatures were in the 80's at the base and 50 at the top.  Johnson, a cross-country skier, narrowly (2 seconds) edged the 1968 time of fellow skier Mike Gallagher to post the second fastest winning time.

Tom Derderian and John Cederholm finished a close fifth and sixth, the pair tied later that year at the Mt Greylock race.  Beating a field, that included Mt Washington champion, Roland Cormier, and top five finisher Peter Crisci.  Other notable finishers included 19-year-old Bob Hodge whose 1:10:19 still stands as the second fastest junior (under age 20) time.  Fourteenth place finisher John Estle had shown his mountain running ability by taking third place at the Killington Hill run earlier that year.  Many of the top finishers at Mt Washington had run the Boston Marathon earlier that year including Derderian (2:19), Rick Bayko (2:21), Ken Mueller (2:22), Ralph Thomas (2:23), Vin Fleming (2:28) and Ray Currier (2:29).

On the ladies' side, Hester Ford Sargent beat 1972 winner Charlotte Lettis by nearly 15 minutes and broke the course record by nearly nine minutes.  She finished 110th in a record field of 276 finishers.  According to the *Union Leader,* "the top women's finisher was Hester Sargent of Boston, the niece of former Mass. Governor Francis Sargent."   Lettis had won the New York Central park mini-marathon, which at the time was the world's largest all-women race, in May. *Hugh Sweeney's* article about the mini-marathon noted, "Charlotte utilized her 59 second 440 speed to pull away to a course record 35:56 and a 7 second victory in the last 200 yards".  Lettis noted on her training, "I run with (husband) Tom on some of his slower workouts, but he runs 120 miles per week and I do 60 so we usually don't train together."

The race was timed by Gloria Ratti, Bob MacVeigh, Bev Whitney, and Fred Brown, Sr. and was also sanctioned by the New England AAU.   Team results were unavailable.  Multiple time Mt Washington finisher George Waterhouse of the North Medford Club died in September. *Yankee runner* noted "His ashes were scattered into the wind from the top of Mt. Washington, a place where he often ran good races to the surprise of his fellow runners."

## Top 25 Finishers

| Place | Name | Team | Time | Age | |
|---|---|---|---|---|---|
| 1 | Gary Johnson | NCAC | 1:06:01 | | |
| 2 | Tom Dowling | BAA | 1:07:15 | | |
| 3 | Vin Fleming | GBTC | 1:07:58 | 21 | |
| 4 | Joe McNulty | | 1:08:29 | | |
| 5 | Tom Derderian | SMAC | 1:08:44 | 26 | |
| 6 | John Cederholm | BAA | 1:09:07 | 32 | **FW** |
| 7 | Malcolm Hunter | LRR | 1:09:20 | | |

| Place | Name | Team | Time | Age | |
|---|---|---|---|---|---|
| 8 | Dan Penza | CSU | 1:09:37 | | |
| 9 | Bob Hodge | LT | 1:10:19 | 19 | FW |
| 10 | Dean Colprit | LRTC | 1:11:08 | | |
| 11 | Sam Winebaum | SS | 1:11:18 | | |
| 12 | Tony Wilcox | SMAC | 1:12:01 | | |
| 13 | Ralph Thomas | | 1:12:18 | | |
| 14 | John Estle | NCAC | 1:12:28 | | |
| 15 | Shaun O'Connor | | 1:12:41 | | |
| 16 | Bob Fowler | | 1:12:50 | | |
| 17 | Tom Atherton | TTAC | 1:13:06 | | |
| 18 | Gaetan Breton | CAPS | 1:13:29 | | |
| 19 | Phil Kalar | SS | 1:13:41 | | |
| 20 | Gil Kemp | MAA | 1:13:51 | | |
| 21 | Brian Reinhold | BRU | 1:14:11 | 21 | |
| 22 | Larry Reed | TTAC | 1:14:17 | | |
| 23 | Wayne Lamothe | NMC | 1:14:23 | | |
| 24 | Bennett Beach | | 1:14:27 | | |
| 25 | John Pfeil | LAC | 1:14:57 | | |

## Women

| Place | Name | Team | Time | Age |
|---|---|---|---|---|
| 110 | Hester Sargent | | 1:31:13 **Course Record** | |
| 202 | Charlotte Lettis | | 1:46:40 | FW |
| 242 | Carol Aucoin | | 2:03:54 | |

Lettis in the 1976 Olympic Trials 1500

# 16<sup>th</sup> Mt Washington Road Race

June 27, 1976
Sunday
225 Finishers


Conditions for the race were 80 degrees at the base and 50 at the summit and the race director noted, "The road was the best I have ever seen it, with a new stretch of blacktop." Two hundred forty eight runners took the starters call, with Bob Hodge gaining his first victory. Hodge's time was the second fastest, behind only Fred Norris.  Hodge also tied as the youngest winner of the race at age 20.

Hodge and third place finisher Vin Fleming had dueled earlier that year in the National AAU 30K championships where they finished seventh and eight in 1:34:03 to 1:34:09 respectively.  Bill Rodgers won the race in a World record time of 1:29:04.

Ellie Mendonca representing the CSU won the ladies race finishing 119<sup>th</sup> overall in 1:35:05.  The 5'5" 120 lb. originally from Brazil noted in a *New England Runner Magazine* article "my mileage is from 60 to 75 or more per week."  She "received an MS in Physical Education and has been involved in athletics for a long period of time."  She had been "running since 1972 and competitively since 1975."  The average time for women toped 1:50 with a 1:50:16 average for women finishers.

Team scoring had Hodge leading the Greater Boston Track Club over the North Country Athletic Club and BAA with a score of 10 points to 17 and 26 respectively.  If scored by top five finisher on time (as is done now) the NCAC would prevail with a fine 6:08:41 followed by the BAA (6:30:00) and NMC (6:47:19).

Tenth place finisher Peter Cresci won the Mt Greylock race later that year.  John Cederholm continued to finish in the top ten with a ninth place finish.   A record eight men finished under 1:10.


## Top 25 Finishers

| Place | Name | Club | Time | Age | |
|---|---|---|---|---|---|
| 1 | Robert Hodge | GBTC | 1:05:31 | 20 | |
| 2 | Norman Patenaude | Laurentian U TC | 1:07:29 | | |
| 3 | Vin Fleming | GBTC | 1:07:56 | 22 | |
| 4 | Gary Johnson | NCAC | 1:08:54 | | FW |
| 5 | Keith Woodward | NCAC | 1:10:11 | 25 | FW |
| 6 | Tony Wilcox | SMAC | 1:10:18 | | |
| 7 | Tom Dowling | BAA | 1:10:36 | | |
| 8 | Charles Riley | GBTC | 1:11:29 | | |
| 9 | John Cederholm | BAA | 1:11:52 | 33 | FW |
| 10 | Peter Cresci | SMAC | 1:12:12 | | |
| 11 | John Heslin | | 1:12:33 | | |

| Place | Name | Club | Time | Age | |
|---|---|---|---|---|---|
| 12 | Will Winebaum | | 1:12:45 | | |
| 13 | Bill Norris | OTC | 1:13:01 | | |
| 14 | Joe McNulty | NCAC | 1:13:52 | | |
| 15 | Paul Thompson | NMC | 1:14:57 | | |
| 16 | Ken Dawson | BAA | 1:15:15 | | |
| 17 | M Hunter | Larigmac RR | 1:15:54 | | |
| 18 | John Brown | | 1:16:17 | | |
| 19 | Robert Lux | | 1:16:34 | | |
| 20 | Seth Bergman | Plausted Harriers | 1:17:11 | | |
| 21 | John Estle | NCAC | 1:17:22 | | |
| 22 | Mark Berman | | 1:17:30 | 18 | |
| 23 | Robert Treadwell | | 1:17:48 | | |
| 24 | Gaetan Breton | CAPS | 1:17:38 | 28 | |
| 25 | Martin Kittell | Cenleona RC | 1:18:01 | | |
| 77 | Jim Capezzuto | BAA | 1:29:03 | | FW |

## Women Finishers

| Place | Name | Club | Time | Age |
|---|---|---|---|---|
| 119 | Ellenora Mendonca | CSU | 1:35:05 | |
| 222 | Sarah Dumas | CSU | 1:59:39 | |

Hodge (left) & Mendonca (right)

17<sup>th</sup> Mt Washington Road Race

June 19, 1977
Sunday
256 Finishers

Bob Hodge won again, this time in a course record as he sneaked under the old record of 64:57 by Fred Norris in 1962.   Hodge beat Ray Currier by over three minutes as he led six men under 1:10.  *Yankee Runner* had only the top 10 listed and lamented that "unfortunately the people with the complete results have decided since the Yankee Runner position regarding the AAU does not agree with their own, that Yankee Runner will no longer receive race results that they are responsible for."

Ellen Mendonca won for the second straight year, finishing 112<sup>th</sup> overall.  She won by more than 12 minutes over Lisa Powers as 11 women finished.   Earlier in the year Mendonca placed ninth at the Bonnie Bell 10K for women in 36:59 and also got seventh at the BAA Marathon in 2:52:49. Lisa Powers lead the Seacoast team to the first verifiable team title in 5:26:16.  It is not recorded whether women's team scoring was done.  Jane Goodman became the first woman to be recorded in the 40+ age group.

Team results had North Country AC (NCAC) winning with 12 points over the BAA (24 points) and NMC (33 points).  The NCAC's combined time of 5:59:28 represents the first time a team ran under six hours and still ranks in the top 25 all time.  The BAA was second with 6:20:31.

The average time for men was 1:32:56 and for women it was 1:51:51.  This was the largest gap recorded between men and women's average finishing time.

## Top 25 Finishers

| Place | Name | Club | Time | Age | |
|---|---|---|---|---|---|
| 1 | Bob Hodge | GBTC | 1:04:44 | 21 | Course Record |
| 2 | Ray Currier | BAA | 1:07:51 | 33 | |
| 3 | Keith Woodward | NCAC | 1:08:15 | 26 | FW |
| 4 | Joseph McNulty | NCAC | 1:08:28 | | |
| 5 | James Crawford | NYAC | 1:08:54 | | |
| 6 | Larry Olsen | NMC | 1:09:33 | | |
| 7 | Ed Sandifer | SMAC | 1:10:30 | | |
| 8 | Henry Phelan | Keene State | 1:11:52 | | |
| 9 | Mark Berman | | 1:12:11 | 19 | |
| 10 | Joseph Doran | NCAC | 1:13:02 | 28 | |
| 11 | Ken Dawson | BAA | 1:13:40 | | |
| 12 | Sean Cummings | Keene State | 1:13:46 | | |
| 13 | Chris Stockdale | | 1:14:02 | | |
| 14 | Breton Gaetan | CAPS | 1:14:10 | 29 | |
| 15 | Martin Kittell | Cenleona RC | 1:14:13 | | |
| 16 | James Smith | NCAC | 1:14:42 | | |

| Place | Name | Club | Time | Age | |
|---|---|---|---|---|---|
| 17 | John Estle | NCAC | 1:15:01 | | |
| 18 | Peter Hanrahan | NMC | 1:15:23 | | |
| 19 | Robert Wilson | CSU | 1:15:36 | | |
| 20 | Yvan Bolduc | CAPS | 1:15:42 | | |
| 21 | Joseph Noel | ECSC | 1:15:50 | | |
| 22 | Robert Teschek | BAA | 1:15:52 | 31 | |
| 23 | Dana Poole | TTAC | 1:16:06 | 18 | |
| 24 | David Duval | NMC | 1:16:48 | | |
| 25 | John Fahey | NMC | 1:17:05 | | |

**Women Finishers**

| Place | Name | Club | Time | Age | |
|---|---|---|---|---|---|
| 1 | Ellen Mendonca | CSU | 1:30:05 | | Course record |
| 2 | Lisa Powers | Seacoast | 1:42:44 | | |
| 3 | Jane Goodman | | 1:45:13 | 42 | Age Group record |
| 4 | Paula Davenport | Seacoast | 1:49:20 | | |
| 5 | Jessica Brandt | Lucky TC | 1:49:35 | | |
| 6 | Patricia Nice | CSU | 1:49:39 | | |
| 7 | Nancy Laferriere | | 1:54:09 | | |
| 8 | Dorothy Bergman | | 1:55:35 | 45 | |
| 9 | Judy McCrone | Seacoast | 1:54:12 | | |
| 10 | Katherine Kirsch | Seacoast | 1:57:19 | | |
| 11 | Linda Binney | | 2:00:11 | | |

Runner-up Lisa Power (left) and Sugarloaf runners leading a pack (right)

June 18, 1978
Sunday
363 Finishers

Bob Hodge won his third straight with another course record as he beat Keith Woodward of the NCAC by over two minutes.  Woodward would eventually finish an incredible 15 times in the top 10 from 1973-1991.  The weather was cloudy and windy as 386 started and a record 363 finished.  *Fred Brown* notes in his race recap regarding finisher certificates, "if you didn't receive yours, contact me at races or at home and you will get it.  Just what you need in your old age to prove you were not always helpless."

Hodge led from the start and stated in *Yankee Runner,* "Usually at the halfway house the wind picks up and blows you around, but it wasn't bad this time."  *Fred Brown* wrote "A new record for Hodges *(sic)*.  Who will be the first to break an hour?"

Team scoring had NCAC and GBTC tied with 17 points followed closely by the BAA with 19 and SMAC with 27.  The result was a close battle of four teams with 10 minutes, using the top five on time, NCAC ran 6:09:59, GBTC 6:14:07, SMA 6:16:52 and BAA 6:19:16.

Ellie Mendonca won her third straight in a course record of 1:28:39 for 108<sup>th</sup> overall.  Karen Dunn and Linda Schneider closely followed her.  Patricia Robinson (1:37:03) was highlighted in *New England Running Magazine.*  She had finished 39<sup>th</sup> at the 1978 BAA marathon in 3:05:45.  She noted "my mileage varies between 65 and 89 miles for 6 weeks before Boston.  My average training runs are 6 to 12 miles at 7 – 7:45 pace."  Robinson beat 1977's runner-up Lisa Powers by just over a minute.

Although no official team results were given for women, the CSU team dominated the women's scoring with a time of 4:54:21 to SSTC's 5:18:37.

The first 200 finishers got certificates and according to an anonymous account in *Yankee Runner,* everyone got "one sandwich (ham/cheese or egg salad) and one Coke back at the base" and "the sandwiches were like this years' stew at Boston…tasted awful and didn't fill you up.  Does Jock handle the cooking too?"  *Fred Brown* noted the problems faced with timing the event, "As usual we had runners crossing the finish line again after finishing.  My mistake was in yelling at them 'are you finishing' which they likely took to mean have you finished, hence when they said yes they got recorded again."

**Top 25 Finishers**

| Place | Name | Club | Time | Age | |
|---|---|---|---|---|---|
| 1 | Robert Hodge | GBTC | 1:04:13 | 22 | **Course Record** |
| 2 | Keith Woodward | NCAC | 1:06:50 | 27 | **FW** |
| 3 | Brian Reinhold | | 1:07:48 | 24 | |
| 4 | Walt Chadwick | BAA | 1:08:55 | | |

| Place | Name | Club | Time | Age | |
|---|---|---|---|---|---|
| 5 | Martin Kittell | Onteora | 1:09:38 | | |
| 6 | John Cederholm | BAA | 1:09:50 | 35 | FW |
| 7 | Tony Wilcox | SMAC | 1:10:16 | | |
| 8 | David Ezersky | GBTC | 1:10:55 | 21 | |
| 9 | John Savoie | | 1:11:08 | | |
| 10 | William Holland | | 1:11:34 | | |
| 11 | Peter Gamble | | 1:11:53 | | |
| 12 | Hank Pfeifle | NCAC | 1:12:19 | 26 | |
| 13 | Joe Doran | NCAC | 1:12:33 | 29 | |
| 14 | Jay Smith | | 1:12:46 | | |
| 15 | Samuel Winebaum | | 1:12:48 | | |
| 16 | David Landry | Onteora | 1:13:16 | | |
| 17 | Howie Bean | | 1:13:43 | | |
| 18 | Ed Sandifer | SMAC | 1:13:51 | | |
| 19 | Albert Fereshetian | TTAC | 1:13:59 | | |
| 20 | Mark Berman | | 1:14:23 | 20 | |
| 21 | James Durkin | GBTC | 1:14:30 | | |
| 22 | Dana Poole | | 1:14:33 | | |
| 23 | John Chandler | | 1:15:07 | | |
| 24 | Jeff Sanborn | | 1:15:20 | | |
| 25 | Ed Burgess | | 1:15:33 | | |

**Top 10 Women**

**Note:** Generally women were not recorded separately from men in the results. I was unable to determine from the information if certain runners were in fact female finishers and noted them with a question mark.

| Place | Name | Club | Time | |
|---|---|---|---|---|
| 1 | Ellie Mendonca | CSU | 1:28:39 | **Course Record** |
| 2 | Karen Dunn | | 1:29:45 | |
| 3 | Linda Schneider | | 1:32:57 | |
| 4 | Pat Carroll    ? | | 1:35:08 | |
| 5 | Patricia Robinson | CSU | 1:37:03 | |
| 6 | Lisa Powers | SSTC | 1:38:23 | |
| 7 | Joan Tomasi | Vermont RR | 1:39:35 | |
| 8 | B R Stepp    ? | | 1:41:56 | |
| 9 | Barbara Regan | State College | 1:42:56 | |
| 10 | Dale Quinlan  ? | | 1:46:28 | |
| 11 | R Gonzales    ? | YMCA | 1:48:27 | |
| 12 | Judith Paine | CSU | 1:48:39 | |
| 13 | Cheryl Newhouse | SSTC | 1:50:02 | |
| 14 | Judith McCrone | SSTC | 1:50:12 | |

37

<u>Teams</u>

| Name | Place | Points |
| --- | --- | --- |
| North Country AC | 2-7-8 | 17 points |
| Greater Boston TC | 1-6-10 | 17 points |
| Boston AA | 3-4-12 | 19 points |
| Sugarloaf Mt AC | 5-9-13 | 27 points |
| No. Medford Club | 11-14-15 | 40 points |
| Cambridge Sports Union | 16-17-18 | 51 points |

19<sup>th</sup> Mt Washington Road Race

June 17, 1979
Sunday Noon
403 Finishers

Bob Hodge, who finished third earlier in the year at the BAA marathon (2:12), won a record tying fourth straight as he set his third course record.  Hodge beat future Olympian Peter Pfitzinger (Pfitz) by just over two minutes as Pfitzinger ran the fastest non-winning time.  A record 11 runners finished under 1:10.

There was a drenching downpour just before the start, but conditions were good during the race.  Hodge blazed to the halfway house in 28:15 with Pfitz next in 29:40 followed by Phelan and Capezzuto in 30:00.  Cross-country skier Don Nelson overtook the 1974 winner, Capezzuto, during the second half of the race.  Hodge was regarded with awe in *New England Running Magazine* "Just after crossing the finish line Bobby's pulse rate was 126.  'Boy, I must be getting out of shape' he averred in all seriousness."

The ladies' race was just as excellent as cross-country ski ace Martha Rockwell cracked the top 50 overall in 1:19:14.  Her time broke the course record by nearly 10 minutes.  Rockwell dominated the field, beating CSU's Patricia Robinson by nearly 13 minutes.  *New England Running* magazine noted, "Mt Washington was only Martha's second race, and she does not as yet train on a regular basis."  Rockwell was on the US Olympic team in 1972 and 1976 and won 18 National Championships in Nordic skiing

Five hundred and four runners entered including 117 post entries, 427 started with 403 finishing.  *Fred Brown* said "national Geographic had a man covering the event so maybe in the future they will have an article on it."  The women's field made up a record 12.41% of finishers, the first time they topped ten percent.

Team scoring was not listed however; the GBTC lead by Hodge and Pfitz ran 5:35:50 beating the BAA by 12 minutes.  This was the first time two clubs broke six hours.  CSU scored a victory for the women with a 5:15:18 to the Manchester Y's 5:45:40

John Cederholm finished 11<sup>th</sup>, breaking 1:10.  He would, later in the year, win the 50,000-meter National championships in 2:56:43, a national record.  Seventeen year-old Mike Casner ran his first Mt Washington in 1:25:28.  He would go on to finish 14 times in the top ten from 1984 through 2001.  Long time Mt Washington runner Fred Ross organized a race up Mt Equinox, which would become a favorite tune-up for runners preparing for Mt Washington.  It was first run on May 20, 1979, and was won that year by Keith Woodward who took the 5.25 mile 3,150 foot climb by eight seconds over John Arthur.

## Top 25 Finishers

| Place | Name | Club | Time | Age | |
|---|---|---|---|---|---|
| 1 | Robert Hodge | GBTC | 1:02:08 | 23 | Course Record |
| 2 | Peter Pfitzinger | GBTC | 1:04:12 | 21 | |
| 3 | Henry Phelan | BAA | 1:05:03 | | |
| 4 | Donald Nelson | Strafford AA | 1:06:29 | | |
| 5 | James Capezzuto | BAA | 1:06:58 | 25 | FW |
| 6 | Tom Dowling | BAA | 1:07:10 | | |
| 7 | Mark Berman | | 1:07:39 | 21 | |
| 8 | Brian Reinhold | | 1:08:13 | 25 | |
| 9 | Duncan Scott | GBTC | 1:08:42 | | |
| 10 | Tom Derderian | GBTC | 1:09:22 | 29 | |
| 11 | John Cederholm | BAA | 1:09:44 | 36 | FW |
| 12 | Jim Fredericks | Craftsbury | 1:11:04 | | |
| 13 | Richard Bonner | GBTC | 1:11:25 | | |
| 14 | Brad Hurst | GBTC | 1:11:29 | 25 | |
| 15 | Dave Ezersky | GBTC | 1:11:35 | 22 | |
| 16 | Stephen Lavorgna | | 1:11:45 | | |
| 17 | Neil Blayney | NZL | 1:11:49 | | |
| 18 | Edward Strabel | N Carolina TC | 1:12:01 | | |
| 19 | Keith Woodward | NCAC | 1:12:30 | 28 | FW |
| 20 | Leonard Hall | NCAC | 1:12:31 | | |
| 21 | Peter Cruise | SMAC | 1:13:05 | | |
| 22 | John Estle | NCAC | 1:13:28 | | |
| 23 | Chuck Riley | GBTC | 1:13:51 | | |
| 24 | Joseph Doran | NCAC | 1:14:19 | 30 | |
| 25 | William Holland | | 1:14:25 | | |

## Top 10 Women

| Place | Name | Club | Time | Age | |
|---|---|---|---|---|---|
| 1 | Martha Rockwell | | 1:19:14 | 35 | Record |
| 2 | Patricia Robinson | CSU | 1:32:00 | 26 | |
| 3 | Ruby Weiner | Wolfpack | 1:35:03 | | |
| 4 | Liz Carey | NCAC | 1:36:17 | | |
| 5 | Chris Kelley   ? | | 1:36:50 | | |
| 6 | Sue Medaglia | | 1:37:07 | | |
| 7 | Laurie Munson | | 1:37:41 | | |
| 8 | Chris Anderson  ? | | 1:38:30 | | |

| Place | Name | Club | Time | Age |
|-------|------|------|------|-----|
| 9 | Abbi Fisher | US Ski Team | 1:39:08 | |
| 10 | Dale Norton  ? | | 1:41:06 | |
| 11 | Linda Holton | | 1:41:11 | |
| 12 | Raphael Linehan | Strafford AA | 1:41:14 | |
| 13 | Blanche Paine NMC | | 1:41:44 | |

A Sugarloaf AC finisher (left) and Hodge duels with Randy Thomas a week before Mt Washington (Right)

20<sup>th</sup> Mt Washington Road Race

June 15, 1980
Sunday Noon
471 Finishers

Bob Hodge continued his streak with a record fifth consecutive victory. Durham's Gary Crossan pressed him in the early going. The field was again the largest to date with over 500 starters and 471 finishers were recorded. It was 78 degrees at the base and 35 degrees with wind and drizzle at the finish. Hodge was again just over 28 minutes at the halfway house, but was unable to improve on his 1:02:08 course record of the previous year. He now held the four fastest times ever as he led a record 12 runners under 1:10. Hodge was in excellent form as displayed earlier in the year when he set an American Record for 15 Kilometers in Stanford CA. He ran 44:00.2 to beat Gary Tuttle's record by 53 seconds.

Cathy Hodgdon of Franklin NH and a member of the UNH track team took the women's race in 1:26:50. Liz Cunningham and Leslie Thompson followed close behind as the top three broke 1:30. Thompson's time remains (as of 2005) the third fastest for a junior runner (under the age of 20). Her time would hold up as the record for another 19 years.

Team scoring was not listed however, if the combined times of the top five runners was used, BAA would have edged GBTC 5:50:41 to 5:51:52. This remains one of the closest team finishes ever, and as one of only four times when two teams broke six hours (1979, 1999, 2005).

Bill McNulty writing in *Frontrunner* said, "You've got to like hill work for this one. You'll also need good concentration. It would help if you are in your best marathon shape, if you plan on running all the way and to finish well." He also noted, "The year you run hard all the way, you will win the race over Mt Washington no matter what time or place you finish."

Jock Semple directed the race and complete results were printed in *New England Running* courtesy of Fred Brown Sr., the NEAC Long Distance running chairman. Fred Ross made a deal with a sports printer to produce numbers for the race. He borrowed a bumper sticker from Doug Philbrick (the Auto road manager) to get "Mt Washington" on the numbers.

**Top 25 Finishers**

| Place | Name | Team | Time | |
|---|---|---|---|---|
| 1 | Robert Hodge | GBTC | 1:04:29 | |
| 2 | Gary Crossan | CTAC | 1:05:27 | FW |
| 3 | Brian Reinhold | | 1:06:02 | |
| 4 | David Ezersky | GBTC | 1:06:08 | |
| 5 | Mark Berman | BAA | 1:06:29 | |
| 6 | Hank Pfeifle | TTAC | 1:07:11 | |
| 7 | Keith Woodward | GMAC | 1:07:52 | FW |
| 8 | Tom Dowling | BAA | 1:08:17 | |
| 9 | Duncan McLena | | 1:08:36 | |

| Place | Name | Team | Time | |
|---|---|---|---|---|
| 10 | Gary Johnson | | 1:08:40 | FW |
| 11 | Steve Lavorgna | BAA | 1:09:26 | |
| 12 | John Cederholm | BAA | 1:09:50 | FW |
| 13 | J Smith | | 1:10:19 | |
| 14 | Steven Bratt | CSU | 1:11:10 | |
| 15 | Martin Kittell | ORC | 1:11:16 | |
| 16 | Jim Fredericks | CRC | 1:11:19 | |
| 17 | Kirk Siegel | DOC | 1:12:56 | |
| 18 | Chuck Riley | GBTC | 1:13:04 | |
| 19 | Andy Halpin | UH | 1:13:33 | |
| 20 | John Darsinos | GBTC | 1:13:41 | |
| 21 | Ray Nelson | JWAC | 1:14:11 | |
| 22 | Donald Powers | GCS | 1:14:18 | |
| 23 | Dana Poole | | 1:14:23 | |
| 24 | Brad Hurst | GBTC | 1:14:30 | |
| 25 | Charles Moeser | GRC | 1:14:33 | |
| 198 | Angus Wooten | | 1:35:41 | FW |

## Top Women

| Place | Name | Team | Time | Age |
|---|---|---|---|---|
| 1 | Catherine Hodgdon | TTAC | 1:26:44 | 21 |
| 2 | Liz Cunningham | BAA | 1:29:41 | |
| 3 | Leslie Thompson | CRC | 1:29:57 | 16 |
| 4 | D Hochschartner | ? | 1:31:23 | |
| 5 | Pat Robinson | | 1:33:18 | 27 |
| 6 | P Papadopoulos | ? | 1:33:39 | |
| 7 | Roberta Abeyta | | 1:36:12 | |
| 8 | C Anderson | ? | 1:36:16 | |
| 9 | Dale Norton | ? | 1:37:17 | |
| 10 | Carol Bickford | | 1:37:27 | |
| 11 | Abby Spring | | 1:37:30 | |
| 12 | Cary Grinold | | 1:37:59 | |
| 13 | Chris Cherella | ? | 1:39:27 | |
| 14 | R McCready | ? | 1:39:45 | |
| 15 | Aean Donovan | ? | 1:40:47 | |
| 16 | J Cunningham | ? | 1:40:48 | |
| 17 | Misha Kirk | ? | 1:41:00 | |
| 18 | Marcia Dowling | | 1:42:45 | |

<h1 style="text-align:center">21<sup>st</sup> Mt Washington Road Race</h1>

June 14, 1981
Sunday
500 Finishers


Not much information was available from the 1981 race.  Almost 700 registered for the 21<sup>st</sup> running.  Second place finisher from 1980, Gary Crossan, took the victory and became only the second runner under 1:03.   Crossan led a record tying 12 runners under 1:10.  Three of the top five (Crossan, Ezersky, and Capezzuto) were former UNH runners, all represented the BAA.


Ezersky took the early lead in 80-degree temperatures.  Crossan overtook him in the early miles and led for most of the race.  Crossan noted in the *Union Leader* that the hardest part for him was the early going.  "You just have to get your mind used to the fact that you're going to be running uphill for the next hour."


Cathy Hodgdon of Franklin, NH took the win in 1:22:57 over Marge Podgajny of Pittsburgh PA.  Hodgdon took three minutes off her winning time from 1980 and said, "It's painful every time, especially the first $7\frac{3}{4}$ miles."  She led from the start to the finish where it was 40 degrees.  In *John Lorway's* article on the race she said, "I'm glad I didn't know (how close Podgajny was)".  She continued, "I knew what to expect.  I figured I'd just take the pain."


Crossan noted in the same article, "I think maybe someone can run under 60 minutes in the next few years." and "Maybe Hodge has been taking it easy."  Lorway longed for the days when Mt Washington wasn't the "in thing to do" saying "Everybody and his mother runs it now...when I ran it there were 50 of us".


The Podgajny's (Steve 11<sup>th</sup> place and Marjorie second place) became the fastest recorded husband/wife team with a combined time of 2:33:35.  Ronald Johnston (112<sup>th</sup> place) began his streak at Mt Washington (25 as of 2005).  He started running in 1981 and Mt Washington was his first race!  Johnston told *New England Runner,* "John (Jock) Semple was the director, Douglas A. Philbrook was the Race Chairman, and Rose B. Cordanelli was the Judge.  I still have my finisher's certificate in mint condition.  It was my very first race of any kind.  I was running about five miles per week, downhill skiing like a nut including Tuckerman's Ravine, and doing some serious hiking.  Always looking for a challenge, someone at the Pinkham Lodge mentioned after a day of skiing Tuck's, "You need to run up the mountain.  They have a race in June."  So I made up a fake AAU number and registered for the race.  I was worried sick because Bob Brown of the Rochester Runners' Club told me some horror stories about the intense incline and weather.  I had on a fanny pack, gloves, jacket, etc.  Now 25 years later, I just run up the mountain in the bare minimum...and turn immediately to run back down the mountain (broke 60 minutes for the downhill run 2 years ago).  I will say this however..."Running Mt. Washington is tougher than racing a marathon.  It hurts from the fourth minute until you stop at the top.  Furthermore, racing the mountain does not get any easier with each year!"

Although team results were not printed, the BAA placed four in the top ten to take the team title.  All of the top four finishers had been in the top five in the previous year.  The BAA's combined time of 5:31:07 would remain the team record for another 12 years.

 For the first time (in print), the event was called the "Race to the Clouds."  The race was listed in a New England race schedule as an 8 mile run with a 1 PM start time.  The entry fee was $3, with a post entry fee of $6 after June 7.  John D. Semple was listed as the race contact.

**All Available results**

| Place | Name | Team | Time | Age | |
|---|---|---|---|---|---|
| 1 | Gary Crossan | BAA | 1:02:51 | 23 | |
| 2 | Mark Berman | BAA | 1:03:49 | 23 | |
| 3 | David Ezersky | GBTC | 1:04:27 | 24 | |
| 4 | Brian Reinhold | | 1:05:12 | 27 | |
| 5 | Jim Capezzuto | BAA | 1:06:20 | 27 | **FW** |
| 6 | Keith Woodward | NCAC | 1:06:45 | 32 | **FW** |
| 7 | Tom Derderian | GBTC | 1:07:52 | 34 | |
| 8 | Brian Taylor | | 1:08:02 | 24 | |
| 9 | Jay Smith | BAA | 1:08:44 | 24 | |
| 10 | Jose Solurzano | | 1:08:47 | | |
| 11 | Steve Podgajny | | 1:08:52 | | |
| 12 | Pete Foley | | 1:09:12 | | |
| 13 | Unknown | | 1:09:?? | | |
| 14 | Len Hall | NCAC | 1:09:52 | 28 | |

**Women**

| Place | Name | Team | Time | Age |
|---|---|---|---|---|
| 1 | Cathy Hodgdon | | 1:22:57 | 22 |
| 2 | Marjorie Podgajny | | 1:23:43 | 28 |
| 3 | Karen Dunn | | 1:25:38 | |

### 22<sup>nd</sup> Mt Washington Road Race

June 13, 1982
Sunday, 11:00 AM
552 Finishers
The big news in 1982 was a new course record and the race management changing hands.  Bob Teschek took over as the race director and also finished a respectable 32nd place.   Gary Crossan ran 1:01:40 to become the first to break 62 minutes.  J Smith followed four minutes behind and led five more runners under 1:10 despite 29-degree temperatures and 30 mph winds at the summit.  The men's average finishing time crept to 1:40:28, the first time it was over 1:40.  The average age for a male finisher was 33.08 years.

Catherine Hodgdon won with an excellent 1:22:40.  Patti Sherry was second just under three minutes back.  The average age for a female finisher was 29.5 years.  The age gap between men and women would typically be three to four years.

For the first time, ages were listed in the results and teams were scored by used the best times of each club's top five finishers.  BAA was the top team with a very fast 5:40:47 to CSU's 6:01:26.  Teams were required to declare in advance, presenting a list to the race organizers.

Major sponsors for the RRCA-sanctioned event included Kronenburg beer, Fitness Resources, and the Auto Road management.  The race entry fee was $4 ($6 post) and the start time was moved to 11:00.  The race was limited to 600 and post race included "soft drinks, light snacks, and beer from Europe's number one bottle of beer."  Bowls were awarded to the top ten, first women, and first 40+, and top two teams.  Medals were given for 11-30th place, the second/third woman, and second/third in the 40+ age group.  All finishers received a certificate.

Bill Morse of the Highland City Striders began a 22 year streak.  He has worn the same Nike Spiridon shoes every year.  He uses them for just this one race a year and has had to re-glue the soles in the last few years.  He said "these shoes are lighter than air and only have a couple of hundred miles on them."

## Top 25 Finishers

| Place | Name | Team | Time | Age | |
|---|---|---|---|---|---|
| 1 | Gary Crossan | BAA | 1:01:40 | 24 | **Course Record** |
| 2 | J Smith | BAA | 1:05:46 | 23 | |
| 3 | G Montero | CSU | 1:06:27 | 28 | |
| 4 | Don Nielsen | | 1:07:11 | 30 | |
| 5 | Keith Woodward | NCAC | 1:07:37 | 31 | **FW** |
| 6 | Brian Taylor | | 1:07:46 | 23 | |
| 7 | Mark Berman | BAA | 1:08:05 | 24 | |
| 8 | Len Hall | NCAC | 1:10:10 | 28 | |
| 9 | Mark Asaro | | 1:10:48 | 26 | |
| 10 | Todd Webber | CSU | 1:11:10 | 26 | |
| 11 | Tom Derderian | GBTC | 1:12:11 | 33 | |

| Place | Name | Team | Time | Age | |
|---|---|---|---|---|---|
| 12 | Robert Wilson | BAA | 1:12:22 | 25 | |
| 13 | Mark Bashour | | 1:12:44 | 22 | |
| 14 | John Cederholm | BAA | 1:12:54 | 39 | FW |
| 15 | Tim Reever | | 1:13:03 | 24 | |
| 16 | Peter Stipe | | 1:13:13 | 35 | |
| 17 | Don Tromblay | | 1:13:32 | 29 | |
| 18 | Greg Nelson | | 1:13:39 | 34 | |
| 19 | Mike Slavin | | 1:14:08 | 22 | |
| 20 | Henry Finch | CSU | 1:14:18 | 33 | |
| 21 | Bernard Rate | CSU | 1:14:32 | 30 | |
| 22 | Thomas Gilligan | | 1:14:47 | 32 | |
| 23 | Robert Haydock | CSU | 1:14:59 | 29 | |
| 24 | Dale Rogers | | 1:15:37 | 34 | |
| 25 | James Doucett | CSU | 1:16:30 | 28 | |

## Top 10 Women

| Place | Name | Team | Time | Age |
|---|---|---|---|---|
| 1 | Catherine Hodgdon | | 1:22:40 | 23 |
| 2 | Patti Sherry | | 1:25:39 | 27 |
| 3 | Karen Henry | DOC | 1:33:06 | 25 |
| 4 | Diana Shannon | | 1:34:35 | 19 |
| 5 | Sherry Haydock | CSU | 1:35:16 | 28 |
| 6 | Lisa Dollman | | 1:36:29 | 26 |
| 7 | Elizabeth Emmons | | 1:37:07 | 25 |
| 8 | Pat Robinson | | 1:38:35 | 29 |
| 9 | Sharon O'Hagan | | 1:38:11 | 34 |
| 10 | Terry Hersh | | 1:38:27 | 29 |

## 5 Year age groups

| Place | Name | Club | Time | Age | Category |
|---|---|---|---|---|---|
| 4 | Diana Shannon | | 1:34:35 | 19 | Under 20 |
| 1 | Catherine Hodgdon | | 1:22:40 | 23 | 20-24 |
| 9 | Sharon O'Hagan | | 1:38:11 | 34 | 30-34 |
| 27 | Priscilla Reinerston | | 1:50:15 | 39 | 35-39 |
| 28 | Helen Hamilton | | 1:50:15 | 51 | 50+ |
| | | | | | |
| 37 | Gary Stanhope | | 1:19:18 | 17 | Under 20 |
| 1 | Gary Crossan | BAA | 1:01:40 | 24 | 20-24 |
| 3 | G Montero | CSU | 1:06:27 | 28 | 25-29 |
| 4 | Don Nielsen | | 1:07:11 | 30 | 30-34 |
| 14 | John Cederholm | BAA | 1:12:54 | 39 | 35-39 |
| 55 | Robert Wright Jr. | | 1:22:24 | 42 | 40-44 |

46

| Place | Name | Club | Time | Age | Category |
|---|---|---|---|---|---|
| 63 | Bob Landry | | 1:24:33 | 45 | 45-49 |
| 90 | Dana Sumner | | 1:28:03 | 50 | 50-54 |
| 314 | Dick Blackman | | 1:45:49 | 58 | 55-59 |
| 193 | Carlton Mendell | | 1:36:19 | 60 | 60-64 |
| 398 | Fred Hackett | | 1:51:24 | 65 | 65+ |

## 23rd Mt Washington Road Race

06-19-1983
Sunday
641 Finishers

With past champion Gary Crossan not competing, the pre-race favorites included second place finisher Jay Smith and perennial top finisher Keith Woodward. A few weeks before the Mt Washington race, Smith, Woodward, and Matt Cull dueled at the Equinox Mountain race in Vermont. Smith prevailed with Woodward second and newcomer Cull close behind. On the ladies' side, Anna Sonnerup looked to be the favorite as she won at Equinox by three minutes over Leslie Thompson.

*Boston Running News* noted, "Last year it was much too cold, this year it was much too hot, but such are the vagaries of scaling the grandest peak east of the Rockies and north of the Great Smokies".

Woodward's persistence finally paid off as he reached the summit first with a 35 second win over Matthew Cull, with Smith in fourth a little over a minute back. Leonard Hall took third 23 seconds up on Smith.

*New England Runner*, in a later profile of Keith Woodward, called Woodward "Vermont's true road warrior." In 1980 he was forced to cut back his mileage due to an Achilles injury. "It really did hurt my mileage, every time I would get it back up there, I would aggravate the injury. I started doing more cross country skiing because it didn't take such a toll on my body." Woodward's personal records ranged from 4:19 for the mile to 30:20 for the 10K and 2:29 for the marathon.

Sonnerup, a cross country skier at Dartmouth College took a three-minute victory over Terry Hersh. Her time was the second fastest, behind only Martha Rockwell's 1:19:14 course record from 1979. Sonnerup led a record five women under 1:30. The average time for a women finisher was 1:49:31, just ten minutes behind the men's average.

There were 641 finishers with 69 of whom were women. Temperatures ranged from the 70s at the base to 50s on top. Team scoring of the top five times for men and the top three times for women was done, with women's teams recorded for the first time. The BAA won in 5:59:28 to CSU (a) 6:07:49 and CSU (b) 6:39:20. The Dartmouth Outing Club won the women's team category in a record 4:23:00 to CSU's 4:45:24. The Dartmouth club's time broke the course record, previously set by CSU in 1978, by over thirty minutes.  For the fist time men and women in the 40+ age group were noted.  Peter Van Garden and Anne Edwards topped the category.

Dean Rasmussen and Ron Paquette, two "streakers" (those running numerous consecutive races) began traveling to the race together.  The two drove from Waterville, Maine, representing the Central Maine Striders.  Paquette and Rasmussen have 24 and 23 consecutive finishes respectively as of 2005.

*New England Runner's* inaugural year of publication included a "First Ascent" account of the race by Bob Fitzgerald.  Fitz admits, "The highlight was being on the shoulder of eventual fifth place finisher (CSU's Steve Bratt) through two miles before going into oxygen debt."  Fitz went on to finish 42nd in 1:17:02 and offered "two points of advice 1. Don't run with a 10K stride 2. Take solace in Dostoevsky's axiom that 'reason is a slave to passion'."

**Top 25 Finishers**

| Place | Name | Time | Age | |
|---|---|---|---|---|
| 1 | Keith Woodward | 1:06:38 | 32 | |
| 2 | Matthew Cull | 1:07:13 | 22 | |
| 3 | Leonard Hall | 1:08:04 | 30 | |
| 4 | Jay Smith | 1:08:27 | 24 | |
| 5 | Steven Bratt | 1:08:42 | 26 | |
| 6 | Mark Ramsay | 1:09:05 | 23 | |
| 7 | James Emmons | 1:09:41 | 24 | |
| 8 | Shawn Gardner | 1:09:52 | 20 | |
| 9 | Eric Weyman | 1:09:54 | 26 | |
| 10 | James Kent | 1:10:02 | 22 | |
| 11 | Casey Gawlak | 1:11:13 | 26 | |
| 12 | Peter Van Garden | 1:11:25 | 42 | |
| 13 | Mike Casner | 1:11:43 | 21 | |
| 14 | Thomas Gilligan | 1:11:58 | 33 | |
| 15 | Charles Gunn | 1:12:05 | 29 | |
| 16 | Todd Webber | 1:12:16 | 27 | |
| 17 | John Cederholm | 1:12:48 | 40 | **FW** |
| 18 | Robert Haydock | 1:13:35 | 30 | |
| 19 | Robert Enright | 1:13:35 | 33 | |
| 20 | Gregory Nelson | 1:13:45 | 35 | |
| 21 | Dale Rodgers | 1:13:49 | 35 | |
| 22 | Bret Cartwright | 1:13:50 | 16 | |
| 23 | John Fiola | 1:13:57 | 20 | |
| 24 | Andrew Kaplan | 1:13:58 | 26 | |
| 25 | Neil Moynihan | 1:14:08 | 24 | |

**Top 10 Women**

| Place | Name | Time | Age |
|---|---|---|---|
| 1 | Anna Sonnerup | 1:22:19 | 22 |
| 2 | Terry Hersh | 1:25:25 | 30 |
| 3 | Karen Henry | 1:27:23 | 26 |
| 4 | Sharon O'Hagan | 1:27:31 | 33 |
| 5 | C Jean McNerny | 1:29:52 | 30 |
| 6 | Bunny Brauns | 1:31:09 | 36 |
| 7 | Peg Pingitore | 1:32:05 | 28 |
| 8 | Winifred Pisarz | 1:32:43 | 22 |
| 9 | Lynn Murray | 1:32:45 | 24 |
| 10 | Leslie Thompson | 1:33:18 | 19 |

**5-Year Age Groups**

| Place | Name | Time | Age | Category | |
|---|---|---|---|---|---|
| 10 | Leslie Thompson | 1:33:18 | 19 | Under 20 | |
| 1 | Anna Sonnerup | 1:22:19 | 22 | 20-24 | |
| 3 | Karen Henry | 1:27:23 | 26 | 25-29 | |
| 2 | Terry Hersh | 1:25:25 | 30 | 30-34 | |
| 6 | Bunny Brauns | 1:31:09 | 36 | 34-39 | |
| 15 | Anne Edwards | 1:37:10 | 41 | 40-44 | |
| 32 | Sally Goodhue | 1:47:28 | 49 | 45-49 | |
| 45 | Dorothy Bergen | 1:55:51 | 51 | 50-54 | |
| | | | | | |
| 22 | Bret Cartwright | 1:13:50 | 16 | Under 20 | |
| 2 | Matthew Cull | 1:07:13 | 22 | 20 - 24 | |
| 5 | Steven Bratt | 1:08:42 | 26 | 25 - 29 | |
| 1 | Keith Woodward | 1:06:38 | 32 | 30-34 | |
| 20 | Gregory Nelson | 1:13:45 | 35 | 35-39 | |
| 12 | Peter Van Garden | 1:11:25 | 42 | 40-44 | |
| 90 | Robert Landry | 1:24:26 | 46 | 45-49 | |
| 70 | Dick Church | 1:22:25 | 51 | 50-54 | |
| 271 | Donald Tillatson | 1:37:09 | 56 | 55-59 | |
| 266 | Carlton Mendell | 1:36:54 | 61 | 60-64 | |
| 401 | Warren Steckmost | 1:47:24 | 68 | 65-69 | |
| 572 | Rudy Fahl | 3:14:35 | 85 | 80+ | Age Group Record |

<h1 align="center">24<sup>th</sup> Mt Washington Road Race</h1>

June 17, 1984
Sunday
605 Finishers

This marked the first time that the race was called the 'Run to the clouds'. Race day had 70 degrees at the start and 50 at the summit with 14 mph winds, which boded well for the more than 600 starters. Gary Crossan and Betsey Haydock took advantage of the conditions, leading the way with a course record, and the second fastest time respectively. Crossan had tuned up on May 20 by shattering Keith Woodward's record at Mt Equinox. A record 162 competed in the race directed by long-time Mt Washington runner Fred Ross. Crossan became the first recorded finisher at Mt Washington to receive money for his victory. He was presented $100 for setting the course record.

The Mt Washington race application noted "the road surface is alternately dirt and paved and covers 7.6 miles (Rolatype measuring Wheel)." This was the first documented time the event was not called 8 miles, despite the course remaining unchanged throughout the years. The field was limited by Race Director Bob Teschek to 800 runners, and it was noted, "Entries have closed well before race day each of the last 2 years." The race entry fee climbed to $8 or $14 if ordering a t-shirt. Sanctioning was provided by the RRCA and a 3-hour time limit was set using the "electric (chronomix) timing system." Certificates were given to all finishers and bowls to the top ten, first 40+, and medals were given to the top 50 and the top five women and top ten 40+ men.

Earlier in the year Teschek started his own business, forming the Granite State Race Services, timing 20 races in 1984. Before taking over as Race Director at Mt Washington Teschek said in New England Runner "I heard rumors the race would be discontinued because it was essentially managed just for the day and the facilities were being taxed. I just couldn't imagine not having the race." He called Mt Washington his favorite race and "my labor of love."

The CSU ladies took the team title by three minutes over the Granite State Racing Team, and on the men's side CSU won by nearly 50 minutes in running a combined 6:00:15. Team Gloucester finished in seventh and are pictured on page 52 – (Kneeling) Mike Gillis, Dave Gallagher, Bob Gillis, John Connors, (Middle Row) Austin Connors, Frank Aiello, (Back Row) Eric Saulnier, Mark Asaro, Gus Saulnier, and Paul Neimi.

Medical staff at the race included Dr Wriss and the Gorham Ambulance service. Doug Philbrook and the Auto Road Crew provided radio contact and official transport. Refreshments provided included, Coke, Busch beer, Eagle snacks, and Colombo yogurt.

Teschek noted after the race that he received 100 requests for entry into the 25<sup>th</sup> running of the event and "helpers will receive an official race t-shirt and may be eligible for a cash award if your group has sufficient numbers." The Auto Road staff charged $9 for each car being driven to the summit and an extra $2 per person for passengers.

Top 25 Finishers

| Place | Name | Time | Age | State | |
|---|---|---|---|---|---|
| 1 | Gary Crossan | 1:01:13 | 26 | CO | Course record |
| 2 | Matthew Cull | 1:03:41 | 23 | VT | |
| 3 | Keith Woodward | 1:08:06 | 33 | VT | FW |
| 4 | Mike Casner | 1:09:20 | 22 | NH | |
| 5 | John Fiola | 1:09:34 | 21 | MA | |
| 6 | Bernard Rate | 1:10:14 | 32 | MA | |
| 7 | Charles Gunn | 1:10:19 | 29 | NH | |
| 8 | Kirk Siegel | 1:10:40 | 23 | MA | |
| 9 | Jo Miles | 1:10:53 | 20 | NH | |
| 10 | Peter Van Gardener | 1:11:19 | 43 | NY | |
| 11 | Richard Weinstein | 1:11:34 | 28 | MA | |
| 12 | Sumner Brown | 1:11:49 | 40 | MA | |
| 13 | Henry Finch | 1:12:19 | 35 | MA | |
| 14 | Brendan Sullivan | 1:12:26 | 21 | NH | |
| 15 | Karl Meltzer | 1:12:29 | 16 | NH | |
| 16 | David Roberts | 1:13:11 | 29 | ME | |
| 17 | Thomas Gilligan | 1:13:48 | 34 | MA | |
| 18 | Leonard Hall | 1:14:07 | 30 | NH | |
| 19 | Robert Haydock | 1:14:19 | 31 | MA | |
| 20 | Robert Sullivan | 1:14:21 | 30 | MA | |
| 21 | Stephen Moser | 1:14:22 | 27 | ME | |
| 22 | Jeffrey Walter | 1:14:27 | 29 | CT | |
| 23 | Gordon Pitt | 1:14:30 | 23 | NH | |
| 24 | Mark Asaro | 1:14:48 | 28 | MA | |
| 25 | Robert Enright | 1:14:54 | 34 | CT | |
| 50 | John Cederholm | 1:19:11 | 41 | MA | FW |
| 220 | Angus Wooten | 1:35:07 | 44 | CT | FW |

Top 10 Women

| Place | Name | Time | Age | State | |
|---|---|---|---|---|---|
| 1 | Betsey Haydock | 1:20:46 | 28 | MA | |
| 2 | Peg Pingitore | 1:24:11 | 29 | NH | |
| 3 | Anna Sonnerup | 1:25:41 | 22 | NH | FW |
| 4 | Kimberly Beaulieu | 1:25:48 | 28 | ME | |
| 5 | Leslie Thompson | 1:26:49 | 20 | VT | |
| 6 | Anne McLean | 1:30:45 | 42 | NH | |
| 7 | Jeannie MacDonald | 1:32:53 | 32 | NH | |
| 8 | Lisa Doucett | 1:33:02 | 28 | MA | |
| 9 | Marsha Giglio | 1:34:18 | 40 | ME | |
| 10 | Lynda Dunn | 1:34:25 | 19 | ME | |

## 5-Year Age Groups

| Place | Name | Time | Age | State | Category |
|---|---|---|---|---|---|
| 207 | Lynda Dunn | 1:34:25 | 19 | ME | Under 20 |
| 94 | Anna Sonnerup | 1:25:41 | 22 | NH | 20-24 |
| 60 | Betsey Haydock | 1:20:46 | 28 | MA | 25-29 |
| 183 | Jeannie MacDonald | 1:32:53 | 32 | NH | 30-34 |
| 212 | Bunny Brauns | 1:34:34 | 37 | NH | 35-39 |
| 159 | Anne McLean | 1:30:45 | 42 | NH | 40-44 |
| 305 | Diana Avery | 1:41:19 | 46 | NH | 45-49 |
| 479 | Dorothy Bergman | 1:54:53 | 52 | MA | 50-54 |
| 356 | Hildy Fosse | 1:45:03 | 55 | NH | 55-59 |
| | | | | | |
| 15 | Karl Meltzer | 1:12:29 | 16 | NH | Under 20 |
| 2 | Matthew Cull | 1:03:41 | 23 | VT | 20-24 |
| 1 | Gary Crossan | 1:01:13 | 26 | CO | 25-29 |
| 3 | Keith Woodward | 1:08:06 | 33 | VT | 30-34 |
| 13 | Henry Finch | 1:12:19 | 35 | MA | 35-39 |
| 10 | Peter Van Garderen | 1:11:19 | 43 | NY | 40-44 |
| 46 | Daniel Ellison | 1:19:00 | 45 | NH | 45-49 |
| 58 | Dick Church | 1:20:29 | 52 | NH | 50-54 **Age group record** |
| 199 | Bill Brace | 1:33:48 | 57 | MA | 55-59 |
| 243 | Carlton Mendell | 1:37:10 | 62 | ME | 60-64 |
| 378 | Warren Steckmost | 1:46:15 | 69 | NH | 65-69 |
| 605 | Rudy Fahl | 3:13:01 | 86 | NH | 80+ |

52

### 25<sup>th</sup> Mt Washington Road Race

June 22, 1985
Saturday
670 Finishers

Great conditions with temperatures in the 70s at the base and clear in the 50s at the summit greeted the racers in the silver anniversary running of the Mt Washington Road Race.  Visibility was 70 miles, and it was noted that the following week it snowed on the summit.  The race was nearly cut short when a small MG automobile caught on fire at the 5 mile mark and the auto road personnel were still attempting to extinguish it when the racers went by.  This was the first year the event was held on Saturday and Race Director *Bob Teschek* noted, "The change to Saturday was very popular, many stayed in the area and attended the party at the Eagle Mountain House."

Five-time winner Bob Hodge set a new personal record of 1:01:32, but came up short on Gary Crossan's 1:01:13 from last year.  Hodge, Crossan and Keith Woodward were the favorites going into the race.  Crossan was returning from a knee injury and Hodge was nursing a sore calf muscle.  Woodward had recently tuned up with a victory at Mt Equinox, beating Pete Farwell by over two minutes.  Hodge told Karen Cummings of the *Mountain Ear,* "The only way to run this race is to go out determined to win."  He also noted "At halfway I knew I still had a shot at it (the course record)."  Crossan and Woodward kept Hodge in sight after he pulled into the lead after the first mile.  Hodge kept waving for the press vans to move ahead of him as he was having trouble with the exhaust fumes.  Woodward moved into second after the 5-mile mark and ran a personal best 1:03:04.  Woodward's time was the sixth fastest ever run, behind only Crossan and Hodge, it was also the fastest non-winning time.  Woodward would go on to break 1:10 an incredible fifteen times.   Crossan finished in the thirteenth fastest time despite his injury woes.  Mike Casner in sixth place picked up his second sub-1:10 on his way to twelve in his Mt Washington career.  A record thirteen runners finished under 1:10.  The average age for a male finisher passed 35 with 35.34 being the average.

Christ Maisto won the women's race in a course record of 1:14:45, taking nearly five minutes off Martha Rockwell's record from 1979.  Maisto was fresh off her victory (2:45:50) at the Maine Coast Marathon in the previous month.  Kim Moody, who had come in second at Maine, took second in 1:23:16.  Maisto had never been up Mt Washington before and noted in the *Mountain Ear,* "I haven't been training on hills and didn't know what to expect."   Maisto became the first woman to break into the top 50, with her thirty-first place overall finish.  She took home $500 for the win and a sub-1:15 time.  Other prize money winners were Bob Hodge who was given $50 for winning and another $50 for leading at the half way point, Sumner Brown and Marsha Giglio each received $100 for winning the 40+ age group.

Marathon Tours Racing Team earned top-Team honors in an excellent 5:41:50 followed by CSU, over 20 minutes back.  Willimantic AC was the top women's team in 4:55:15 over CSU's 5:00:52.  Teams were required to submit a team roster prior to the race and women were allowed to run for a women's team or an open team, but not both.

Bill Teschek video taped the race for the first time and sold the VHS or Beta (!) copies for $20. Sponsors for the race included Puma USA and associate sponsor Numerica Bank which helped to double the prize money.  Others included Coke, Hood, Colombo, and Eagle Snacks.  Dr. Riss and the Gorham ambulance services provided medical assistance.  The total prize purse was $1800 with most of it for sub 60/75 minute performances for men and women respectively. The entry fee was $10 and the entry limit was 800.  The race was electronically timed and a Digital clock was added at the exact halfway point.  The three hour time limit was in place with an exception for Rudy Fahl.  Fahl, the 87-year-old founder and former director of the Pikes Peak marathon said in the *Mountain Ear,* "running up mountains is part of the secret of a long life."

Hodge summed up his feelings on the race in the *Mountain Ear:* "It's really a personal challenge. You are running against yourself more than anybody else.  If someone went by me I wouldn't give a damn."  Maisto called the race "spacey above the treeline, the second half you feel like you're running on another planet."  Steve Schlicting called the race "an object lesson in humility" and continued, "There are old men who go flying by you and you say 'My God how can they do that?', but they can."

Added bonuses this year included showers and a whirlpool available for $2 at the Mountain Valley Court Club in North Conway, a post-race party at the Eagle Mountain House featuring a "Boston Dance band" and a viewing of the race video, and a special runner's rate at the Eagle Mountain House of $20 per person for Bed and Breakfast.

## Top 25 Finishers

| Place | Name | Team | Time | Age | City and State | |
|---|---|---|---|---|---|---|
| 1 | Bob Hodge | | 1:01:31 | 29 | Wellesley, MA | |
| 2 | Keith Woodward | | 1:03:06 | 34 | Craftsbury Com., VT | **FW** |
| 3 | Gary Crossan | | 1:04:45 | 27 | Amherst, MA | **FW** |
| 4 | Joseph Stanley Jr. | | 1:05:33 | 32 | Prospect, CT | |
| 5 | Matthew Cull | | 1:06:13 | 24 | Middlebury, VT | |
| 6 | Philip Brock | Mara Tours | 1:06:28 | 25 | Ithaca, NY | |
| 7 | Vincent Fleming | | 1:07:16 | 31 | Brighton, MA | |
| 8 | Mike Casner | | 1:07:36 | 23 | Keene, NH | |
| 9 | Brad Hurst | Mara Tours | 1:07:52 | 31 | Chelmsford, MA | |
| 10 | Duncan Scott | Mara Tours | 1:08:43 | 28 | Cambridge, MA | |
| 11 | David Ezersky | Mara Tours | 1:09:19 | 28 | Sandwich, MA | |
| 12 | Rodney Pearson | Mara Tours | 1:09:28 | 31 | Brookline, MA | |
| 13 | Richard Weinstein | CSU | 1:09:35 | 29 | Brighton, MA | |
| 14 | Kirk Siegel | | 1:10:33 | 24 | Bethel, ME | |
| 15 | Malcolm Page | CSU | 1:10:39 | 26 | Boston, MA | |
| 16 | Sumner Brown | CSU | 1:10:53 | 41 | Belmont, MA | |
| 17 | Karl Meltzer Jr. | | 1:11:17 | 17 | Auburn, NH | |
| 18 | David Roberts | | 1:11:37 | 30 | Kennebunk, ME | |
| 19 | Douglas Sweazey | | 1:11:53 | 28 | Jamaica Plain, MA | |

| Place | Name | Team | Time | Age | City and State |
|---|---|---|---|---|---|
| 20 | James Kent | | 1:11:56 | 25 | N Easton, MA |
| 21 | Charles Gunn | | 1:12:11 | 31 | Henniker, NH |
| 22 | Gregory Nelson | | 1:12:12 | 37 | Gardiner, ME |
| 23 | Paul Rabenold | | 1:12:15 | 32 | Bristol, CT |
| 24 | John Fiola | | 1:12:18 | 22 | Bloomington, IN |
| 25 | Leonard Hall | WMM | 1:13:09 | 32 | Monroe, NH |
| 30 | John Cederholm | | 1:14:24 | 42 | Boston, MA  **FW** |

**Top 25 Women**

| Place | Name | Team | Time | Age | City and State |
|---|---|---|---|---|---|
| 1 | Christine Maisto | | 1:14:44 | 25 | Concord, NH **Course Record** |
| 2 | Kimberly Moody | | 1:23:16 | 30 | Portland, ME |
| 3 | Sally Zimmer | | 1:24:34 | 26 | Cambridge, MA |
| 4 | Marsha Giglio | | 1:29:48 | 41 | Augusta, ME |
| 5 | Patricia Swim | | 1:29:53 | 31 | Noank, CT |
| 6 | Jeannie MacDonald | | 1:30:03 | 33 | Windham, NH |
| 7 | Sharon O'Hagan | | 1:30:14 | 37 | Cambridge, MA |
| 8 | Eliza Deery | | 1:32:09 | 24 | Hanover, NH |
| 9 | Renee DiCicco | | 1:32:43 | 24 | Hyde Park, MA |
| 10 | Frannie Fisher | | 1:33:02 | 30 | Wellesley, MA |
| 11 | Nancy McKenney | Willimantic | 1:33:07 | 21 | Tolland, CT |
| 12 | Donna Dearborn | | 1:33:55 | 32 | Lyme, NH |
| 13 | Dianne Menard | | 1:35:20 | 33 | Taunton, MA |
| 14 | Bette Davis | | 1:36:59 | 41 | Cambridge, MA |
| 15 | Bernadette Brauns | | 1:37:38 | 38 | Gilford, NH |
| 16 | Diana Shannon | | 1:37:46 | 22 | Hanover, NH |
| 17 | Ann Dunham | | 1:38:39 | 27 | Portsmouth, RI |
| 18 | Gayle Richards | | 1:38:46 | 23 | N Conway, NH |
| 19 | Anne McLean | | 1:39:21 | 43 | Laconia, NH |
| 20 | Amy Morse-Leeds | Willimantic | 1:39:50 | 28 | Willimantic, CT |
| 21 | Mary Beth Lawlor | | 1:42:10 | 25 | N Andover, MA |
| 22 | Beth Hudson-Hankins | Willimantic | 1:42:18 | 25 | Storrs, CT |
| 23 | Kersten Sonnerup | | 1:42:22 | 26 | Hanover, NH |
| 24 | Diana Avery | | 1:43:23 | 47 | Loudon, NH |
| 25 | Priscilla Reinerston | | 1:43:54 | 42 | Concord, NH |

**5 Year Age group winners**

| Place | Name | Time | Age | City and State | Category |
|---|---|---|---|---|---|
| 178 | Eliza Deery | 1:32:09 | 24 | Hanover, NH | 20-24 |
| 31 | Christine Maisto | 1:14:44 | 25 | Concord, NH | 25-29 |
| 77 | Kimberly Moody | 1:23:16 | 30 | Portland, ME | 30-34 |

| 155 | Sharon O'Hagan | 1:30:14 | 37 | Cambridge, MA | 35-39 |
| 146 | Marsha Giglio | 1:29:48 | 41 | Augusta, ME | 40-44 |
| 367 | Diana Avery | 1:43:23 | 47 | Loudon, NH | 45-49 |
| 445 | Linda Bradley | 1:48:33 | 54 | Sweden, ME | 50-54 |
| 478 | Hildy Fosse | 1:50:38 | 56 | Holderness, NH | 55-60 |
|  |  |  |  |  |  |
| 17 | Karl Meltzer Jr. | 1:11:17 | 17 | Auburn, NH | Under 20 |
| 5 | Matthew Cull | 1:06:13 | 24 | Middlebury, VT | 20-24 |
| 1 | Bob Hodge | 1:01:31 | 29 | Wellesley, MA | 25-29 |
| 2 | Keith Woodward | 1:03:06 | 34 | Craftsbury Com. VT | 30-34 |
| 22 | Gregory Nelson | 1:12:12 | 37 | Gardiner, ME | 35-39 |
| 16 | Sumner Brown | 1:10:53 | 41 | Belmont, MA | 40-44 |
| 48 | Robert Wright | 1:18:25 | 45 | Bradford, NH | 45-49 |
| 57 | Dick Church | 1:20:03 | 53 | Plymouth, NH | 50-54 **Age Group Record** |
| 245 | Bill Brace | 1:35:20 | 58 | Concord, MA | 55-59 |
| 348 | Larry Wilbers | 1:42:19 | 60 | Cincinnati, OH | 60-64 |
| 565 | Rufus Reed | 1:58:58 | 66 | Gorham, NH | 65-69 |
| 670 | Rudy Fahl | 3:09:51 | 87 | Exeter, NH | 80+ **Age Group Record** |

## 26th Mt Washington Road Race

06-28-1986
Saturday
700 Finishers

The race was again referred to as the "Run to the clouds" and in a new move the race named Weeks Dairy as the official dairy of the Mt Washington Road race. The race started at 11 a.m. and had a strong field running at the substantial prize-money pot. Conditions may have slowed everyone down, as it was warm/muggy at the base and 49 degrees with 34 mph winds at the summit. Gary Crossan was the favorite going in, as Bob Hodge was absent; he was getting married on race day. The challengers looked to be newcomers Domingo Tibaduiza and Sheldon Larson. Tibaduiza had finished seventh at the Boston Marathon and run a 44:38 for 15k, while Larson was the holder of many course records for mountain races in Colorado.

Crossan took the lead in the early going and had a 65 second lead at halfway (in 29:12). He went on to win in 1:02:10, which ranked fifth on the all time list. Tibaduiza came to the race with a 2:11 personal best for the marathon. Sheldon Larson, a mountain runner from Colorado, caught Tibaduiza just as the duo reached the finish line. Both were given a time of 63:12, Tibaduiza's time was the fastest run by a first-timer. Al Waquie, the course record holder at Pikes Peak, finished seventh in his first Mt Washington.

The women's race had a repeat as Chris Maisto again finished in the top 50, with a 1:19:26. Maisto won despite being injured for most of the spring. She won by nearly four minutes over Leslie Thompson. Former champion Martha Rockwell was fourth and top master with a 40+ course record run of 1:28:39.

CSU took the team title in 6:07:53 with Granite State Racing Team first in the ladies team category with a 4:49:16.  Age groups were officially expanded to include those under 20, and 10-year categories up to 60+.  The winners in each age group received Puma wind suits.

Prize money winners included Crossan who won $250 for the victory and $100 for leading at halfway, and Maisto who earned $250 for topping the ladies field.

Miscellaneous: For the first time it appears that the auto road was at least partially closed to traffic, as the road was closed at the bottom from 10:45 a.m. to 12:30 p.m.  Auto Road charges increased to $10 per car and $3 per passenger.  Sponsors for the race included Puma USA and Numerica Savings bank.  They helped to increase the prize pool to a total of $1000 plus time bonuses of $1000 for a sub-hour run and $100 for a team record and $100 for a master's record.  Free entry for the following year was granted to the top 10 and top 5 women and the first man and woman in the 40+.  The 800-runner limit was reached in a record 21 days.  *Boston Running News* named the race the "Race of the Month."  Crossan won the Pickering Wharf 10K two weeks later in 29:59.  The official race hotel, the Eagle Mountain House, underwent a $4 million renovation, but still offered rooms to runners at a discounted rate of $47.50 plus $15 for each person.  The post race party was held at the Eagle Mountain House with the viewing of the race video, which was also for sale (VHS only).  The first video from the previous year showed the start, Hodge leading, and everyone finishing.  This year the press truck stopped to get a view of some of the other runners before rushing to the finish to catch everyone crossing the line.

**Top 25 Finishers**

| Place | Name | Team | Time | Age | City & State |
|---|---|---|---|---|---|
| 1 | Gary Crossan | | 1:02:10 | 28 | Amherst, MA |
| 2 | Domingo Tibaduiza | | 1:03:12 | 36 | Reno, NV |
| 3 | Sheldon Larson | | 1:03:12 | 25 | Boulder, CO |
| 4 | Buck Logan | GBTC | 1:06:55 | 26 | Charlestown, MA |
| 5 | Joseph Stanley | | 1:07:43 | 33 | Prospect, CT |
| 6 | Sean Hanley | | 1:07:59 | 25 | N Attleboro, MA |
| 7 | Al Waquie | | 1:08:19 | 35 | Jemez Pueblo, NM |
| 8 | Mike Casner | | 1:08:34 | 24 | Bristol, NH |
| 9 | John Fitzgerald | | 1:08:38 | 22 | Lewiston, ME |
| 10 | Jay Smith | | 1:09:34 | 27 | St Louis Park, MN |
| 11 | Peter Farwell | | 1:09:45 | 35 | Williamstown, MA |
| 12 | Shawn Gardner | | 1:10:07 | 23 | Georgetown, MA |
| 13 | James Kent | | 1:11:26 | 26 | N Easton, MA |
| 14 | Neil Moynihan | | 1:11:39 | 27 | Farmington, CT |
| 15 | Jeffrey Robie | | 1:11:57 | 29 | Kingston, NH |
| 16 | Richard Weinstein | CSU | 1:12:06 | 30 | Newton, MA |
| 17 | Uriel Rivera | | 1:12:10 | 22 | Williamstown, MA |
| 18 | Art Sorrell | BAA | 1:12:12 | 26 | Laconia, NH |

| 19 | Malcolm Page | CSU | 1:12:17 | 28 | Allston, MA | |
| 20 | Sumner Brown | CSU | 1:12:26 | 42 | Belmont, MA | |
| 21 | Bruce Ellis | | 1:13:11 | 34 | Exeter, NH | |
| 22 | Sam Palistine | | 1:13:19 | 35 | New Bedford, MA | |
| 23 | John Fiola | BAA | 1:13:27 | 23 | Dedham, MA | |
| 24 | Leonard Hall | | 1:13:44 | 33 | Monroe, NH | |
| 25 | Jon Waldron | CSU | 1:13:59 | 28 | Newton, MA | |
| 35 | John Cederholm | BAA | 1:17:48 | 43 | Boston, MA | FW |
| 479 | Angus Wooten | | 1:50:21 | 46 | Willimantic | FW |

**Top 25 Women**

| Place | Name | Team | Time | Age | City & State | |
| --- | --- | --- | --- | --- | --- | --- |
| 1 | Chris Maisto | | 1:19:26 | 26 | Concord, NH | |
| 2 | Leslie Thompson | | 1:23:18 | 22 | Hanover, NH | |
| 3 | Peg Donovan | GSRT | 1:25:06 | 31 | Auburn, NH | FW |
| 4 | Martha Rockwell | | 1:28:39 | 42 | Strafford, VT | FW |
| 5 | Bunny Brauns | | 1:30:31 | 39 | Gilford, NH | |
| 6 | Jeannie MacDonald | GSRT | 1:30:50 | 34 | Windham, NH | |
| 7 | Theresa young | | 1:31:45 | 24 | Jackson, NH | |
| 8 | Sharon O'Hagan | | 1:32:24 | 38 | Charlestown, MA | |
| 9 | Lisa Doucett | | 1:32:53 | 30 | Watertown, MA | |
| 10 | Anne McLean | | 1:33:29 | 44 | Laconia, NH | |
| 11 | Patricia Robinson | GSRT | 1:36:07 | 33 | Waban, MA | |
| 12 | Jennifer Elberty | | 1:36:37 | 24 | Wolfeboro, NH | |
| 13 | Doris Medina | | 1:36:45 | 32 | Woonsocket, RI | |
| 14 | Beth Walker-Corkery | | 1:37:27 | 26 | Jamaica Plain, MA | |
| 15 | Elaine McGrevey | | 1:38:01 | 33 | Manchester, NH | |
| 16 | Marsha Giglio | | 1:39:12 | 42 | Augusta, ME | |
| 17 | Joann Ranslow | | 1:39:22 | 28 | Pepperell, MA | |
| 18 | Amy Morss-leeds | | 1:39:23 | 29 | Storrs, CT | |
| 19 | Beth Hudson-Hankins | | 1:39:24 | 26 | Willimantic, CT | |
| 20 | Mary Beth Lawlor | | 1:39:47 | 26 | N Andover, MA | |
| 21 | Carol Bickford | | 1:41:08 | 31 | Somersworth, NH | |
| 22 | Sharon Crawford | | 1:41:20 | 41 | Concord, MA | |
| 23 | Cindy Jacoby | | 1:41:35 | 39 | Newton Falls, MA | |
| 24 | Peg Crocker | | 1:42:35 | 33 | Brighton, MA | |
| 25 | Patti Hickey | | 1:44:26 | 26 | Laconia, NH | |

<u>Team Results:</u>

| Women | | Men | |
|---|---|---|---|
| 1 GSRT | 4:49:16 | 1 CSU | 6:07:53 |
| 2 CSU | 4:50:20 | 2 GBTC | 6:21:00 |
| 3 Willimantic | 5:08:18 | 3 BAA | 6:36:18 |
| 4 BAA | 5:09:50 | 4 Willimantic | 6:39:16 |
| 5 WMM | 5:20:31 | 5 MVS | 6:42:53 |

## 5 Year Age group winners

| Place | Name | Time | Age | City & State | Category |
|---|---|---|---|---|---|
| 669 | Brenda Sweeney | 2:17:38 | 17 | Nottingham, NH | Under 20 |
| 80 | Leslie Thompson | 1:23:18 | 22 | Hanover, NH | 20-24 |
| 49 | Chris Maisto | 1:19:26 | 26 | Concord, NH | 25-29 |
| 95 | Peg Donovan | 1:25:06 | 31 | Auburn, NH | 30-34 |
| 175 | Bunny Brauns | 1:30:31 | 39 | Gilford, NH | 35-39 |
| 146 | Martha Rockwell | 1:28:39 | 42 | Strafford, VT | 40-44 |
| 496 | Sandra Hayes | 1:51:10 | 48 | Chelmsford, MA | 45-49 |
| 560 | Joyce Hals | 1:57:01 | 53 | Lexington, MA | 50-54 |
| 532 | Hildy Fosse | 1:54:23 | 57 | Holderness, NH | 55-59 |

| Place | Name | Time | Age | City & State | Category |
|---|---|---|---|---|---|
| 26 | Sean Livingston | 1:15:43 | 17 | Conway, NH | Under 20 |
| 8 | Mike Casner | 1:08:34 | 24 | Bristol, NH | 20-24 |
| 1 | Gary Crossan | 1:02:10 | 28 | Amherst, MA | 25-29 |
| 5 | Joseph Stanley | 1:07:43 | 33 | Prospect, CT | 30-34 |
| 2 | Domingo Tibaduiza | 1:03:12 | 36 | Reno, NV | 35-39 |
| 20 | Sumner Brown | 1:12:26 | 42 | Belmont, MA | 40-44 |
| 33 | Peter Van Garderen | 1:17:14 | 45 | Hudson Falls, NY | 45-49 |
| 60 | Dick Church | 1:20:56 | 54 | Plymouth, NH | 50-54 |
| 139 | Robert Shelton | 1:28:00 | 56 | Bradford, VT | 55-59 |
| 307 | Carlton Mendell | 1:38:55 | 64 | Portland, ME | 60-64 |
| 600 | Charley Reed | 2:01:00 | 65 | Gorham, NH | 65-69 |
| 682 | David Torlon | 2:24:27 | 70 | S Hadley, MA | 70-74 |
| 700 | Rudy Fahl | 3:18:12 | 88 | Exeter, NH | 80+ |

06-20-1987
Saturday
732 Finishers

The race was dedicated to the four-time winner and course record holder, Gary Crossan who, while on a training run was struck and killed by a train. Bob Hodge returned and took aim at Crossan's course record. The weather, although clear, was windy with gusts up to 50 mph above the treeline. As was the case in 1985, Hodge had trouble with the press vans. He almost ran into a van that was parked on the edge of one of the small parking lots. Hodge waved at the vans to move forward and at one time can be heard on the race video yelling "move up!" The commentator on the video also noted that "He has a shot at winning…If he stays ahead." Hodge stormed through an incredible 28:08 for the first half and went on to defeat 1996 runner-up Domingo Tibaduiza with a 1:01:13. His time tied Crossan's mark however, when going to tenths of a second Crossan prevailed .3 to .7. Hodge was awarded $250 for winning and another $100 for leading at the half. Tibaduiza ran the fastest non-winning time and set a new record for the 35-39 age group. Only Hodge and Crossan had run faster. A record tying thirteen runners broke 1:10.

Peg Donovan took an amazing nine minutes off of her personal record to run the second fastest time for a female with a 1:15:05. Donovan also cracked the top 50 with a thirty-seventh place finish and led the Granite State Racing Team to a team record. She noted in *New England Runner* that she was a triathlete until two years prior. She recently placed first at the New England Athletic Congress (NEAC) 10K in 34:36 and was victorious at the NEAC 10 mile in 56:42. Donovan won $250 for the victory and another $100 for being the top female New Hampshire finisher. A record nine female runners broke 1:30, which nearly doubled the previous best; in addition for the first time two women broke 1:20.

Granite State Racing Team took the women's team title running 4:00:33, defeating CSU by 35 minutes. The GSRT smashed the Dartmouth Outing Club's course record by nearly 23 minutes. The US Biathlon team led by Keith Woodward edged the GLRR team 5:57:33 to 6:00:07.

Jack Coakley, a wheelchair athlete and friend of Gary Crossan, pushed himself to the top in 2:48.

Primary sponsors were the Numerica Savings Bank and Homebank. The Crossan cup was awarded to the top male and female finishers from New Hampshire. Roger and Sandra Smith donated a cash prize to the Crossan Cup recipients, Peg Donovan and Mike Casner. The entry fee rose to $12 and the number of prizes was increased to cover the top ten women, ten male and two female masters' three open teams, and the top women's team. The total prize purse was $1,300 plus time incentives. Prize money was given to both the men and women for finishing in the top three, the top 40+, and the top New Hampshire runner.

## Top 25 Finishers

| Place | Name | Team | Time | Age | City and State | |
|---|---|---|---|---|---|---|
| 1 | Bob Hodge | GLRR | 1:01:14 | 31 | Clinton, MA | |
| 2 | Domingo Tibaduiza | | 1:02:52 | 37 | Reno, NV | |
| 3 | Matt Ebiner | | 1:05:03 | 26 | W Covina, CA | |
| 4 | Sheldon Larson | | 1:05:36 | 26 | Boulder, CO | |
| 5 | Mike Casner | | 1:06:10 | 25 | Bristol, NH | |
| 6 | Sean Hanley | | 1:06:41 | 26 | Sharon, MA | |
| 7 | Matthew Cull | | 1:07:29 | 26 | Bristol, VT | |
| 8 | Keith Woodward | US BI | 1:07:48 | 36 | Craftsbury Com., VT | FW |
| 9 | Richard Surace | | 1:07:55 | 21 | Syracuse, NY | |
| 10 | Jay Smith | | 1:08:36 | 28 | Grand Rapids, MI | |
| 11 | Peter Farwell | | 1:08:53 | 36 | Williamstown, MA | |
| 12 | John Fiola | | 1:09:00 | 24 | Dedham, MA | |
| 13 | Sean Livingston | | 1:09:14 | 18 | Conway, NH | |
| 14 | Mark Will-Weber | | 1:10:21 | 32 | Bethlehem, PA | |
| 15 | Rick Oliver | US BI | 1:10:46 | 26 | Essex Junction, VT | |
| 16 | Duncan Douglas | US BI | 1:10:46 | 22 | Essex Junction, VT | |
| 17 | Christopher Moulton | | 1:11:00 | 21 | Keene, NH | |
| 18 | Lyle Nelson | US BI | 1:11:24 | 38 | Essex Jct., VT | |
| 19 | Sumner Brown | | 1:11:27 | 43 | Belmont, MA | |
| 20 | Richard Weinstein | | 1:11:33 | 31 | Newton, MA | |
| 21 | Bob Chasen | | 1:11:46 | 32 | Weymouth, MA | |
| 22 | Rob Hurlbutt | | 1:12:00 | 28 | Keene, NH | |
| 23 | Walter Murphy | GLRR | 1:12:07 | 33 | Boxboro, MA | |
| 24 | Leonard Hall | | 1:12:43 | 34 | Monroe, NH | |
| 25 | Jeffrey Robie | | 1:12:45 | 30 | Kingston, NH | |
| 30 | Jim Capezzuto | | 1:13:10 | 33 | E Boston, MA | FW |
| 44 | John Cederholm | BAA | 1:16:30 | 44 | Boston, MA | FW |

## Top 25 Women

| Place | Name | Club | Time | Age | City and State | |
|---|---|---|---|---|---|---|
| 1 | Peg Donovan | GSRT | 1:15:05 | 32 | Auburn, NH | |
| 2 | Christine Maisto | GSRT | 1:15:38 | 27 | Concord, NH | FW |
| 3 | Patricia Shiffert | | 1:24:21 | 32 | Philadelphia, PA | |
| 4 | Martha Rockwell | | 1:25:57 | 43 | Strafford, VT | FW |
| 5 | Susan Marchant | | 1:26:07 | 27 | Concord, MA | |
| 6 | Theresa Young | | 1:27:46 | 25 | Jackson, NH | |
| 7 | Nanci Carlson | | 1:27:57 | 31 | W Milford, NJ | |
| 8 | Melissa Smedley | CSU | 1:28:42 | 24 | Cambridge, MA | |
| 9 | Terry Hersh | GSRT | 1:29:50 | 34 | Laconia, NH | |
| 10 | Julie Westland-Litus | | 1:32:02 | 29 | Lakewood, CO | |
| 11 | Debbie Crow | | 1:32:41 | 36 | Stowe, CT | |
| 12 | Anne Kuklinski | | 1:33:39 | 28 | Niskayuna, NY | |

| Place | Name | Club | Time | Age | City and State |
|-------|------|------|------|-----|----------------|
| 13 | Beth Walker-Corkery | | 1:35:19 | 27 | Jamaica Plain, MA |
| 14 | Melissa Sandifer | | 1:36:36 | 25 | S Hadley, MA |
| 15 | Doris Medina | | 1:36:53 | 33 | Woonsocket, RI |
| 16 | Martha Hatch | | 1:37:44 | 30 | N Conway, NH |
| 17 | Lucia Greenough | | 1:38:53 | 31 | Ipswich, MA |
| 18 | Jennifer Rood | | 1:38:56 | 26 | Kittery, ME |
| 19 | Jeannie MacDonald | | 1:39:06 | 35 | Windham, NH |
| 20 | Lisa Hals | | 1:39:16 | 23 | Lexington, MA |
| 21 | Gail Kinney | | 1:40:24 | 35 | Conway, NH |
| 22 | Patricia Robinson | | 1:41:08 | 34 | Waban, MA |
| 23 | Anne Schmitt | | 1:41:15 | 40 | Boston, MA |
| 24 | Amy Morss | | 1:41:40 | 30 | Storrs, CT |
| 25 | Carol Crafts | | 1:42:26 | 42 | Providence, RI |

Peg Donovan

5-Year Age Groups

| Place Name | Time | Age | City and State | Category |
|---|---|---|---|---|
| 630 Lucie Hager | 2:01:28 | 15 | Concord, NH | Under 20 |
| 175 Melissa Smedley | 1:28:42 | 24 | Cambridge, MA | 20-24 |
| 40 Christine Maisto | 1:15:38 | 27 | Concord, NH | 25-29 |
| 37 Peg Donovan | 1:15:05 | 32 | Auburn, NH | 30-34 |
| 226 Debbie Crow | 1:32:41 | 36 | Stowe, CT | 35-39 |
| 138 Martha Rockwell | 1:25:57 | 43 | Strafford, VT | 40-44 |
| 476 Judith Davis | 1:49:28 | 47 | Hollis Ctr., ME | 45-49 |
| 499 Hildy Fosse | 1:50:59 | 58 | Holderness, NH | 50-59 |
| | | | | |
| 13 Sean Livingston | 1:09:14 | 18 | Conway, NH | Under 20 **AGR** |
| 9 Richard Surace | 1:07:55 | 21 | Syracuse, NY | 20-24 |
| 3 Matt Ebiner | 1:05:03 | 26 | W Covina, CA | 25-29 |
| 1 Bob Hodge | 1:01:14 | 31 | Clinton, MA | 30-34 |
| 2 Domingo Tibaduiza | 1:02:52 | 37 | Reno, NV | 35-39 |
| 19 Sumner Brown | 1:11:27 | 43 | Belmont, MA | 40-44 |
| 81 Bob Emerson | 1:21:37 | 47 | N Reading, MA | 45-49 |
| 139 Grant Avery | 1:26:01 | 50 | Loudon, NH | 50-54 |
| 168 Robert Shelton | 1:27:58 | 57 | Bradford, VT | 55-59 |
| 355 Earl Stetson | 1:40:34 | 61 | N Conway, NH | 60-64 |
| 401 Carlton Mendell | 1:44:10 | 65 | Portland, ME | 65-69 |
| 650 Howard Kellogg | 2:04:29 | 71 | Holderness, NH | 70-74 |
| 709 Clarke Gilbert | 2:18:50 | 77 | Lake Peekskill, NY | 75-79 |

## Teams

| Women | | Men | |
|---|---|---|---|
| 1 GSRT | 4:00:33 | 1 US BI | 5:57:33 |
| 2 CSU | 4:35:57 | 2 GLRR | 6:00:07 |
| 3 CSU | 4:45:54 | 3 WMM - A | 6:08:22 |
| 4 BAA | 5:08:42 | 4 CSU - A | 6:10:52 |
| | | 5 Club NEast | 6:18:36 |
| | | 6 BAA | 6:38:27 |
| | | 7 Willimantic | 6:45:52 |
| | | 8 GNB | 6:49:11 |
| | | 9 WCRC | 7:17:49 |
| | | 10 GMAA | 7:18:56 |

June 18, 1988
Saturday
800 Finishers

A record field of 800 runners turned out for the newly dubbed "Race to the Sky" (also called the "Run to the Sky" this year).  Temperatures of 70 degrees at the base and 47 at the summit with winds a mild 25 mph made for some fast times.  Runners turned out from 17 states, DC, Canada, and Great Britain.

Invited runners included the 1987 World Mountain trophy champion Jay Johnson of Boulder, Colorado, Sheldon Larson, and Janine Aiello.  Johnson had also recently won the Big Sur Marathon.  Sheldon Larson was returning to Mt Washington for a third time, and he had captured the 1987 Pikes Peak race.  Janine Aiello of San Rafael, California, looked to be the women's favorite.  She was a three-time winner and the course record holder of the Empire State Building run-up.

Johnson and Dave Dunham stayed together for the first two miles before Dunham pulled away.  Just before three miles Dunham was nearly hit by a car coming down the mountain.  Dunham was unfazed as he set a course record of 1:00:50, becoming the first person to break 1:01.  Johnson followed a little over two minutes back with Larson taking third.  Eleven runners broke 1:10 in the favorable conditions.  Johnson noted in the *Union Leader,* "The race was harder than I expected.  I'm just pleased to get second."  Aiello, who led from start to finish took the women's race.  Aiello noted in the *Union Leader*, "It's really hard.  I've never experience anything like it in my life.  It's and incredible race."  Dunham was quoted in the *Mountain Ear,* "after the half, it just seemed to go on and on."  He earned $500 for winning the race, and an additional $500 for setting a course record, along with $100 for leading at the half.  Aiello earned $500 for the win.

The team victory went to the GLRR in 5:48:56, which was the fifth fastest time.  The women's champion team was the WMM over the BAA 4:36:47 to 4:56:56.
Numerica Savings Bank sponsored the race and increased the prize purse.  The total prize purse was $2550 plus time incentives.  Entry fees remained at $12, and the fee was now waived for former winners along with the top ten men and top five women and the top 40+ man/woman.  Awards were expanded to the top finishers in the under 20, and all 10 year age groups starting at 40-49.  Women were no longer allowed to score on an "open" team.  Entries for the race closed in 10 days.  Plans for 1988 included restricting traffic at the start to allow up to one thousand competitors to run.

## Top 25 Finishers

| Place Name | Team | Time | Age | City and State | |
|---|---|---|---|---|---|
| 1 Dave Dunham | GLRR | 1:00:50 | 24 | Lowell, MA | **Course Record** |
| 2 Jay Johnson | | 1:03:09 | 28 | Boulder, CO | |
| 3 Sheldon Larson | | 1:04:25 | 27 | Boulder, CO | |

| Place Name | Team | Time | Age | City and State |
|---|---|---|---|---|
| 4 Martin Kryska | | 1:06:11 | 23 | Hanover, NH |
| 5 Keith Woodward | | 1:06:40 | 37 | E Corinth, VT    FW |
| 6 John Fiola | | 1:07:53 | 25 | Arlington, MA |
| 7 Sean Hanley | | 1:08:46 | 27 | Sharon, MA |
| 8 Mike Casner | CNE | 1:09:00 | 26 | Bristol, NH |
| 9 Joseph Stanley Jr. | | 1:09:08 | 35 | Prospect, CT |
| 10 Steve Peterson | GLRR | 1:09:11 | 22 | Lowell, MA |
| 11 Tom Carroll | GLRR | 1:09:53 | 37 | Lowell, MA |
| 12 James McAvoy | | 1:10:05 | 28 | Goffstown, NH |
| 13 Art Sorrell | CNE | 1:10:10 | 28 | Laconia, NH |
| 14 Bill O'Mara | | 1:10:18 | 30 | Acushnet, MA |
| 15 Michael Beeman | | 1:10:43 | 32 | Derry, NH |
| 16 Sean Livingston | WMM | 1:10:54 | 19 | Conway, NH |
| 17 Sumner Brown | | 1:11:10 | 44 | Belmont, MA |
| 18 David Byrnes | | 1:11:32 | 37 | Chapel Essex |
| 19 Paul Merrill | | 1:11:56 | 34 | Portland, ME |
| 20 Len Hall | WMM | 1:12:00 | 34 | Monroe, NH |
| 21 Richard Surace | WMM | 1:12:32 | 22 | Syracuse, NY |
| 22 Walter Murphy | GLRR | 1:12:38 | 34 | Boxboro, MA |
| 23 James Kent | | 1:12:57 | 27 | Norton, MA |
| 24 George Frost | CNE | 1:13:05 | 34 | Laconia, NH |
| 25 Chris Moulton | CNE | 1:13:05 | 22 | Keene, NH |
| 29 John Cederholm | | 1:15:05 | 45 | Boston, MA    **FW** |

## Top 25 Women

| Place  Name | Team | Time | Age | City and State |
|---|---|---|---|---|
| 1 Janine Aiello | | 1:20:48 | 28 | San Rafael, CA |
| 2 Ruth Hall | | 1:21:09 | 30 | Gorham, NH |
| 3 Lynn Achee | WMM | 1:30:37 | 32 | Manchester Ctr., NH |
| 4 Beth Walker-Corkery | | 1:30:48 | 28 | Jamaica Plain, MA |
| 5 Terry Young | WMM | 1:32:06 | 26 | Intervale, NH |
| 6 Janet Perkins | | 1:32:12 | 26 | Merrimac |
| 7 Carol Bickford | | 1:32:30 | 33 | Somersworth |
| 8 Gretchen Walthers | | 1:32:47 | 17 | Northfield |
| 9 Sharon Gilligan | | 1:33:19 | 40 | Charlestown |
| 10 Gayle Richards | WMM | 1:34:04 | 26 | Jackson, NH |
| 11 Gail Turner | | 1:34:45 | 28 | Newtonville, NH |
| 12 Barbara Scott | | 1:34:50 | 32 | N Conway, NH |
| 13 Leslie Brown | | 1:35:14 | 30 | Prospect, CT |
| 14 Debbie Crow | | 1:36:52 | 37 | Stowe, CT |
| 15 Bette Davis | | 1:37:02 | 44 | Cambridge, MA |
| 16 Marsha Giglio | | 1:38:07 | 44 | Hallowell, ME |
| 17 Martina Quinn | | 1:39:23 | 38 | Exeter, NH |

| Place | Name | Team | Time | Age | City and State |
|---|---|---|---|---|---|
| 18 | Dotty Fine | | 1:41:04 | 43 | Boston, MA |
| 19 | Lynne Smith | | 1:41:58 | 28 | Hillsboro, NH |
| 20 | Melissa Sandifer | | 1:42:08 | 26 | S Hadley, MA |
| 21 | Anne Schmitt | | 1:42:28 | 41 | Boston, MA |
| 22 | Gail Kinney | | 1:42:39 | 36 | Conway, NH |
| 23 | Sharon Crawford | | 1:43:02 | 43 | Concord |
| 24 | Vickie Sears | | 1:43:13 | 30 | Nashua, NH |
| 25 | Connie Gilman | | 1:43:18 | 41 | Meredith, NH |

## 5-Year Age Groups

| Place | Name | Time | Age | City and State | Category | |
|---|---|---|---|---|---|---|
| 254 | Gretchen Walthers | 1:32:47 | 17 | Northfield | Under 20 | |
| 460 | Pam Moore | 1:46:03 | 24 | Hillsborough | 20-24 | |
| 88 | Janine Aiello | 1:20:48 | 28 | San Rafael, CA | 25-29 | |
| 92 | Ruth Hall | 1:21:09 | 30 | Gorham, NH | 30-34 | |
| 325 | Debbie Crow | 1:36:52 | 37 | Stowe, CT | 35-39 | |
| 263 | Sharon Gilligan | 1:33:19 | 40 | Charlestown | 40-44 | |
| 609 | Suzanne Lemieux | 1:55:24 | 47 | Springfield, MA | 45-49 | |
| 517 | Sandy Hayes | 1:49:21 | 50 | Chelmsford, MA | 50-54 | |
| 587 | Hildy Fosse | 1:54:03 | 59 | Holderness, NH | 55+ | |
| 16 | Sean Livingston | 1:10:54 | 19 | Conway, NH | Under 20 | |
| 1 | Dave Dunham | 1:00:50 | 24 | Lowell, MA | 20-24 | **Age Group Record** |
| 2 | Jay Johnson | 1:03:09 | 28 | Boulder, CO | 25-29 | |
| 14 | Bill O'Mara | 1:10:18 | 30 | Acushnet, MA | 30-34 | |
| 5 | Keith Woodward | 1:06:40 | 37 | E Corinth, VT | 35-39 | |
| 17 | Sumner Brown | 1:11:10 | 44 | Belmont, MA | 40-44 | |
| 29 | John Cederholm | 1:15:05 | 45 | Boston, MA | 45-49 | |
| 149 | Henry Golet | 1:25:16 | 51 | Old Lyme, CT | 50-54 | |
| 178 | Robert Shelton | 1:27:15 | 58 | Bradford, VT | 55-59 | |
| 395 | Earl Stetson | 1:42:11 | 62 | N Conway, NH | 60-64 | |
| 424 | Carlton Mendell | 1:44:11 | 66 | Portland, ME | 65-69 | |
| 658 | Howard Kellogg | 1:59:29 | 72 | Philadelphia, PA | 70+ | **Age Group Record** |

Dave Dunham setting a new course record

**29<sup>th</sup> Mt Washington Road Race**

June 17, 1989
Saturday
820 Finishers

Numerica savings Bank, Bridgton Academy and the radio station WZPK, sponsored the race. WZPK had recently placed a tower on the summit. The weather was 50 degrees at the base and rain and fog for the last two miles. The record field of 820 finishers from 19 states and Canada were greeted by 40 mph winds and visibility of 40 feet in places.

Seven-time winner Bob Hodge shared the lead with 1988 winner and course record holder Dave Dunham. Within the first two minutes of the race they broke away from the chase pack. The duo had multiple run-ins with press vans. They were nearly hit by a van in the first mile and at three miles a van was blocking the tangent. Hodge called out to the van driver "You're just making this whole thing more difficult." Dunham took the lead on the steep final section to take the win by 1.5 seconds. Hodge, who had run a 2:16 marathon in the Olympic trials the previous year (sixth place), made this the closest finish in race history. Dunham can be heard on the race video saying "Hodgie, sorry" as the teammates made their way through the finish chute. Keith Woodward finished in third, nearly four minutes back. Hodge and Dunham would duke it out two weeks later at the New England Athletic Congress (NEAC) 5K championships. Dunham again edged Hodge in a time of 14:24 to 14:27.

Peg Donovan passed through the halfway in a very fast 34:07 and finished the race sixteenth overall. Her effort was not good enough for the win as 1980 BAA Marathon winner Jacqueline Gareau finished first in a new course record. Gareau was 17 seconds back at the half and overtook Donovan in the last two miles. Julie Peterson ran 1:19:24 in her first attempt, becoming only the fifth woman to break 80 minutes. Gareau noted in the *Mountain Ear* that when she saw the final steep climb "I said 'shit' in English. I thought it was more stronger than French." This was the first time three women broke 1:20. The average age for a female finisher passed 35 with an average age of 35.99.

The team title was awarded to the Greater Lowell Road Runners over CSU, 5:50:24 to 6:33:50. GLRR also took the ladies' title in 4:24:17 over the BAA (4:40:08).

Denis Hager stated in the *Union Leader* "It's the most fun of any races I've run. It's a great sense of accomplishment." Karen Cumming's wrote in the *Mountain Ear* that "I had been run/walking with a guy named Bill from Taunton MA and he was beginning to falter. In true expedition fashion, with our heads lowered against the wind and rain, Bill touched my arm and said 'Karen it's all right, go ahead without me'. I never saw him again."

The entry fee rose to $15 with a limit of 900 runners, which was reached in seven days. The cost of driving up the road increased to $11 per car and $4 per passenger.

Teams had to provide a list of team members prior to June 1.  Ten-year age groups were recognized up to 80+.  Prize money (which fell under TAC trust rules) totaled $2,450 plus time incentives.  The road was again closed "at the bottom" from 10:45 AM until 1:00 PM.  Aid stations provided Poland Springs water.

## Top 25

| Place Name | Team | Time | Age | City and State | |
|---|---|---|---|---|---|
| 1 Dave Dunham | GLRR | 1:02:59 | 25 | Lowell, MA | |
| 2 Bob Hodge | GLRR | 1:03:01 | 33 | Clinton, MA | FW |
| 3 Keith Woodward | | 1:06:57 | 38 | E Corinth, VT | FW |
| 4 Sean Hanley | | 1:07:05 | 28 | Sharon, MA | |
| 5 Sheldon Larson | | 1:07:56 | 28 | Boulder, CO | |
| 6 Chris Cameron | | 1:09:10 | 22 | Methuen, MA | |
| 7 Joel Sumrall | | 1:09:59 | 27 | W Townsend, MA | |
| 8 Jeffrey Robie | | 1:10:45 | 32 | Kingston, NH | |
| 9 John Fiola | | 1:11:23 | 26 | Arlington, MA | |
| 10 Rick Stuart | CMeS | 1:12:25 | 31 | Phoenix, AZ | |
| 11 Paul Shepardson | | 1:12:41 | 32 | Pittsfield, MA | |
| 12 Paul Merrill | | 1:12:54 | 35 | Portland, ME | |
| 13 Sumner Brown | CSU | 1:13:00 | 45 | Belmont, MA | |
| **14 Jacqueline Gareau** | | **1:13:13** | **36** | **St Bruno, CAN** | |
| 15 Joe Stanley | | 1:13:16 | 36 | Prospect, CT | |
| **16 Peg Donovan** | **GLRR** | **1:13:26** | **34** | **Auburn, NH** | |
| 17 Bern Kohler | | 1:13:41 | 25 | Cambridge, MA | |
| 18 John Swartz | | 1:13:43 | 41 | Breckenridge, CO | |
| 19 Arthur Demers | GLRR | 1:13:53 | 28 | Pelham, NH | |
| 20 Peter Gallenz | | 1:14:23 | 24 | Hanover, NH | |
| 21 David Johnston | | 1:14:36 | 35 | Brattleboro, VT | |
| 22 Bill O'Mara | | 1:14:40 | 31 | Acushnet, MA | |
| 23 Stephen Peterson | GLRR | 1:14:53 | 23 | Lowell, MA | |
| 24 Chuck Moeser | | 1:15:10 | 37 | Campton, NH | |
| 25 Joseph Daly | | 1:15:27 | 27 | Columbia, MD | |
| 26 Neil Moynihan | Willimantic | 1:15:36 | 30 | Storrs, CT | |
| 27 Thomas Carroll | GLRR | 1:15:38 | 39 | Dunstable, MA | |
| 64 John Cederholm | | 1:21:04 | 46 | Boston, MA | FW |

## Top 25 Women

| Place Name | Team | Time | Age | City and State | |
|---|---|---|---|---|---|
| 1 Jacqueline Gareau | | 1:13:13 | 36 | St Bruno, CAN | **Course Record** |
| 2 Peg Donovan | GLRR | 1:13:26 | 34 | Auburn, NH | FW |
| 3 Julie Peterson | | 1:19:24 | 29 | Beverly, MA | |
| 4 Leslie Maerki | | 1:25:42 | 32 | Southampton, MA | |
| 5 Maureen Sullivan | GLRR | 1:26:13 | 32 | Concord, MA | |

| Place Name | Team | Time | Age | City and State | |
|---|---|---|---|---|---|
| 6 Melissa Smedley | | 1:27:46 | 26 | Cambridge, MA | |
| 7 Gail Turner | | 1:29:12 | 29 | Newtonville, MA | |
| 8 Libby Greaney | | 1:30:49 | 26 | Concord, NH | |
| 9 Anne Kuklinski | | 1:31:18 | 30 | Schenectady, NY | |
| 10 Yvonne Swartz | | 1:31:44 | 27 | Manchester, MA | |
| 11 Pam Moore | | 1:33:24 | 25 | Keene, NH | |
| 12 Marcy Schwam | BAA | 1:34:27 | 36 | Natick, MA | |
| 13 Sharon Barbano | BAA | 1:34:27 | 35 | Newtonville, MA | |
| 14 Alana Larrivee | | 1:34:42 | 25 | Agawam, MA | |
| 15 Beth Walker-Corkery | BAA | 1:35:14 | 29 | Jamaica Plain, MA | |
| 16 Jennifer Calder | | 1:36:18 | 42 | New Canaan, CT | |
| 17 Martha Hatch | WMM | 1:38:27 | 32 | N Conway, NH | |
| 18 Barbara Scott | WMM | 1:38:42 | 33 | N Conway, NH | |
| 19 Lynne Achee | WMM | 1:38:50 | 33 | Middletown Spring, VT | |
| 20 Ann McGrath | | 1:39:08 | 28 | Nyack, NY | |
| 21 Mary Beth Lawlor | | 1:39:20 | 29 | N Andover, MA | |
| 22 Cathy Hodgdon | | 1:39:24 | 30 | Boulder, CO | FW |
| 23 Vickie Sears | | 1:39:39 | 31 | Nashua, NH | |
| 24 Leslie Brown | | 1:39:50 | 31 | Prospect, CT | |
| 25 Angela Giampaolo | | 1:40:53 | 26 | Andover, NH | |

## 5-Year Age Groups

| Place | Name | Time | Age | City and State | Category | |
|---|---|---|---|---|---|---|
| 477 | Lori Paelinck | 1:47:53 | 24 | Merrimack, NH | 20-24 | |
| 42 | Julie Peterson | 1:19:24 | 29 | Beverly, MA | 25-29 | |
| 16 | Peg Donovan | 1:13:26 | 34 | Auburn, NH | 30-34 | |
| 14 | Jacqueline Gareau | 1:13:13 | 36 | St Bruno, CAN | 35-39 | |
| 275 | Jennifer Calder | 1:36:18 | 42 | New Canaan, CT | 40-44 | |
| 436 | Marsha Giglio | 1:45:00 | 45 | Hallowell, ME | 45-49 | |
| 518 | Diana Avery | 1:50:42 | 51 | Loudon, NH | 50-54 | |
| 684 | Hildy Fosse | 2:03:21 | 60 | Holderness, NH | 60+ | |
| 820 | Frances Kellogg | 3:00:50 | 70 | Holderness, NH | 70+ | Age Group Record |
| 56 | Terrence White | 1:20:44 | 19 | Chelmsford, MA | Under 20 | |
| 6 | Chris Cameron | 1:09:10 | 22 | Methuen, MA | 20-24 | |
| 1 | Dave Dunham | 1:02:59 | 25 | Lowell, MA | 25-29 | |
| 2 | Bob Hodge | 1:03:01 | 33 | Clinton, MA | 30-34 | |
| 3 | Keith Woodward | 1:06:57 | 38 | E Corinth, VT | 35-39 | |
| 18 | John Swartz | 1:13:43 | 41 | Breckenridge, CO | 40-44 | |
| 13 | Sumner Brown | 1:13:00 | 45 | Belmont, MA | 45-49 | |
| 69 | Gil Emery | 1:21:20 | 50 | Amesbury, MA | 50-54 | |
| 215 | Robert Shelton | 1:32:50 | 59 | Bradford, VT | 55-59 | |
| 446 | Bill Brace | 1:46:15 | 62 | Concord, MA | 60-64 | |

| 472 | Carlton Mendell | 1:47:35 | 67 | Portland, ME | 65-69 |
| 765 | Howard Kellogg | 2:13:18 | 73 | Holderness, NH | 70+ |

**Teams**

| **Women** | | **Men** | |
| --- | --- | --- | --- |
| 1 GLRR | 4:24:17 | 1 GLRR | 5:50:24 |
| 2 BAA | 4:44:08 | 2 CSU | 6:33:54 |
| 3 WMM | 4:55:59 | 3 WCRC | 6:36:22 |
| 4 CSU | 4:56:54 | 4 CMeS | 6:41:56 |
| 5 Willimantic | 5:04:55 | 5 Willimantic | 6:43:56 |
| | | 6 GCS | 6:45:17 |
| | | 7 MTC | 6:53:50 |
| | | 8 BAA | 6:54:42 |
| | | 9 GLRR B | 7:15:53 |
| | | 10 WMM | 7:33:01 |

Dunham (left) and Hodge (right)

June 16, 1990
Saturday, 10:00 AM
839 Finishers

Pre-race favorites included seven time winner Bob Hodge, reigning champion Dave Dunham, Derek Froude, and Smartex Tambala.  Froude, a New Zealand resident and member of the 1984 New Zealand Olympic marathon team, was training part of the year in Boulder, Colorado, and had recently run a 28:50 for 10 Kilometers.  Tambala from Malawi, Africa had recently won a half-marathon in Canada.  The field appeared to be wide open on the women's side as last years top two finisher were out.  Jacqueline Gareau decided to remain home because of a lingering cold, and Peg Donovan was sidelined with a hip injury.

The weather was a bit warm in the early stages of the race, with temperatures in the 70s.  It cooled to 54 at the summit and winds were only 2-3 mph.  Runners came from 22 states, D.C., and six countries.  The field had a record 839 finishers.

Derek Froude became the first person to crack the one-hour barrier with his victory in 59:16.  He took home $2,000 for the win and record.  Froude ran an even race, passing the half way mark in 28:28 and slowing to only 30:18 for the second half.  Froude, who has run a 2:11 marathon, established a lead after four miles and extended his lead over the chase group.  Dave Dunham held second from the early going and beat Pike's Peak ascent winner and Empire State Building run-up winner, Scott Elliot.  Bob Hodge was hampered by a knee and thigh injury but still managed to place tenth.

Froude related to John Stifler in *New England Runner,* "I used to run hilly legs of relays in New Zealand.  When I read about Mt Washington I said to myself, 'Gee an uphill race.  I think I could do that.'"  Froude prepared for the race by running "some of it on Wednesday at 7:50's."  Dunham conceded, "I ran as hard as I could, the other guy ran faster."  A record 16 runners broke 1:10.

Lynn Brown of Durango Colorado bested a record field of 137 women, winning in 1:19:57.  Brown was the 1988 Pike's Peak ascent champion and had mountain-raced in Europe.  Her splits also showed a steady run as she ran 38:15 and 41:42 for the first and second half of the race.  In *New England Runner,* Brown called it, "the hardest mountain race I've ever run.  Colorado races may go up to 14,000 feet, but there are switchbacks.  They're mild compared to this." A record 16.33% of the finishers were women.

Team competition featured the Greater Lowell Road Runners again taking both the men's and women's titles.  The ladies topped the Winner's Circle by ten minutes, 4:39:42 to 4:49:26.  The men ran the third fastest team time with a 5:39:23.  This placed them behind only the 1979 GBTC (5:35:50) and the 1981 BAA (5:31:07).  Lynn (1:19:57) and Brent Brown (1:09:11) teamed up for a very fast time for a married couple with a 2:29:08.  "Pick-up teams", or teams formed specifically for the race, were allowed this year but weren't eligible for awards.

Sandy Ackerman summed up her experience in a *Derry News* article saying "every year I do it I swear I'll never do it again.  But a month or so after the race I say 'There must be some way these people do it in just over an hour' and I decide to do it again".  Bob Romer, who works in the physics department at Amherst (Massachusetts) College, ran his first Mt Washington race in 1990.  He "trained repeatedly running all the steep roads I could find in my neighborhood, getting their slopes from the topo maps and making graphs of time (minutes/mile) versus slope (feet/mile).  By race day, I knew what price I had to pay for every vertical foot, in my case about .6 seconds per foot, and I quite accurately predicted 1:45 finishing time."  He continued "weather can be a real problem...I hear there is a great view from the summit.  I've never seen it but maybe in another seven years when I turn 80."

New check-in procedures this year required every runner to pick up their own number (numbers were non-transferable) and the entry fee was $15.  The Auto Road would now be closed at the bottom from 9:45 AM until noon.  Autos heading to the summit were now charged $12 per car and $5 per passenger.   Aid stations now provided Monadnock Springs water for the 1,000 runners allowed into the race via a new lottery system.  Consideration was given to top men and women and elite "contenders" along with those who had a consecutive streak of at least six years (beginning with 1983).  Medals were no longer given to the top 50, but to age groups based on previous participation.  The prize purse was $2550 plus time based incentives.

This year marked the return of the Auto Hill climb, which had been last run in 1961.  A field of 50 cars was expected.

**Top 25 finishers**

| Place | Name | Club | Time | Age | City & State | |
|---|---|---|---|---|---|---|
| 1 | Derek Froude | | 0:59:17 | 31 | Boulder, CO (NZL) | **Course Record** |
| 2 | Dave Dunham | GLRR | 1:01:37 | 26 | Londonderry, NH | **FW** |
| 3 | Scott Elliott | | 1:01:53 | 26 | Boulder, CO | |
| 4 | Brian Reinhold | | 1:05:36 | 36 | Akersberga, SWE | |
| 5 | Keith Woodward | | 1:06:12 | 39 | E Corinth, VT | **FW** |
| 6 | Erich Wilbrech | | 1:06:26 | 28 | Jackson, WY | |
| 7 | Joel Somerall | GCS | 1:06:32 | 28 | W Townsend, MA | |
| 8 | Matthew Cull | | 1:07:22 | 29 | Bristol, VT | |
| 9 | Peter Heesen | | 1:07:24 | 35 | Bethlehem, PA | |
| 10 | Robert Hodge | GLRR | 1:07:35 | 34 | Clinton, MA | **FW** |
| 11 | Daniel Verrington | WCRC | 1:07:58 | 27 | Bradford, MA | |
| 12 | Peter Farwell | BRR | 1:08:49 | 39 | Williamstown, MA | |
| 13 | John Fiola | | 1:08:58 | 27 | Arlington, MA | |
| 14 | Stephen Peterson | GLRR | 1:09:08 | 29 | Lowell, MA | |
| 15 | Brent Brown | | 1:09:11 | 35 | Durango, CO | |
| 16 | Thomas Carroll | GLRR | 1:09:52 | 40 | Dunstable, MA | |
| 17 | Rick Stuart | | 1:10:21 | 32 | Phoenix, AZ | |
| 18 | Randal Sightler | | 1:10:23 | 31 | Winooski, VT | |

| 19 John Swartz | | 1:10:30 | 42 | Breckenridge, CO | |
| 20 Joseph Daly | WAC | 1:10:37 | 28 | Columbia, MD | |
| 21 Jeffrey Robie | | 1:10:48 | 33 | Kingston, NH | |
| 22 Tom Bowmaster | | 1:11:05 | 30 | Morristown, NJ | |
| 23 Robert Colantuono | BRR | 1:11:07 | 37 | N Adams, MA | |
| 24 David Lapierre | GLRR | 1:11:11 | 26 | Lowell, MA | |
| 25 Sumner Brown | | 1:11:41 | 46 | Belmont, MA | |
| 37 John Cederholm | | 1:15:40 | 47 | Boston, MA | FW |

**Top 25 Women**

| Place  Name | Club | Time | Age | City & State |
|---|---|---|---|---|
| 1 Lynn Brown | | 1:19:57 | 29 | Durango, CO |
| 2 Kelly Brinkmema | | 1:22:11 | 26 | Amherst, NH |
| 3 Libby Greaney | | 1:22:42 | 27 | Henniker, NH |
| 4 Maureen Sullivan | GLRR | 1:23:16 | 33 | Concord, MA |
| 5 Yvonne Swartz | | 1:28:46 | 28 | Manchester, MA |
| 6 Catherine Lifschultz | | 1:29:11 | 27 | Brookline, MA |
| 7 Nancy Sutton | | 1:29:31 | 29 | Manchester, NH |
| 8 Nixie Raymond | CSU | 1:30:04 | 30 | Watertown, MA |
| 9 Sue Passler | WCRC | 1:30:51 | 34 | Amesbury, MA |
| 10 Liz Kellogg | | 1:31:38 | 42 | Portland, OR |
| 11 Jeryl Simpson | | 1:32:27 | 32 | Delmar, NY |
| 12 Jennifer Calder | | 1:32:32 | 43 | New Canaan, CT |
| 13 Anne Kuklinski | | 1:32:44 | 31 | Schenectady, NY |
| 14 Beth Walker-Corkery | | 1:33:35 | 30 | Needham, MA |
| 15 Carol Bickford | | 1:33:54 | 35 | Gonic, NH |
| 16 Sharon Gilligan | | 1:34:05 | 42 | Charlestown, MA |
| 17 Barbara Scott | | 1:34:23 | 34 | Whitefield, NH |
| 18 Donna Kasianchuk | | 1:34:30 | 33 | Wolfeboro Falls, NH |
| 19 Kelly Goddard | | 1:35:21 | 26 | Gorham, NH |
| 20 Merrill Cray | | 1:35:41 | 37 | Lake Elmore, VT |
| 21 Katie Modeen | | 1:36:05 | 34 | Waterbury, CT |
| 22 Stella McCormick | WCRC | 1:36:11 | 30 | Salem, MA |
| 23 Ann Kucharski | | 1:36:31 | 38 | N Andover, MA |
| 24 Leslie Brown | | 1:37:48 | 32 | Prospect, CT |
| 25 Patty Girouard | GLRR | 1:37:51 | 42 | Stowe, VT |

**Teams:**

| Men | | Women | |
|---|---|---|---|
| 1 GLRR | 5:39:23 | 1 GLRR | 4:39:42 |
| 2 BRR | 6:16:54 | 2 WCRC | 4:49:26 |
| 3 WCRC | 6:17:39 | 3 CSU | 4:50:57 |
| 4 GCS | 6:27:00 | 4 BAA | 4:51:29 |
| 5 Willimantic | 6:30:21 | 5 WMM | 4:57:08 |

**5-Year Age Groups**

| Place | Name | Time | Age | City and State | Category | |
|---|---|---|---|---|---|---|
| 551 | Melanie Hannon | 1:49:45 | 19 | Concord, MA | Under 20 | |
| 372 | Gail Heinrich | 1:39:36 | 24 | Bedford, MA | 20-24 | |
| 69 | Lynn Brown | 1:19:57 | 29 | Durango, CO | 25-29 | |
| 100 | Maureen Sullivan | 1:23:16 | 33 | Concord, MA | 30-34 | |
| 267 | Carol Bickford | 1:33:54 | 35 | Gonic, NH | 35-39 | |
| 233 | Liz Kellogg | 1:31:38 | 42 | Portland, OR | 40-44 | |
| 375 | Bette Davis | 1:39:38 | 46 | Cambridge, MA | 45-49 | |
| 572 | Diana Avery | 1:51:07 | 52 | Loudon, NH | 50-54 | |
| 690 | Dorothy Bergman | 2:00:03 | 58 | Swampscott, MA | 55-59 | |
| 686 | Hildy Fosse | 1:59:45 | 61 | Holderness, NH | 60-64 | **Age Group Record** |
| 834 | Frances Kellogg | 2:45:04 | 71 | Holderness, NH | 65-69 | |
| | | | | | | |
| 112 | Chad Sutcliffe | 1:24:49 | 17 | Kennebunk, ME | Under 20 | |
| 46 | Smartex Tambala | 1:17:07 | 24 | Bedford NS CAN | 20-24 | |
| 2 | Dave Dunham | 1:01:37 | 26 | Londonderry, NH | 25-29 | |
| 1 | Derek Froude | 0:59:17 | 31 | Boulder, CO (NZL) | 30-34 | |
| 4 | Brian Reinhold | 1:05:36 | 36 | Akersberga SWE | 35-39 | |
| 17 | Thomas Carroll | 1:09:52 | 40 | Dunstable, MA | 40-44 | |
| 26 | Sumner Brown | 1:11:41 | 46 | Belmont, MA | 45-49 | |
| 141 | Henry Golet | 1:26:34 | 53 | Old Lyme, CT | 50-54 | |
| 150 | John Saarinen | 1:27:06 | 55 | Stow, MA | 55-59 | |
| 281 | Leon Beverly | 1:34:26 | 63 | Stamford, VT | 60-64 | **Age Group Record** |
| 499 | Carlton Mendell | 1:46:44 | 68 | Portland, ME | 65-69 | |
| 706 | Howard Kellogg | 2:01:43 | 74 | Holderness, NH | 70+ | |

Ronald Johnston on the final pitch

June 15, 1991
Saturday, 10:00 AM
876 Finishers

As the race entry fee increased to $20 and the 1,000-runner limit required applications to be submitted by March 15 to be eligible for the lottery.  The cash purse increased to $4150 and all award winners were now granted a lottery by-pass for the following year.  For the first time age graded times were listed based on tables from the World Association of Veteran Athletes (WAVA).  Race Director Bob Teschek noted in the race guidelines "Adjusted times allow us to compare our performances…to be compared fairly across the entire age range."  In a somewhat controversial move, prize money for 40+ runners would be awarded based on the WAVA times.  A new sponsor for the race was Haagen-Dazs, who provided frozen yogurt after the race for the record crowd of 876 finishers from 23 states and Canada.

Derek Froude returned and ran history's second fastest time.  He led through the half in 28:25 (three seconds faster than last year) gapping runner-up Dave Dunham by one minute.  He finished with a 1:31 margin of victory over Dunham.  Seven-time champion Bob Hodge took third place in 65:32.  Dunham and Hodge finished third and fourth in the NEAC 10K championships the week before.  Froude may have been feeling the aftereffects of a 2:16 marathon he had run in the previous month.  The men's average finishing time was 1:39:42, the first time it dipped under 1:40 since 1983.

Conditions were windy with light rain and cold temperatures in the second half with 40-50 MPH winds and 45- degree summit temperatures.  Chris Maisto came back after a three-year absence to take nearly a minute off of the course record with a 1:12:15.  Julie Peterson led through the half in 34:02 with Maisto 24 seconds back.  Peterson's 1:14:19 and Peg Donovan (1:16:51) made for the fastest top three women as they led a record field of 147 to the finish line.  Donovan had won in 1987 and was second in 1989 and was also the NEAC 30K champion.  Maisto noted in *New England Runner*, "my legs were giving way at the end, but other than that I felt good the whole way."  Maisto won $600 for the victory and an additional $500 for running under 1:15. A record 13 women broke 1:30 and this was only the second time that three women broke 1:20.

The female team champions were Liberty AC over the Greater Lowell Road Runners 4:19:52 to 4:24 as six teams broke five hours.  The GLRR men ran the second fastest team time, behind only the BAA's 1981 time of 5:31 winning by 36 minutes in 5:33:53.  Former champion Keith Woodward won $250 for leading the age adjusted scoring as did Liz Kellogg on the ladies age adjusted.

Steve Peterson, GLRR's third man in eight place ran 1:08:01 and had a unique experience.  In his race story from the *GLRR Newsletter* he recounts, "Never, I repeat never, run the mountain with shoes that you think do not fit snug in the heel.  I did and will never again.  My right heel was not snug in the heel for most of the race.  I cherished the semi-flat stretches of road when I could hit the ground with my whole foot and let the heel feel support.  Sure enough as I turned into the final stretch in a really good mood, I felt the right and then the left shoe give way.  I did not even break stride, proceeding up the hill in my good ole socks.  I crossed the line with a huge smile on my face and my fingers pointing down at my white socks."

ESPN broadcast clips of the race on an episode of *Running and Racing* later in the summer.

**Top 25 Finishers**

| Place Name | Team | Time | Age | City and State | |
|---|---|---|---|---|---|
| 1 Derek Froude | | 1:00:35 | 32 | Boulder, CO | |
| 2 Dave Dunham | GLRR | 1:02:07 | 27 | Londonderry, NH | **FW** |
| 3 Bob Hodge | GLRR | 1:05:32 | 35 | Clinton, MA | **FW** |
| 4 Mike Casner | | 1:06:03 | 29 | Keene, NH | |
| 5 Matthew Cull | | 1:07:22 | 30 | Bristol, VT | |
| 6 Sean Hanley | | 1:07:42 | 30 | Watertown, MA | |
| 7 Joe Stanley | | 1:07:51 | 38 | Prospect, CT | |
| 8 Stephen Peterson | GLRR | 1:08:01 | 25 | Lowell, MA | |
| 9 Daniel Verrington | WCRC | 1:08:29 | 28 | Bradford, MA | |
| 10 Keith Woodward | | 1:08:32 | 40 | E Corinth, VT | **FW** |
| 11 David Lapierre | GLRR | 1:08:45 | 27 | Lowell, MA | |
| 12 Jeffery Robie | MVS | 1:09:04 | 34 | Kingston, NH | |
| 13 Randal Sightler | | 1:09:15 | 32 | Winooski, VT | |
| 14 Thomas Carroll | GLRR | 1:09:28 | 41 | Dunstable, MA | |
| 15 Mark Asaro | GLRR | 1:09:51 | 35 | Gloucester, MA | |
| 16 Robert Colantuono | Berks | 1:10:06 | 39 | N Adams, MA | |
| 17 Richard Marion | | 1:10:14 | 29 | Sterling, MA | |
| 18 Paul Shepardson | Berks | 1:11:20 | 34 | Pittsfield, MA | |
| 19 Paul Merrill | METC | 1:11:26 | 37 | Portland, ME | |
| 20 Nelson Lebo | | 1:11:36 | 23 | Mount Hermon, MA | |
| 21 Rick Stuart | CMeS | 1:11:48 | 33 | Phoenix, AZ | |
| 22 Peter Lessard | CMeS | 1:11:52 | 29 | Oakland, ME | |
| 23 John Shanley | | 1:11:54 | 31 | Hamden, CT | |
| **24 Christine Maisto** | | **1:12:15** | **31** | **Morristown, NJ** | |
| 25 Bill O'Mara | | 1:12:26 | 33 | Acushnet, MA | |
| 26 Pete Farwell | Berks | 1:12:36 | 40 | Williamstown, MA | |

**Top 25 Women**

| Place Name | Team | Time | Age | City and State | |
|---|---|---|---|---|---|
| 1 Christine Maisto | | 1:12:15 | 31 | Morristown, NJ | **Course record** |
| 2 Julie Peterson | LAC | 1:14:19 | 31 | Beverly, MA | |
| 3 Peg Donovan | GLRR | 1:16:51 | 36 | Auburn, NH | **FW** |
| 4 Jo Gathercole | | 1:24:23 | 37 | Jackson Hole, WY | |
| 5 Sue Lachance | CSU | 1:24:37 | 31 | Shirley, MA | |
| 6 Gail Turner | METC | 1:27:19 | 31 | Yarmouth, ME | |

| Place | Name | Team | Time | Age | City and State |
|---|---|---|---|---|---|
| 7 | Yvonne Swartz | LAC | 1:27:56 | 29 | Essex, MA |
| 8 | Libby Greaney | BC/BS | 1:28:12 | 28 | Henniker, NH |
| 9 | Nanci Sirois | | 1:28:31 | 33 | Windham, NH |
| 10 | Patti Laliberte | GCS | 1:28:37 | 36 | Merrimack, NH |
| 11 | Mary Beth Evans | | 1:28:57 | 31 | New York, NY |
| 12 | Catherine Lifschultz | BAA | 1:29:03 | 28 | Brookline MA |
| 13 | Anne Davee | CMeS | 1:29:20 | 35 | Bowdoinham, ME |
| 14 | Lucia Greenough | | 1:31:45 | 35 | Ipswich, MA |
| 15 | Linda Waitkun | | 1:31:50 | 38 | N Conway, NH |
| 16 | Deb Brazil | | 1:32:59 | 36 | S Boston, MA |
| 17 | Eileen Dunfey | | 1:33:10 | 35 | Cape Elizabeth, ME |
| 18 | Mary Jane Boyd | GLRR | 1:33:15 | 28 | Cambridge, MA |
| 19 | Liz Kellogg | | 1:33:32 | 42 | Portland, OR |
| 20 | Ann Kucharski | MVS | 1:33:42 | 39 | N Andover, MA |
| 21 | Karen Connor | BC/BS | 1:34:09 | 30 | Bow, NH |
| 22 | Anne Kuklinski | | 1:34:23 | 32 | Portsmouth, RI |
| 23 | Sue Maslowski | GLRR | 1:34:38 | 38 | Billerica, MA |
| 24 | Leslie Brown | | 1:35:22 | 33 | Prospect, CT |
| 25 | Sarah Sauvayre | | 1:35:50 | 30 | New York, NY |

## 5-Year Age Groups

| Place | Name | Team | Time | Age | City and State | |
|---|---|---|---|---|---|---|
| 705 | Livvy Williams | | 1:54:57 | 16 | Manoment, MA | Under 20 |
| 347 | Ginger Robber | | 1:36:27 | 23 | Glen, NH | 20-24 |
| 188 | Yvonne Swartz | | 1:27:56 | 29 | Essex, MA | 25-29 |
| 24 | Christine Maisto | | 1:12:15 | 31 | Morristown, NJ | 30-34 |
| 47 | Peg Donovan | | 1:16:51 | 36 | Auburn, NH | 35-39 |
| 290 | Liz Kellogg | | 1:33:32 | 42 | Portland, OR | 40-44 |
| 493 | Jane Levesque | | 1:43:31 | 49 | Nashua, NH | 45-49 |
| 476 | Louisa Dunlap | | 1:42:54 | 50 | Belfast, ME | 50-54 **Age Group Record** |
| 731 | Maggie Solomon | | 1:57:01 | 57 | Conway, NH | 55-59 |
| 796 | Hildy Fosse | | 2:05:32 | 62 | Holderness, NH | 60-64 |
| 868 | Frances Kellogg | | 2:29:49 | 72 | Holderness, NH | 70+ **Age Group Record** |
| 65 | Jeremy Brooks | | 1:18:43 | 19 | Salem, NH | Under 20 |
| 20 | Nelson Lebo | | 1:11:36 | 23 | Mt Hermon, MA | 20-24 |
| 2 | Dave Dunham | | 1:02:07 | 27 | Londonderry, NH | 25-29 |
| 1 | Derek Froude | | 1:00:35 | 32 | Boulder, CO | 30-34 |
| 3 | Bob Hodge | | 1:05:32 | 35 | Clinton, MA | 35-39 |
| 10 | Keith Woodward | | 1:08:32 | 40 | E Corinth, VT | 40-44 |
| 27 | Sumner Brown | | 1:12:37 | 47 | Belmont, MA | 45-49 |
| 122 | Eric White | | 1:24:16 | 50 | N Adams, MA | 50-54 |
| 144 | Bruce Brinkema | | 1:25:52 | 56 | Amherst, NH | 55-59 |

| Place | Name | Team Time | | Age | City and State | |
|---|---|---|---|---|---|---|
| 250 | Robert Shelton | 1:31:06 | | 61 | Bradford, VT | 60-64 **Age Group Record** |
| 440 | Earl Stetson | 1:41:22 | | 65 | Conway, NH | 65-69 |
| 755 | Charley Reed | 1:59:39 | | 70 | Gorham, NH | 70-74 |
| 766 | Howard Kellogg | 2:01:51 | | 75 | Holderness, NH | 75+ |

## Top Teams

**Women's Open**

| 1 Liberty AC | 4:19:52 |
|---|---|
| 2 GLRR | 4:24:44 |
| 3 CSU | 4:47:46 |
| 4 BC/BS | 4:50:22 |
| 5 BAA | 4:50:34 |

**Men's Open**

| 1 GLRR | 5:33:53 |
|---|---|
| 2 Berkshire | 6:09:04 |
| 3 WCRC | 6:15:04 |
| 4 CMeS | 6:23:27 |
| 5 Maine TC | 6:29:11 |

**Men's 40+**

| 1 Berkshire | 7:05:15 |
|---|---|
| 2 MVS | 7:05:45 |
| 3 CMeS | 7:09:39 |
| 4 WCRC | 7:34:32 |

**Women's 40+**

| 1 White Mtn | 6:11:41 |
|---|---|

**Men's 50+**

| 1 Berkshire | 4:38:44 |
|---|---|
| 2 Bridgton | 5:17:51 |
| 3 RICH | 5:19:13 |
| 4 White Mtn | 5:24:54 |
| 5 Maine TC | 5:31:03 |
| 6 MVS | 5:31:27 |

## 32nd Mt Washington Road Race

June 20, 1992
Saturday, 10:00 AM
881 Finishers

Runners from 25 states, D.C. and Canada filled out the record field of 881 finishers. Favorites included course record holder Derek Froude, Dave Dunham who was still recovering from a twentieth place 2:21 in the Olympic Trials marathon, and Bob Hodge who finished third in the previous year. Matthew Cull had warmed up for the race by winning the Prospect Mountain race in Lake George, NY in a course record. He followed that up a week later with a win at the 3186-foot climb up Mt Equinox. At Equinox, Cull pulled another top Mt Washington runner Keith Woodward, to a master's record second place finish. Others of note included Tomasz Gnabel of Poland and Matt Carpenter a two-time Pike's Peak ascent champion. Carpenter noted in the *Union Leader*, "I think we'll (Colorado runners) be right in there as far as the record goes. Maybe we'll show you guys how to really run a mountain."

Carpenter and Derek Froude pushed each other until three miles when Carpenter pulled ahead. He passed the half in 29:00 with Froude 30 seconds back. Froude slowed to a walk at one point but was able to maintain a lead over GLRR teammates Dunham and Hodge. Dunham caught Froude at 5 miles but Froude was able to regroup and pull away. Carpenter took the victory by nearly two minutes with a fine 1:00:42. He led 15 men under 1:10 and a record three men under

1:05 in favorable conditions of 51 degrees at the summit with 10 mph winds and 72 degrees at the base.

J'Ne Day-Lucore, the Pike's Peak ascent record holder broke the women's course record by 30 seconds.  Julie Peterson led through the half in 34:05 with Day-Lucore a few seconds back.  As Day-Lucore powered to a 1:11:45, Peterson continued on to take second in 1:14:41.  Day-Lucore won $600 for the victory and an additional $500 for running under 1:15.  Peterson was awarded $400 for finishing second and $100 for leading the women's field at half-way.   After the race Day-Lucore stated in *New England Runner* that she "saved too much" despite setting the record.  Carpenter was quoted in the *Union Leader,* "I think this course is doable in 55 minutes."

Chuck Smead ran the second fastest time in the 40+ age group finishing eight overall in 1:07:16, slightly more than two minutes behind the record he was shooting for.  Other finishers included Gnabel, who took sixth and 1991 Pike's Peak winner Steve Smalez, who finished fifteenth in 1:09:06.

For the first time, master (40+) men's and women's teams were scored.  The combined times of the top three runners were used to score the teams.   Maine TC won the female 40+ team title in 5:22:21 and Green Mountain AC won the men's in 3:58:51.  Three runners combined times were used.  The Central Mass. Striders made their first appearance and ran an excellent 5:41:36 to win by nearly 46 minutes over the Berkshire Road Rats.  The Boston Running Club took the women's title in 4:18:28, besting Liberty AC by 23 minutes.

Blue Cross / Blue Shield of NH came on as a new sponsor along with New Dartmouth Bank.

**Top 25 Finishers**

| Place  Name | Club | Time | Age | City and State |
|---|---|---|---|---|
| 1 Matt Carpenter | | 1:00:42 | 27 | Colorado Springs, CO |
| 2 Derek Froude | | 1:02:27 | 33 | Boulder, CO   (NZL) **FW** |
| 3 Dave Dunham | CMS | 1:03:18 | 28 | Londonderry, NH   **FW** |
| 4 Bob Hodge | | 1:04:31 | 36 | Clinton, MA   **FW** |
| 5 Sean Livingston | | 1:04:56 | 23 | Conway, NH |
| 6 Tomasz Gnabel | | 1:06:02 | 25 | Alamosa, CO  (POL) |
| 7 Mike Casner | CMS | 1:06:57 | 30 | Keene, NH |
| 8 Chuck Smead | | 1:07:16 | 40 | Mosca, CO |
| 9 James Seefeldt | | 1:07:25 | 26 | Alamosa, CO |
| 10 Matthew Cull | | 1:07:28 | 31 | Manchester Ctr., VT |
| 11 Keith Woodward | GMAA | 1:08:16 | 41 | E Corinth, VT   **FW** |
| 12 Joe Stanley | | 1:08:18 | 39 | Prospect, CT |
| 13 Daniel Verrington | CMS | 1:08:35 | 29 | Bradford, MA |
| 14 Art Sorrell | | 1:08:45 | 32 | Laconia, NH |
| 15 Stephen Smalez | | 1:09:06 | 27 | Boulder, CO |
| 16 Jim Garcia | CMS | 1:10:09 | 33 | Leominster, MA |
| 17 Stephen Peterson | | 1:10:28 | 26 | Clinton, MA |

| Place | Name | Club | Time | Age | City and State | |
|-------|------|------|------|-----|----------------|---|
| 18 | Ernesto Riano | | 1:10:36 | 35 | Lowell, MA | |
| 19 | David Johnston | | 1:10:40 | 38 | Brattleboro, VT | |
| 20 | Brian Stevens | | 1:10:59 | 28 | New Boston, NH | |
| 21 | Randal Sightler | | 1:11:11 | 33 | Winooski, VT | |
| 22 | Robert Colantuono | BRR | 1:11:15 | 40 | N Adams, MA | |
| 23 | Sean Hanley | | 1:11:40 | 31 | Salem, MA | |
| 24 | J'Ne Day-Lucore | | 1:11:45 | 31 | Denver, CO | Course Record |
| 25 | Peter Lessard | CMeS | 1:12:09 | 30 | Winslow, ME | |
| 26 | Peter Blomquist | CMS | 1:12:37 | 40 | Worcester, MA | |
| 51 | John Cederholm | | 1:18:33 | 49 | Boston, MA | FW |
| 837 | Angus Wooten | | 2:15:11 | 52 | Willimantic, CT | FW |

## Top 25 Women

| Place | Name | Club | Time | Age | City and State | |
|-------|------|------|------|-----|----------------|---|
| 1 | J'Ne Day-Lucore | | 1:11:45 | 31 | Denver, CO | Course Record |
| 2 | Julie Peterson | LAC | 1:14:41 | 32 | Beverly, MA | |
| 3 | Pam Moore | | 1:20:22 | 28 | Keene, NH | |
| 4 | Catherine Lifschultz | BRC | 1:21:03 | 29 | Brookline, MA | |
| 5 | Kim Marie Goff | BRC | 1:24:03 | 31 | Greenville, RI | |
| 6 | Ann Benoit | GCS | 1:26:18 | 28 | Waterville Valley, ME | |
| 7 | Libby Greaney | | 1:27:18 | 29 | Henniker, NH | |
| 8 | Karen Powers | | 1:31:58 | 37 | Concord, MA | |
| 9 | Debbie Greenslit | | 1:32:26 | 36 | Worcester, MA | |
| 10 | Sharon Barbano | BRC | 1:33:22 | 38 | Newtonville, MA | |
| 11 | Lucia Greenough | LAC | 1:33:23 | 36 | Ipswich, MA | |
| 12 | Karen Knuepfer | | 1:34:35 | 40 | York, PA | |
| 13 | Patricia Crane | | 1:34:55 | 31 | Dalton, MA | |
| 14 | Liz Kellogg | | 1:35:04 | 43 | Portland, OR | |
| 15 | Deborah Sheedy | | 1:35:54 | 36 | Waltham, MA | |
| 16 | Paula Holm | | 1:36:12 | 39 | Newburyport, MA | |
| 17 | Kimberly Carlson | | 1:36:22 | 29 | Boston, MA | |
| 18 | Dorothy Helling | | 1:37:33 | 42 | Montpelier, VT | |
| 19 | Janet Bradley | | 1:39:02 | 40 | Windsor, MA | |
| 20 | Elaine Stoeckle | | 1:39:07 | 44 | Barrington, RI | |
| 21 | Allie McGuinness | | 1:39:43 | 40 | Newburyport, MA | |
| 22 | Karen Saunders | | 1:39:46 | 39 | Manchester, CT | |
| 23 | Vicki Bush | | 1:40:45 | 37 | Plaistow, NH | |
| 24 | Jennifer Noyes | GCS | 1:40:59 | 28 | Pepperell, MA | |
| 25 | Joan Lavin | MTC | 1:41:09 | 44 | Portland, ME | |

**Top 5 Teams**

| Women's Open | | | Women's 40+ | | |
|---|---|---|---|---|---|
| 1 BRC | 4:18:28 | | 1 MTC | 5:22:21 CR | |
| 2 LAC | 4:41:33 | | 2 RIRR | 5:41:16 | |
| 3 GCS | 4:49:52 | | 3 AA | 5:43:59 | |
| 4 WCRC | 4:56:40 | | 4 WMM | 5:50:39 | |
| 5 BRR | 5:02:34 | | 5 MVS | 6:24:38 | |

| Men's Open | | | Men's 40+ | | |
|---|---|---|---|---|---|
| 1 CMS | 5:41:36 | | 1 GMAA | 3:58:51 | |
| 2 BRR | 6:27:30 | | 2 BRR | 4:02:32 | |
| 3 CMeS | 6:29:17 | | 3 WCRC | 4:12:23 | |
| 4 HTC | 6:32:18 | | 4 MVS | 4:18:15 | |
| 5 WCRC | 6:36:44 | | 5 WMM | 4:24:50 | |

**5-Year age groups**

| Place | Name | Time | Age | City and State | Category |
|---|---|---|---|---|---|
| 543 | Livvy Williams | 1:48:19 | 17 | Manomet, MA | Under 20 |
| 448 | Kristin Wilkes | 1:43:40 | 20 | Narragansett, RI | 20-24 |
| 65 | Pam Moore | 1:20:22 | 28 | Keene, NH | 25-29 |
| 24 | J'Ne Day-Lucore | 1:11:45 | 31 | Denver, CO | 30-34 |
| 227 | Karen Powers | 1:31:58 | 37 | Concord, MA | 35-39 |
| 274 | Karen Knuepfer | 1:34:35 | 40 | York, PA | 40-44 |
| 525 | Sharon Crawford | 1:47:44 | 47 | Concord, MA | 45-49 |
| 394 | Louisa Dunlap | 1:41:16 | 51 | Belfast, ME | 50-54 **Age Group Record** |
| 617 | Jeannette Cyr | 1:51:32 | 57 | Kensington, CT | 55-59 |
| 657 | Dorothy Bergman | 1:54:29 | 60 | Marblehead, MA | 60-64 **Age Group Record** |
| 878 | Frances Kellogg | 2:36:42 | 73 | Holderness, NH | 65-69 |
| 50 | Seth Williams | 1:18:33 | 14 | Manomet, MA | Under 20 |
| 5 | Sean Livingston | 1:04:56 | 23 | Conway, NH | 20-24 |
| 1 | Matt Carpenter | 1:00:42 | 27 | Colorado Spgs, CO | 25-29 |
| 2 | Derek Froude | 1:02:27 | 33 | Boulder, CO | 30-34 |
| 4 | Bob Hodge | 1:04:31 | 36 | Clinton, MA | 35-39 |
| 8 | Chuck Smead | 1:07:16 | 40 | Mosca, CO | 40-44 |
| 51 | John Cederholm | 1:18:33 | 49 | Boston, MA | 45-49 |
| 118 | Doug Ludewig | 1:25:11 | 52 | Monmouth, ME | 50-54 |
| 176 | John Saarinen | 1:29:28 | 57 | Stow, MA | 55-59 |
| 182 | Jay Sturdevant | 1:29:48 | 61 | Ridgefield, CT | 60-64 **Age Group Record** |
| 357 | Leon Beverly | 1:39:34 | 65 | Stamford, VT | 65-69 |
| 661 | Carlton Mendell | 1:54:42 | 70 | Portland, ME | 70-74 **Age Group Record** |
| 799 | Howard Kellogg | 2:06:35 | 76 | Holderness, NH | 75+ |

### 33<sup>rd</sup> Mt Washington Road Race

June 19, 1993
Saturday, 10:00 AM
888 Finishers

New Dartmouth Bank and Blue Cross/Blue Shield joined Bridgton Academy as race sponsors. The 1,000-person lottery was held on March 15 (with a $20 entry fee).  This was the first year that the women's 65-69 age group was scored.  Another addition that was favorably received was the pre and post-race massages by Mark Mills and his team of Therapists.

Leading into the race, Matt Carpenter, J'Ne Day-Lucore, and Chuck Smead were aiming to defend their titles.  In a *Boston Globe* article, Race Director Bob Teschek said of Carpenter and Day-Lucore "Both of them are going for a course record."  Carpenter had smashed the Pike's Peak ascent record the previous spring and was a definite favorite to repeat.  The previous year's third-place finisher, Dave Dunham, was recovering from tendonitis and, when asked about his chances noted "It's so hard to tell, I was as fit as I ever was in my life last year.  I had my worst Mt Washington."  Sub-4-minute miler Eric Morse of Vermont was another New England favorite.  Neji Makhlouf, a Tunisian marathoner with a 2:12 personal best training in Fort Collins, CO also looked to be in the mix.  Local women to watch included Pam Moore from Keene, who was on the mend from an appendectomy and Libby Greaney, who had finished seventh in 1992.

Conditions were difficult as the upper part of the road was closed to traffic at one point because of rain, fog, and slick mud.  The record field of 888 finishers from 21 states, Canada, Tunisia, Poland, and Bermuda were undeterred by the 50-foot visibility, 40-degree temperatures and 32 mph winds.

Carpenter won for the second straight year with the second fastest time run.  He became the second person to break one hour with his 59:49.  Dunham ran the fastest non-winning time to take second in 1:00:44.  Neji Makhlouf pushed Carpenter for the first 1.5 miles before falling back and taking third in 1:02:35.  Makhlouf and Carpenter passed the mile in 6:10 and 2 miles in 13:00.  At halfway Carpenter had a 16-second lead over Dunham.   Dunham noted in a story in *Runner's World* that after seeing Carpenter drop his hat "I thought, 'I'll grab it, sprint, catch him and hand it back. It'll blow his mind'. Then I thought 'There is no way I can reach him.'  So I stomped it!  It pumped me up a little."  Eric Morse was fourth in 1:03:50 and Chuck Smead finished fifth overall with the second fastest 40+ time of 1:05:20, less than 30 seconds shy of the record.   In the *Mountain Ear* Carpenter was quoted as saying, "I'd rather win the race than get a record any day."  A record 17 men broke 1:10.  The average age of the men's field broke 40 years, at 40.6.

J'Ne Day-Lucore ran unchallenged to a 1:12:59 winning time.  Karen Knuepfer was second master; she removed a cast from her leg prior to the start in order to compete. She had a stress fracture, but was still able to take second behind Susan Maslowski.  A record fifteen women broke 1:30.

CMS broke the 12-year-old team record (BAA 5:31:07), running a 5:30:34.  CMS was lead by Dunham (second), Morse (fourth), Casner (tenth), Verrington (twelfth), and Peterson (sixteenth) taking a third of the sub 1:10 times.  CMS also took the women's team title with a fast 4:08:54.  White Mountain Milers and the Winner's Circle placed first and second in the women's 40+ team category with just over one minute separating the two teams.  The GLRR and the GMAA also had a close race with GLRR on top by two minutes in the 40+ men's team category.  *The Mountain Ear* noted, "A team of teachers from Bermuda...chose to use their winnings from a corporate relay to come to compete."

A few of the changes this year included awarding medals to only the top two in each of the 5-year age groups (up to 75+ for men and 60+ for women).  Certificates were still given to all finishers.  The cash purse was $4,350 plus time incentives.  The cash awards were given to the top five overall, top New Hampshire finisher, and top three master's runners based on the WAVA adjusted times.

*The Hockomock Swamp Rat* (a journal of New England running), known for amusing and sarcastic race reports summed up the race saying, "Two...new age, yuppy, perfect toothed, Rocky Mountain runners successfully defended their titles" and included the "Official race song: Rocky Mountain High – John Denver 1968."

**Top 25 Finishers**

| Place | Name | Club | Time | Age | City and State | |
|---|---|---|---|---|---|---|
| 1 | Matt Carpenter | | 0:59:49 | 28 | Colorado Springs, CO | |
| 2 | Dave Dunham | CMS | 1:00:44 | 29 | Londonderry, NH | **FW** |
| 3 | Neji Makhlouf | | 1:02:35 | 31 | Ft Collins, CO  (TUN) | |
| 4 | Eric Morse | CMS | 1:03:50 | 28 | Moretown, VT | |
| 5 | Chuck Smead | | 1:05:20 | 41 | Mosca, CO | |
| 6 | Matthew Cull | | 1:05:28 | 32 | Dorset, VT | |
| 7 | Bob Hodge | | 1:05:54 | 37 | Clinton, MA | **FW** |
| 8 | Sean Livingston | WMM | 1:07:00 | 24 | Conway, NH | |
| 9 | LJ Briggs | HTC | 1:07:28 | 29 | W Hartford, CT | |
| 10 | Mike Casner | CMS | 1:07:59 | 31 | Keene, NH | |
| 11 | Mark Asaro | | 1:08:33 | 37 | Gloucester, MA | |
| 12 | Daniel Verrington | CMS | 1:08:51 | 30 | Bradford, MA | |
| 13 | Patrick Moreton | CSU | 1:09:00 | 33 | Cambridge, MA | |
| 14 | Peter Pfitzinger | WCRC | 1:09:02 | 35 | Exeter, NH | |
| 15 | Keith Woodward | | 1:09:09 | 42 | E Corinth, VT | **FW** |
| 16 | Stephen Peterson | CMS | 1:09:10 | 27 | Clinton, MA | |
| 17 | Rick Stuart | | 1:09:14 | 35 | Phoenix, AZ | |
| 18 | Rich Marion | | 1:10:05 | 31 | Sterling, MA | |
| 19 | John Dowling | | 1:10:13 | 36 | Warner, NH | |
| 20 | Jim Garcia | | 1:10:21 | 34 | Westford, MA | |
| 21 | Lyford Merrow | | 1:10:24 | 32 | Loudon, NH | |
| 22 | Tomasz Gnabel | | 1:10:34 | 26 | Alamosa, CO | |

| 23 Ernesto Riano | | 1:10:37 | 35 | Lowell, MA | |
| 24 Joe Stanley | | 1:10:41 | 40 | Prospect, CT | |
| 25 Russell Whittaker | | 1:10:42 | 34 | Brookline, MA | |
| 127 John Cederholm | | 1:24:46 | 50 | Boston, MA | **FW** |

## Top 25 Women

| Place  Name | Club | Time | Age | City and State |
|---|---|---|---|---|
| 1 J'Ne Day-Lucore | | 1:12:59 | 32 | Denver, CO |
| 2 Margo Webber | CMS | 1:20:00 | 32 | Boxborough, MA |
| 3 Pam Moore | MCS | 1:20:57 | 29 | Keene, NH |
| 4 Sue Lachance | CSU | 1:21:17 | 33 | Lunenburg, MA |
| 5 Donna Smyers | | 1:22:37 | 35 | Manchester, CT |
| 6 Catherine Lifschultz | | 1:23:57 | 30 | Brookline, MA |
| 7 Maureen Sullivan | | 1:24:21 | 36 | Concord, MA |
| 8 Sandra Natal | | 1:26:17 | 31 | Brooklyn, MA |
| 9 Renee Riedel | WCRC | 1:26:17 | 31 | Newburyport, MA |
| 10 Ann Benoit-Rasmussen | | 1:27:05 | 29 | Waterville Valleys, VT |
| 11 Naoko Ishibe | | 1:27:22 | 24 | Somerville, MA |
| 12 Gail Turner | | 1:27:25 | 33 | Yarmouth, ME |
| 13 Jacqueline Shakar | CMS | 1:27:57 | 33 | Worcester, MA |
| 14 Johanne Brus | | 1:28:45 | 37 | Ayers Cliff, CAN |
| 15 Susan McNatt | CSU | 1:28:57 | 27 | Needham, MA |
| 16 Nixie Raymond | CSU | 1:30:09 | 33 | Watertown, MA |
| 17 Susan Passler | WCRC | 1:31:20 | 37 | Amesbury, MA |
| 18 Suzan Ballmer | | 1:31:28 | 34 | Montreal, CAN |
| 19 Stella McCormick | WCRC | 1:31:35 | 34 | Newburyport, MA |
| 20 Sharon Johnson | | 1:32:25 | 36 | Atkinson, NH |
| 21 Lucia Greenough | | 1:32:28 | 37 | Ipswich, MA |
| 22 Joy Moreton | | 1:33:11 | 33 | Cambridge, MA |
| 23 Susan Maslowski | | 1:33:28 | 40 | Billerica, MA |
| 24 Maureen Mahoney | | 1:33:30 | 28 | Melrose, MA |
| 25 Karen Knuepfer | | 1:33:47 | 41 | York, PA |

**Matt Carpenter**

## Teams

| Female Open | | Female 40+ | | |
| --- | --- | --- | --- | --- |
| 1 CMS | 4:08:54 | 1 WMM | 5:17:27 | **CR** |
| 2 CSU | 4:20:23 | 2 WCRC | 5:18:37 | |
| 3 WCRC | 4:29:12 | 3 MTC | 5:28:02 | |
| 4 MVS | 4:41:24 | 4 GSRT | 5:40:49 | |
| 5 GSRT | 4:41:24 | 5 Mercer | 5:50:59 | |

| Male Open | | Male 40+ | |
| --- | --- | --- | --- |
| 1 CMS | 5:30:34 CR | 1 GLRR | 3:51:23 |
| 2 CSU | 6:05:38 | 2 GMAA | 3:53:55 |
| 3 HTC | 6:22:04 | 3 Educators | 4:06:07 |
| 4 WCRC | 6:23:01 | 4 AA | 4:09:50 |
| 5 WMM | 6:37:56 | 5 RIRR | 4:14:22 |

## 5-Year Age groups

| Place | Name | Time | Age | City and State | Category |
| --- | --- | --- | --- | --- | --- |
| 438 | Livvy Williams | 1:42:22 | 18 | Manomet, MA | Under 20 |
| 161 | Naoko Ishibe | 1:27:22 | 24 | Somerville, MA | 20-24 |
| 81 | Pam Moore | 1:20:57 | 29 | Keene, NH | 25-29 |
| 34 | J'Ne Day-Lucore | 1:12:59 | 32 | Denver, CO | 30-34 |
| 100 | Donna Smyers | 1:22:37 | 35 | Manchester, CT | 35-39 |
| 259 | Susan Maslowski | 1:33:28 | 40 | Billerica, MA | 40-44 |
| 444 | Joan Lavin | 1:42:34 | 45 | Portland, ME | 45-49 |
| 407 | Louisa Dunlap | 1:40:46 | 52 | Belfast, ME | 50-54 **Age Group Record** |
| 596 | Maggie Solomon | 1:50:34 | 59 | Conway, NH | 55-59 |
| 690 | Dorothy Bergman | 1:55:57 | 61 | Marblehead, MA | 60-64 |
| 880 | Molly Hennig | 2:29:27 | 69 | Middle Grove, NY | 65+ |
| 43 | Tim Livingston | 1:16:31 | 19 | Conway, NH | Under 20 |
| 8 | Sean Livingston | 1:07:00 | 24 | Conway, NH | 20-24 |
| 1 | Matt Carpenter | 0:59:49 | 28 | Colorado Sprgs, CO | 25-29 |
| 3 | Neji Makhlouf | 1:02:35 | 31 | Ft Collins, CO | 30-34 |
| 7 | Bob Hodge | 1:05:54 | 37 | Clinton, MA | 35-39 |
| 5 | Chuck Smead | 1:05:20 | 41 | Mosca, CO | 40-44 |
| 28 | Sumner Brown | 1:11:54 | 49 | Belmont, MA | 45-49 |
| 115 | Douglas Ludewig | 1:24:00 | 53 | Monmouth, ME | 50-54 |
| 187 | John Saarinen | 1:28:42 | 58 | Stow, MA | 55-59 |
| 234 | Donald Ross | 1:31:39 | 63 | Marblehead, MA | 60-64 |
| 635 | Earl Stetson | 1:52:47 | 67 | Conway, NH | 65-69 |
| 741 | Harold Luetjen | 1:59:53 | 70 | Rockville, CT | 70-74 |
| 807 | Howard Kellogg | 2:08:12 | 77 | Holderness, NH | 75+ |

### 34th Mt Washington Road Race

June 18, 1994
Saturday, 10:00 AM
884 Finishers

The big guns from Colorado would not be returning this year, leaving the top spots up for grabs. Matt Carpenter pulled out due to injuries he sustained running a mountain marathon.  J'Ne Day-Lucore was out of the running due to the recent birth of her daughter.  Favorites included Kenyans Andrew Musuva and Daniel Kithuka.  Musuva had recently run a 2:16 marathon and Kithuka had run under 1:05 for a half marathon.  Dave Dunham was returning from a back injury suffered while shoveling snow, but seemed in good form.  He was the top finisher at the Dipsea (Mill Valley, CA) trail race the week before.  Former winner Christine Maisto was among the women favored to win.

Hot weather was the theme for this edition of the race, with sweltering temperatures approaching 90 at the base and a near record 66 at the top.  There was little wind to cool the runners in the 87% humidity.  This did not deter a record 884 (167 women) from finishing, although seven ended up in the hospital suffering from heat exhaustion and others dropped out in the early going.  Athletes turned out from 28 states, D.C., Canada, Kenya, Sweden, Tunisia, Germany and the Dominican Republic.

Neji Makhlouf, Abraham Limo and Daniel Kithuka were the early leaders.  Dave Dunham moved into the lead before reaching the half in 30:11, he continued on to win in 1:03:21.  In *New England Runner* Dunham said, "I ran scared.  I knew I could run 64 minutes, but I didn't know if that would be first or tenth."  Over the last two miles Makhlouf, Mike Casner, and Limo each took a turn in second place.  Limo ended up third and told *New England Runner,* "It is very steep! Next year I will win."  He also told the Mountain Ear, "The Mountain, it was too hilly."  The men's average finishing time soared to an all time high of 1:49:02.  The women also had a slow average time coming in at 2:01:39.

In the women's race Canadians took the top two spots, as Jacqueline Gareau was the first female across the line in 1:16:15 with Alayne Adams nearly five minutes back.  Gareau's time was also nine minutes under the old record for 40+ women, besting Martha Rockwell's time.  Rockwell set her own record in the new 50-55 age group.  Christine Maisto dropped out early into the race and walked back to the base of the mountain.  Gareau told the *Boston Globe,* "It was hot. I'm not in that good shape.  I didn't expect to run that fast anyway."

The CMS team continued its winning ways taking the team title by 47 minutes over CSU with a 5:34:37.  CSU took the ladies' title with a 30-second victory over CMS, 4:31:37 to 4:32:07.  This year the number of runners scoring for the male 40+ teams changed from three to five runners. GLRR took the win in 7:27:47.  The women's 40+ (3 still score) had the WCRC taking a 17 minute victory over WMM.

The total purse was $4350 with additional time bonuses as Shawmut Bank and Healthsource NH sponsored the race along with associate sponsor Bridgton Academy. *New England Runner* Magazine named the 1994 Mt Washington race as the "Race of the year." Chuck Smead noted in the *Mountain Ear,* "There's nothing harder than a mountain race, but I love this race – nothing compares to this."

## Top 25 Finishers

| Place Name | Club | Time | Age | City and State | |
|---|---|---|---|---|---|
| 1 Dave Dunham | CMS | 1:03:12 | 30 | Londonderry, MA | |
| 2 Neji Makhlouf | | 1:05:07 | 31 | TUN | |
| 3 Abraham Limo | | 1:05:48 | 32 | KEN | |
| 4 Mike Casner | CMS | 1:06:26 | 32 | Keene, NH | |
| 5 Robert Ratcliffe | | 1:06:35 | 32 | Cambridge, MA | |
| 6 Eric Morse | CMS | 1:07:12 | 29 | Moretown, VT | |
| 7 Scott Clark | CMS | 1:07:40 | 28 | Gilmanton, NH | |
| 8 Daniel Kithuka | | 1:08:03 | 20 | KEN | |
| 9 Karl Meltzer Jr. | | 1:08:45 | 26 | Salt Lake City, UT | |
| 10 Jim Garcia | CMS | 1:09:57 | 35 | Westford, MA | |
| 11 Keith Woodward | | 1:10:03 | 43 | E Corinth, VT | FW |
| 12 Chuck Smead | | 1:11:13 | 42 | Mosca, CO | |
| 13 Stephen Peterson | CMS | 1:11:32 | 28 | Hopkinton, MA | |
| 14 Andrew Musuva | | 1:11:56 | 24 | KEN | |
| 15 Ernesto Riano | | 1:11:58 | 36 | Lowell, MA | |
| 16 Daniel Verrington | CMS | 1:12:22 | 31 | Bradford, MA | |
| 17 Francis Burdett | GLRR | 1:12:27 | 29 | Katonah, NY | |
| 18 Sumner Brown | CSU | 1:12:37 | 50 | Belmont, MA | |
| 19 Rick Stuart | | 1:13:36 | 36 | Phoenix, AZ | |
| 20 David Hannon | GLRR | 1:13:44 | 23 | Chelmsford, MA | |
| 21 David Beauley | GCS | 1:14:01 | 28 | Nashua, NH | |
| 22 Dave Walecka | | 1:14:20 | 40 | Acushnet, MA | |
| 23 Terrance McNatt | CSU | 1:14:57 | 29 | Needham, MA | |
| 24 Thomas Murdock III | | 1:14:59 | 30 | Somerville, MA | |
| 25 Shaun Keenan | | 1:14:59 | 32 | Coopers Mills, ME | |
| 30 Bob Hodge | | 1:15:40 | 38 | Clinton, MA | FW |
| 88 John Cederholm | | 1:25:19 | 51 | Boston, MA | FW |

## Top 25 Women

| Place Name | Club | Time | Age | City and State |
|---|---|---|---|---|
| 1 Jacqueline Gareau | | 1:16:15 | 41 | St Bruno, CAN |
| 2 Alayne Adams | | 1:21:01 | 32 | Cambridge, MA |
| 3 Sandra Natal | | 1:22:58 | 32 | Brooklyn, NY |
| 4 Sue Lachance | CSU | 1:23:55 | 34 | Lunenburg, MA |
| 5 Donna Smyers | | 1:26:40 | 36 | Manchester, CT |
| 6 Renee Riedel | WCRC | 1:26:46 | 32 | Newburyport, MA |

| | | | | | |
|---|---|---|---|---|---|
| 7 Veronica Haskell | | 1:28:07 | 27 | Lafayette, CO | |
| 8 Margo Webber | CMS | 1:28:11 | 33 | Boxborough, MA | |
| 9 Catherine Lifschultz | | 1:28:20 | 31 | Brookline, MA | |
| 10 Kerry Arsenault | AF | 1:28:44 | 29 | Branford, CT | |
| 11 Maureen Sullivan | | 1:29:15 | 37 | Concord, MA | |
| 12 Jacqueline Shakar | CMS | 1:30:40 | 34 | Worcester, MA | |
| 13 Catherine Parbst | AF | 1:30:44 | 26 | Ashford, CT | |
| 14 Susan McNatt | CSU | 1:31:35 | 28 | Needham, MA | |
| 15 Debbie Greenslit | CMS | 1:33:16 | 38 | Worcester, MA | |
| 16 Jean Flanzer | | 1:33:59 | 32 | Warner, NH | |
| 17 Martha Rockwell | | 1:34:39 | 50 | Strafford, VT | **FW** |
| 18 Gail Turner | | 1:34:44 | 34 | Portland, ME | |
| 19 Nixie Raymond | CSU | 1:36:07 | 34 | Watertown, MA | |
| 20 Ann Rasmussen | | 1:36:58 | 30 | Waterville Valley, ME | |
| 21 Heidi Wallis | | 1:37:05 | 29 | Belmont, MA | |
| 22 Anne Marie Davee | | 1:37:31 | 38 | Pownal, ME | |
| 23 Maureen Mahoney | | 1:37:49 | 29 | Andover, MA | |
| 24 Susan Passler | | 1:39:53 | 38 | Amesbury, MA | |
| 25 Donna Kasianchuk | | 1:40:00 | 37 | Wolfeboro Falls, NH | |

**Gareau and Dunham show off their trophies**

Top 5 Teams

| Men | | Men 40+ | |
| --- | --- | --- | --- |
| 1 CMS | 5:34:37 | 1 GLRR | 7:27:47 |
| 2 CSU | 6:21:28 | 2 CMS | 7:33:24 |
| 3 GLRR | 6:22:54 | 3 WCRC | 7:38:59 |
| 4 GCS | 6:31:19 | 4 Willimantic | 7:56:13 |
| 5 WCRC | 6:40:20 | 5 AA | 7:57:02 |

| Women | | Women 40+ | |
| --- | --- | --- | --- |
| 1 CSU | 4:31:37 | 1 WCRC | 5:31:51 |
| 2 CMS | 4:32:07 | 2 WMM | 5:48:10 |
| 3 AF | 4:48:16 | 3 CMS | 6:02:00 |
| 4 WCRC | 4:49:26 | 4 HTC | 6:34:46 |
| 5 MTC | 5:02:00 | 5 OSAC | 6:42:03 |

5-Year age groups

| Place | Name | Time | Age | City and State | Category | |
| --- | --- | --- | --- | --- | --- | --- |
| 410 | Livvy Williams | 1:48:10 | 19 | Manomet, MA | Under 20 | |
| 406 | Amy Pierce | 1:47:57 | 23 | Kennebunkport, ME | 20-24 | |
| 115 | Veronica Haskell | 1:28:07 | 27 | Lafayette, CO | 25-29 | |
| 56 | Alayne Adams | 1:21:01 | 32 | Cambridge, MA | 30-34 | |
| 97 | Donna Smyers | 1:26:40 | 36 | Manchester, CT | 35-39 | |
| 31 | Jacqueline Gareau | 1:16:15 | 41 | St Bruno, CAN | 40-44 | **Age Group Record** |
| 493 | Barbara Brent | 1:52:39 | 47 | Hopewell, NJ | 45-49 | |
| 194 | Martha Rockwell | 1:34:39 | 50 | Strafford, VT | 50-54 | |
| 323 | Carrie Parsi | 1:43:14 | 55 | Lexington, MA | 55-59 | |
| 536 | Maggie Solomon | 1:55:41 | 60 | Conway, NH | 60-64 | |
| 768 | Hildy Fosse | 2:13:46 | 65 | Holderness, NH | 65+ | |
| 37 | Seth Williams | 1:17:28 | 16 | Manomet, MA | Under 20 | |
| 8 | Daniel Kithuka | 1:08:03 | 20 | KEN | 20-24 | |
| 6 | Eric Morse | 1:07:12 | 29 | Moretown, VT | 25-29 | |
| 1 | Dave Dunham | 1:03:12 | 30 | Londonderry, MA | 30-34 | |
| 10 | Jim Garcia | 1:09:57 | 35 | Westford, MA | 35-39 | |
| 11 | Keith Woodward | 1:10:03 | 43 | E Corinth, VT | 40-44 | |
| 60 | Peter Dane | 1:21:55 | 46 | Essex, MA | 45-49 | |
| 18 | Sumner Brown | 1:12:37 | 50 | Belmont, MA | 50-54 | **Age Group Record** |
| 212 | Jim Way | 1:35:59 | 57 | Evanston, WY | 55-59 | |
| 304 | Donald Ross | 1:41:52 | 64 | Marblehead, MA | 60-64 | |
| 356 | Richard Gatto | 1:45:13 | 65 | Candia, MA | 65-69 | |
| 600 | Russell Bradley | 2:00:27 | 70 | Cape Elizabeth, ME | 70-74 | |
| 842 | Howard Kellogg | 2:27:56 | 78 | Holderness, NH | 75+ | |

June 17, 1995
Saturday, 10:00 AM
929 Finishers

Pre-race favorites included Gideon Mutisya, Eddy Hellebuyck, and local runners Dave Dunham and Eric Morse.  Hellebuyck came into the race having recently run a 45:38 15K and had a marathon best of 2:11:50.   He had also won the Litchfield Hills 7.1M race the week before, as did Froude in 1990 when he set the course record at Mt Washington.   Matt Cull and Keith Woodward looked strong after dueling at Mt Equinox, taking first and second in the 3,186' climb.  Dunham and Bob Hodge had recently gone 1-2 at the Wachusett Mountain race with Dunham taking the 1,000' climb over 4.3m in a course record 24:37.  Other possible top runners included Jose Moriera a top mountain runner from Brazil, and Andy Ames from Colorado.  J'Ne Day-Lucore and Jacqueline Gareau looked to be the women's favorites.

A record 929 finishers from 27 states and 6 countries headed out as the cannon fired.  A small pack, fronted by Mutisya, formed early with Dunham, Helleybuyck, Fram, and Robert Pierce staying in the hunt through the mile.  Mutisya then began to pull away by the second mile he had a 50-second lead, which he continued to expand.  He hit the half in 28:30 and continued on to win by 2:40 over Fram and Dunham with a 1:01:41.  Morse was seventeen seconds back with Helleybuyck another minute back as 16 runners broke 1:10.  Mutisya told the *Union Leader* "If not for the wind I would have broken the course record.  I'm very light (98 lbs.) and the wind was throwing me back."  A record tying five men finished under 1:05.

J'Ne Day-Lucore returned after a one-year absence to forge a 1:03 victory over Sandra Natal in 1:17:28.  Day-Lucore led the way, passing the half in 35:54 as a record tying 15 women broke 1:30.  Day-Lucore noted in the *Union Leader* that the race was "just a bit breezy" and "you never know about what the wind is going to be like."  This was the first time four women broke 1:20.  The average age for female finishers topped 40 at 40.08.  The male average age of 41.48 made this the closest age gap between men and women at 1.4 years.

Former champions fared well this year as Dunham (1988, 89, 94) tied for second, Keith Woodward (1982) won the masters title, Bob Hodge (7 wins) was seventeenth, Gary Johnson (1975) finished thirty-sixth and Peg Donovan (1987) was the first women's master.  Hellebuyck, who would go on to finish fifth in the 2000 US Olympic trials marathon, talked about his experience in the *Union Leader* "This is not for me, it was unbelievable.  Every time I came to a flat place, I go vrroomm.  Then – nothing."

CMS lowered the team record to 5:25:57 with five finishers in the top 13.  They won by 57 minutes over CSU.  The CSU women turned the tables, winning the team title in 4:13:38, eight minutes faster than CMS.  The WCRC took the 40+ title by five minutes over CSU.  The WCRC also took the women's 40+ win with a 17-minute victory over LAC.

**Top 25 Finishers**

| Place | Name | Club | Time | Age | City and State | |
|---|---|---|---|---|---|---|
| 1 | Gideon Mutisya | | 1:01:42 | 28 | Amsterdam, NY (KEN) | |
| 2 | Craig Fram | CMS | 1:03:20 | 36 | Hampstead, NH | FW |
| 3 | Dave Dunham | CMS | 1:03:20 | 31 | Londonderry, NH | FW |
| 4 | Eric Morse | CMS | 1:03:37 | 30 | Moretown, VT | |
| 5 | Eddy Hellebuyck | | 1:04:49 | 34 | Albuquerque, NM | |
| 6 | Andy Ames | | 1:05:16 | 32 | Boulder, CO | |
| 7 | Bob Ratcliffe | | 1:05:29 | 37 | Cambridge, MA | |
| 8 | Robert Pierce | | 1:06:44 | 34 | Alfred, ME | |
| 9 | Matthew Cull | | 1:06:55 | 34 | Manchester Ctr., VT | |
| 10 | Scott Clark | CMS | 1:07:00 | 29 | Gilmanton, NH | |
| 11 | Seth McClennen | | 1:07:08 | 23 | Norwich, VT | |
| 12 | Thomas Murdock III | | 1:07:12 | 31 | Somerville, MA | |
| 13 | Mike Casner | CMS | 1:08:40 | 33 | Keene, NH | |
| 14 | Keith Woodward | | 1:09:05 | 44 | E Corinth, VT | FW |
| 15 | Jim Garcia | CMS | 1:09:13 | 36 | Westford, MA | |
| 16 | Karl Meltzer | | 1:09:28 | 27 | Salt Lake, UT | |
| 17 | Bob Hodge | CMS | 1:10:03 | 39 | Clinton, MA | FW |
| 18 | Rick Stuart | | 1:10:34 | 37 | Phoenix, AZ | |
| 19 | Lachlan Campbell | | 1:10:55 | 22 | Groton, CT | |
| 20 | Stephen Peterson | CMS | 1:11:01 | 29 | Lowell, MA | |
| 21 | Seth Williams | | 1:11:10 | 17 | Manomet, MA | |
| 22 | Paul Shepardson | | 1:11:29 | 38 | Pittsfield, MA | |
| 23 | Ernesto Riano | | 1:11:33 | 37 | Lowell, MA | |
| 24 | Terrance McNatt | CSU | 1:11:51 | 30 | Needham, MA | |
| 25 | James Garrett | | 1:11:56 | 30 | Bennington, VT | |
| 36 | Gary Johnson | | 1:14:29 | 44 | Irasburg, VT | FW |

**Top 25 Women**

| Place | Name | Club | Time | Age | City & State | |
|---|---|---|---|---|---|---|
| 1 | J'Ne Day-Lucore | | 1:17:29 | 34 | Denver, CO | |
| 2 | Sandra Natal | | 1:18:31 | 33 | Brooklyn, NY | |
| 3 | Anna Brook | CSU | 1:18:51 | 29 | Somerville, MA | |
| 4 | Kathy Kanes | | 1:19:46 | 33 | Columbia, SC | |
| 5 | Renee Riedel | WCRC | 1:23:02 | 33 | Newburyport, MA | |
| 6 | Donna Smyers | | 1:23:06 | 37 | Manchester, CT | |
| 7 | Sue Lachance | CSU | 1:24:31 | 35 | Lunenburg, MA | |
| 8 | Kerry Arsenault | | 1:25:34 | 30 | Guilford, CT | |
| 9 | Peg Donovan | | 1:26:31 | 40 | Auburn, NH | FW |
| 10 | Jacqueline Shakar | CMS | 1:26:54 | 35 | Worcester, MA | |
| 11 | Cheryl Dube | | 1:27:20 | 38 | South Hadley, MA | |
| 12 | Olga Kennison | CMS | 1:28:41 | 28 | Keene, NH | |
| 13 | Catherine Lifschultz | | 1:28:49 | 32 | Brookline, MA | |

| Place | Name | Club | Time | | Age | City & State |
|---|---|---|---|---|---|---|
| 14 | Lynn Achee | | 1:29:14 | | 39 | Manchester Ctr., VT |
| 15 | Gail Turner | | 1:29:33 | | 35 | Portland, ME |
| 16 | Heidi Wallis | | 1:30:10 | | 30 | Belmont, MA |
| 17 | Susan McNatt | CSU | 1:30:16 | | 29 | Needham, MA |
| 18 | Michelle Pelletier | | 1:33:01 | | 30 | Manchester, NH |
| 19 | Kelley Grautski | | 1:34:58 | | 30 | Franconia, NH |
| 20 | Jean Flanzer | | 1:35:42 | | 36 | Elkins, NH |
| 21 | Linda Waitkun | | 1:36:20 | | 42 | North Conway, NH |
| 22 | Vicki Miller | WCRC | 1:36:53 | | 42 | Durham, NH |
| 23 | Susan Passler | WCRC | 1:38:09 | | 39 | Amesbury, MA |
| 24 | Rachel Berg | | 1:38:31 | | 33 | Salisbury, CT |
| 25 | Eileen Portz-Shovlin | | 1:38:34 | | 47 | Allentown, PA |

## 5-Year age groups

| Place | Name | Time | Age | City & State | Category |
|---|---|---|---|---|---|
| 853 | Ember Brosius | 2:09:07 | 16 | Wayne, ME | Under 20 |
| 470 | Amy Pierce | 1:44:04 | 24 | Stockbridge, MA | 20-24 |
| 64 | Anna Brook | 1:18:51 | 29 | Somerville, MA | 25-29 |
| 55 | J'Ne Day-Lucore | 1:17:29 | 34 | Denver, CO | 30-34 |
| 106 | Donna Smyers | 1:23:06 | 37 | Manchester, CT | 35-39 |
| 147 | Peg Donovan | 1:26:31 | 40 | Auburn, NH | 40-44 |
| 358 | Eileen Portz-Shovlin | 1:38:34 | 47 | Allentown, PA | 45-49 |
| 544 | Marcia Puryear | 1:46:48 | 52 | Concord, MA | 50-54 |
| 446 | Carrie Parsi | 1:42:33 | 56 | Lexington, MA | 55-59 |
| 639 | Maggie Solomon | 1:51:35 | 61 | Conway, NH | 60-64 **Age Group Record** |
| 877 | Hildy Fosse | 2:13:54 | 66 | Holderness, NH | 65+ |
| 21 | Seth Williams | 1:11:10 | 17 | Manomet, MA | Under 20 |
| 11 | Seth McClennen | 1:07:08 | 23 | Norwich, VT | 20-24 |
| 1 | Gideon Mutisya | 1:01:42 | 28 | Amsterdam, NY (KEN) 25-29 | |
| 3 | Dave Dunham | 1:03:20 | 31 | Londonderry, NH | 30-34 |
| 2 | Craig Fram | 1:03:20 | 36 | Hampstead, NH | 35-39 |
| 14 | Keith Woodward | 1:09:05 | 44 | E Corinth, VT | 40-44 |
| 30 | Joseph Nzau | 1:13:22 | 46 | Amsterdam, NY KEN 45-49 | |
| 34 | Sumner Brown | 1:13:56 | 51 | Belmont, MA | 50-54 |
| 214 | Frank Salvatore | 1:30:31 | 55 | Newburyport, MA | 55-59 |
| 298 | John Saarinen | 1:34:53 | 60 | Stow, MA | 60-64 |
| 388 | Donald Ross | 1:39:38 | 65 | Marblehead, MA | 65-69 |
| 741 | Russell Bradley | 1:59:04 | 71 | Cape Elizabeth, ME | 70-74 |
| 885 | George Etzweiler | 2:15:50 | 75 | State College, PA | 75+ |

**Top 5 Teams**

| **Men** | | **Men 40+** | |
|---|---|---|---|
| 1 CMS | 5:25:57 **CR** | 1 WCRC | 6:59:35 **CR** |
| 2 CSU | 6:22:00 | 2 CSU | 7:04:07 |
| 3 WCRC | 6:30:16 | 3 GLRR | 7:06:58 |
| 4 Willimantic 6:36:16 | | 4 GMAA | 7:12:27 |
| 5 HTC | 6:41:13 | 5 Willimantic 7:26:53 | |

| **Women** | | **Women 40+** | |
|---|---|---|---|
| 1 CSU | 4:13:38 | 1 WCRC | 5:07:22 **CR** |
| 2 CMS | 4:21:43 | 2 LAC | 5:24:13 |
| 3 WCRC | 4:38:04 | 3 WMM | 5:33:14 |
| 4 AA | 5:02:07 | 4 AA | 5:39:06 |
| 5 WMM | 5:08:23 | 5 OSAC | 6:04:00 |

(left to right) Dunham, Morse, and Fram of the CMS record setting team

**36<sup>th</sup> Mt Washington Road Race**

June 15, 1996
Saturday, 10:00 AM
911 Finishers


Temperatures were in the seventies at the base and fifties at the summit as 911 lined up for the annual race up the Auto Road.  The lucky starters, including 160 women, were selected in early March via a lottery.  It is commonly noted that only one in three made it into the race.  New Hampshire public television was on hand taping a segment for the "New Hampshire Crossroads" show.  Three-time winner Dave Dunham was wired for sound for the broadcast.

Dunham was among the favorites, which included Daniel Kihara for the men and Jacqueline Gareau for the women.  Kihara came into the race with personal bests of 28:06 for 10K and 43:29 for 15K.  Kihara warmed up with a third place finish at the Litchfield Hills 7.1 mile race the week before.  Gideon Mutisya finished second, Eddy Hellebuyck in sixth and Dunham in seventh at Litchfield.

New Englanders had the opportunity to tune up for Mt Washington in the first USATF Mountain running Grand prix.  The three-race series wrapped up the week before Mt Washington at the Temple Mountain 10 mile.  CMS teammates Dunham, Mike Casner, and Steve Peterson showed their form finishing first, second, and fifth at Temple.

Kihara was unmatched in the race as he pulled away and gapped the field early.  He was near record pace at the halfway mark in 28:10.  Dunham was 1:32 back with Eric Morse and Craig Fram another 15 and 33 seconds farther back.  Kihara powered on to a 58:20, beating the course record by nearly a minute.  He told the *Union Leader,* "I was not surprised to break the record." although he did say "It was much more difficult today than a half marathon.  There is nowhere on this course where you can gear yourself to be comfortable.  You're like a car in low gear."  Kihara won $750 for the victory and an additional $1,000 for setting a new course record.

Julie Peterson led the race early on, but was passed by Gareau who picked up her third win in three attempts.  Gareau told the *Boston Globe,* "I just go the way I feel.  I wasn't feeling that great at first."  Peterson who raced in her fourth Olympic trials marathon earlier in the year, said, "It was no contest once she went by me."  Gareau won by just over 1:30 and was awarded $750 for the victory and another $250 for topping the WAVA age graded masters.

CMS again lowered the team record; led by Dunham, Morse and Fram, to 5:24:15 the team was awarded $500 for setting a new record.  Willimantic AC finished 62 minutes behind in second place.  CSU took the women's victory in 4:26:33, 5 minutes up on CMS.  The men's 40+ went to the WCRC in 6:47:01, 28 minutes ahead of the NMC.  The women's 40+ went to the WCRC as well, with an eight-minute victory over Liberty AC.

The primary sponsor for the race was Healthsource with associate sponsors Bridgton Academy and Polar Beverages.  Changes this year included no longer offering a cash prize for the halfway leader.   The auto road now charged $15 per car and an additional $6 per passenger to drive to the top.   A free entry to the 1997 race was offered to the top ten finishers, the first WAVA finishers, and all race winners.  The total prize purse was $4850 with additional time bonuses, which included a $1,000 prize for a men's course record or women under 1:10.  New on the post-race refreshments was a bowl of vegetarian chili provided by Bearcamp's Tavern.  Polar Beverages provided the water at the various stops along the course and carbonated beverages after the race.  The entry fee was $20, with a registration deadline of March 15.  One thousand entrants were drawn from the lottery.

**Top 25 Finishers**

| Place  Name | Time | Age | City and State | |
|---|---|---|---|---|
| 1 Daniel Kihara | 0:58:21 | 28 | Norristown, PA (KEN) | Course Record |
| 2 Dave Dunham | 1:02:24 | 32 | Bradford, MA | FW |
| 3 Eric Morse | 1:03:46 | 31 | Moretown, VT | |
| 4 Craig Fram | 1:04:22 | 37 | Plaistow, NH | FW |
| 5 Bob Ratcliffe | 1:05:13 | 38 | Auburndale, MA | |
| 6 Daniel Verrington | 1:05:43 | 33 | Bradford, MA | |
| 7 Andy Ames | 1:05:48 | 33 | Boulder, CO | |
| 8 Mike Casner | 1:08:00 | 34 | Marlow, NH | |
| 9 Thomas Murdock III | 1:08:05 | 32 | Somerville, MA | |
| 10 Kip Kemboi Kimeli | 1:08:52 | 29 | Albuquerque, NM | |
| 11 Stephen Peterson | 1:08:59 | 30 | Chelmsford, MA | |
| 12 Ed Sheldon | 1:10:13 | 31 | Manchester, NH | |
| 13 Bob Hodge | 1:10:17 | 40 | Clinton, MA | FW |
| 14 Jose Moriera | 1:11:04 | 28 | Albuquerque, NM | |
| 15 David Beauley | 1:11:08 | 30 | Nashua, NH | |
| 16 Andrew Baird | 1:11:09 | 23 | Foster, RI | |
| 17 Tom Schmiedel | 1:12:11 | 41 | Danbury, CT | |
| 18 Brian Stevens | 1:12:14 | 32 | New Boston, NH | |
| 19 Jeffrey Robie | 1:12:39 | 39 | Kingston, NH | |
| 20 Charlie Gunn | 1:13:00 | 41 | Henniker, NH | |
| 21 Keith Woodward | 1:13:07 | 45 | E Corinth, VT | FW |
| 22 Chip Merrow | 1:13:09 | 35 | Loudon, NH | |
| 23 Adam Eyre-Walker | 1:13:34 | 30 | New Brunswick, NJ | |
| 24 Paul Shepardson | 1:13:39 | 39 | Newton, MA | |
| 25 Rick Stuart | 1:13:49 | 38 | Phoenix, AZ | |

**Top 25 Women**

| Place  Name | Time | Age | City & State |
|---|---|---|---|
| 1 Jacqueline Gareau | 1:17:15 | 43 | St. Bruno, CAN |
| 2 Julie Peterson | 1:18:49 | 36 | Beverly, MA |

| Place | Name | Time | Age | City & State |
|---|---|---|---|---|
| 3 | Alayne Adams | 1:20:02 | 34 | Cambridge, MA |
| 4 | Barbara Higgins-Nelson | 1:22:32 | 32 | Concord, NH |
| 5 | Lori Jorgenson | 1:22:43 | 37 | Purdys, NY |
| 6 | Donna Smyers | 1:23:19 | 38 | Northfield, VT |
| 7 | Margo Webber | 1:23:43 | 35 | Boxborough, MA |
| 8 | Cheryl Dube | 1:23:52 | 39 | S. Hadley, MA |
| 9 | Anna Brook | 1:25:05 | 30 | Somerville, MA |
| 10 | Gail Turner | 1:26:50 | 36 | Portland, ME |
| 11 | Maureen Sullivan | 1:27:17 | 39 | Concord, MA |
| 12 | Dorothy Helling | 1:28:42 | 46 | Montpelier, VT |
| 13 | Renee Riedel | 1:29:59 | 34 | Sekiu, WA |
| 14 | Gail Eberle | 1:30:00 | 36 | Boise, ID |
| 15 | Jacqueline Shakar | 1:30:04 | 36 | Worcester, MA |
| 16 | Johanne Deboer | 1:30:56 | 40 | Ayers Cliff, CAN |
| 17 | Cathy Lifschultz | 1:31:29 | 33 | Sudbury, MA |
| 18 | Mary Collins | 1:32:25 | 37 | Boston, MA |
| 19 | Heather McKeown | 1:33:13 | 43 | Enosburg Falls, VT |
| 20 | Sarah Tabbutt | 1:33:36 | 37 | Newton Center, MA |
| 21 | Nancy Rowe | 1:34:52 | 33 | New York, NY |
| 22 | Karen Palmer | 1:35:06 | 31 | Fitchburg, MA |
| 23 | Beth Dutton | 1:35:29 | 31 | Nashua, NH |
| 24 | Maureen Sproul | 1:35:44 | 40 | New Gloucester, ME |
| 25 | Lisa Hart | 1:36:00 | 33 | Durham, NH |

## 5-Year Age Groups

| Place | Name | Time | Age | Town and State | Category |
|---|---|---|---|---|---|
| 707 | Moira Goegel | 1:58:23 | 19 | Canterbury, NH | Under 20 |
| 287 | Brenda O'Connell | 1:36:48 | 23 | Mystic, CT | 20-24 |
| 319 | Jeanne Marois | 1:38:36 | 27 | Boston, MA | 25-29 |
| 60 | Alayne Adams | 1:20:02 | 34 | Cambridge, MA | 30-34 |
| 51 | Julie Peterson | 1:18:49 | 36 | Beverly, MA | 35-39 |
| 42 | Jacqueline Gareau | 1:17:15 | 43 | St. Bruno CAN | 40-44 |
| 145 | Dorothy Helling | 1:28:42 | 46 | Montpelier, VT | 45-49 |
| 451 | Faye Gagnon | 1:44:36 | 51 | Minot, ME | 50-54 |
| 372 | Carrie Parsi | 1:40:43 | 57 | Lexington, MA | 55-59 |
| 678 | Sally Strazdins | 1:56:46 | 62 | N. Hampton, NH | 60-64 |
| 829 | Hildy Fosse | 2:12:37 | 67 | Holderness, NH | 65+ |
| 32 | James Linton | 1:14:57 | 17 | Media, PA | Under 20 |
| 16 | Andrew Baird | 1:11:09 | 23 | Foster, RI | 20-24 |
| 1 | Daniel Kihara | 0:58:21 | 28 | Norristown, PA | 25-29 |
| 2 | Dave Dunham | 1:02:24 | 32 | Bradford, MA | 30-34 |
| 4 | Craig Fram | 1:04:22 | 37 | Plaistow, NH | 35-39 |

| Place | Name | Time | Age | Town and State | Category |
|---|---|---|---|---|---|
| 13 | Bob Hodge | 1:10:17 | 40 | Clinton, MA | 40-44 |
| 21 | Keith Woodward | 1:13:07 | 45 | E Corinth, VT | 45-49 |
| 37 | Sumner Brown | 1:16:21 | 52 | Belmont, MA | 50-54 |
| 249 | Andrew Lewis | 1:34:37 | 56 | Lexington, MA | 55-59 |
| 190 | Gerald Barney | 1:31:40 | 63 | Swanton, VT | 60-64 |
| 308 | Donald Ross | 1:38:00 | 66 | Marblehead, MA | 65-69 |
| 737 | Carlton Mendell | 2:01:03 | 74 | Portland, ME | 70-74 |
| 865 | Charley Reed | 2:18:04 | 75 | Gorham, NH | 75-79 |
| 902 | Howard Kellogg | 2:36:23 | 80 | Holderness, NH | 80+ **Age Group Record** |

## Top 5 Teams

| Men | | | Men 40+ | | |
|---|---|---|---|---|---|
| 1 CMS | 5:24:15 | | 1 WCRC | 6:47:01 **CR** | |
| 2 Willimantic | 6:26:15 | | 2 NMC | 7:15:53 | |
| 3 GCS | 6:27:49 | | 3 Willimantic | 7:20:29 | |
| 4 WCRC | 6:33:40 | | 4 GMAA | 7:23:46 | |
| 5 CSU | 6:40:57 | | 5 GNBTC | 7:28:54 | |

| Women | | | Women 40+ | | |
|---|---|---|---|---|---|
| 1 CSU | 4:26:33 | | 1 WCRC | 5:02:39 **CR** | |
| 2 CMS | 4:31:51 | | 2 LAC | 5:10:30 | |
| 3 WCRC | 4:46:35 | | 3 CMeS | 5:12:15 | |
| 4 BRC | 4:55:37 | | 4 NMC | 5:38:37 | |
| 5 AA | 4:59:16 | | 5 AA | 5:39:12 | |

The "flag man" (left) and Mike "Caz" Casner (right)

### 37<sup>th</sup> Mt Washington Road Race

June 21, 1997
Saturday, 10:00 AM
929 Finishers

Conditions for the race were not ideal.  It was hot and humid at the start, and the record 929 finishers were met by 55 MPH winds, drizzle, and fog at the summit.  Only seven runners broke 1:10, which was the least since 1989, and only nine women broke 1:30, which was the lowest since 1992 when only seven did so.  The field featured a record 181 women among the runners from 30 states and four countries.

Eric Morse, who tuned up for the race by winning the Wachusett hill climb in near record time and taking the overall USATF New England Mountain running circuit title, built a 30-second lead by the one mile post.  His lead would not hold as his CMS teammate Craig Fram began to close on him after four miles.  Fram passed Morse after the 5-mile mark and went on to win in 1:04:48, fifty seconds up on Morse.

Prolific racer Cathy O'Brien, who was the youngest Olympic trials qualifier at age 16 in the 1980 marathon trials, started the race conservatively.  She passed early leaders Julie Peterson, Joan Samuelson, and Jacqueline Gareau to beat a strong women's field.  Samuelson, the 1984 Olympic marathon champion, went on to break Gareau's master's record by 13 seconds.  Samuelson passed Peterson in the second mile but could not catch O'Brien.  She told *New England Runner,* "This is the first time I've gone into a race saying I don't care about my time, I just want to finish.  This hill doesn't quit!"

CMS took the team title finishing 33 minutes ahead of the GCS.  The BAA women took a 15-minute victory over the WCRC.  Willimantic AC won a close battle with CSU in the men's 40+, winning by just under four minutes in a record 7:06:54.  The WCRC took the women's 40+ title with an 8-minute win over the CMeS in 5:07:47.

Vin Sylvia, a writer for the *Union Leader*, gave his personal account of running the race in *New England Runner* and talked about the draw of racing up Mt Washington.  "Perhaps it was the sheer exultation of having finished, maybe it was the severe lack of oxygen I had inflicted on my brain, but I told myself I could do better.  I told myself I would return to Mt Washington."

Healthsource, Bridgton, and Citizens Bank sponsored the race, which had a total purse of $4650 and additional time bonuses.  Winners of cash prizes were required to have a USATF card, and a Direct Payment License was needed for anyone winning more than $500.  The race information packet proclaimed, "More than half of this year's applicants were rejected in the lottery."  This year you could, however, cancel your entry and by-pass next year's lottery if you could not run the race.  They would still forfeit the entry fee and t-shirt.  The road remained closed at the bottom form 9:45 AM until 12:30 PM and NH AMTA sports massage team again provided complimentary massages.  In a sign of the computer age, the complete results were available within 30 minutes of the last finisher's time being recorded.

Earlier in the year the second annual "Ski to the Clouds" was held.  Thirty-one skiers and six snowshoe racers made their way up to the four mile post.  Matt Bellizzi set a new course record of 38:33.  Chris Graham was the top snowshoe finisher clocking in at 53:48 and winning a pair of Sherpa snowshoes for the victory.  Graham had her best finish in the footrace in 1996, running a 1:37:55.

## Top 25 Finishers

| Place | Name | Club | Time | Age | Town and State | |
|---|---|---|---|---|---|---|
| 1 | Craig Fram | CMS | 1:04:48 | 38 | Plaistow, NH | |
| 2 | Eric Morse | CMS | 1:05:38 | 32 | Montpelier, VT | |
| 3 | Thomas Borschel | GCS | 1:07:09 | 39 | Idaho Falls, ID | |
| 4 | Daniel Verrington | CMS | 1:08:31 | 34 | Bradford, MA | |
| 5 | Thomas Murdock III | IATC | 1:09:26 | 33 | Somerville, MA | |
| 6 | Joel St Louis | | 1:09:37 | 35 | Fleurimont, CAN | |
| 7 | Steve Peterson | CMS | 1:09:52 | 31 | Chelmsford, MA | |
| 8 | Mike Casner | CMS | 1:10:03 | 35 | Keene, NH | |
| 9 | Craig Widnes | | 1:10:24 | 26 | Denver, CO | |
| 10 | Richard Bolt | CMS | 1:10:34 | 26 | Lunenburg, MA | |
| 11 | Fergus Cullen | HTC | 1:11:40 | 25 | Gilford, NH | |
| 12 | Brian Reinhold | HSK | 1:11:44 | 43 | Akersberga, SWE | |
| 13 | Tony Bates | | 1:11:45 | 38 | Salisbury, VT | |
| 14 | Francis Burdett | GLRR | 1:11:52 | 32 | Worcester, MA | |
| 15 | Brian Stevens | GCS | 1:12:03 | 33 | New Boston, NH | |
| 16 | Ian Fallas | BLO | 1:12:18 | 28 | Burlington, CAN | |
| **17** | **Cathy O'Brien** | **NB** | **1:12:24** | **29** | **Durham, NH** | |
| 18 | Thompson Parker | HS | 1:13:42 | 27 | Bow, NH | |
| 19 | Edward Sheldon | GCS | 1:13:44 | 32 | Manchester, NH | |
| 20 | Keith Woodward | GMAA | 1:13:55 | 46 | E Corinth, VT | FW |
| 21 | Bob Hodge | CMS | 1:14:08 | 41 | Clinton, MA | FW |
| 22 | Gary Johnson | | 1:14:34 | 46 | Irasburg, VT | FW |
| 23 | Rick Stuart | CMeS | 1:15:14 | 39 | Santa Fe, NM | |
| 24 | Andrew Baird | WillAC | 1:15:22 | 24 | Foster, RI | |
| 25 | Seth Williams | | 1:15:37 | 19 | Manoment, MA | |
| 26 | Paul Shepardson | | 1:15:59 | 40 | Pittsfield, MA | |
| 94 | John Cederholm | BAA | 1:26:51 | 54 | Boston, MA | FW |

## Top 25 Women

| Place | Name | Club | Time | Age | Town and State | |
|---|---|---|---|---|---|---|
| 1 | Cathy O'Brien | NB | 1:12:24 | 29 | Durham, NH | |
| 2 | Joan Benoit-Samuelson | NIKE | 1:16:03 | 40 | Freeport, ME | |
| 3 | Julie Peterson | BAA | 1:20:07 | 37 | Beverly, MA | |
| 4 | Jacqueline Gareau | | 1:22:32 | 44 | St Bruno, CAN | FW |
| 5 | Kerry Arsenault | AF | 1:25:50 | 32 | Guilford, CT | |

| Place | Name | Club | Time | Age | Town and State |
|---|---|---|---|---|---|
| 6 | Sandra Khannouchi | NB | 1:27:25 | 35 | Brooklyn, NY |
| 7 | Kim Goff | RIRR | 1:27:40 | 36 | Greenville, RI |
| 8 | Donna Smyers | | 1:27:56 | 39 | Northfield, VT |
| 9 | Tara Martin | PFIZR | 1:28:19 | 28 | W Mystic, CT |
| 10 | Jacquelyn Shakar | CMS | 1:30:18 | 37 | Worcester, MA |
| 11 | Christine Braceras | METC | 1:31:45 | 34 | Portland, ME |
| 12 | Lori Lambert | | 1:32:46 | 33 | Nashua, NH |
| 13 | Allison Suchenski | AF | 1:33:53 | 35 | Trumbull, CT |
| 14 | Michele Koski | | 1:34:06 | 31 | Meriden, CT |
| 15 | Donna Hurley | | 1:34:08 | 40 | Sprucehead, ME |
| 16 | Maureen Sullivan | | 1:34:18 | 40 | Concord, MA |
| 17 | Lauren Rhatigan | | 1:35:37 | 33 | Shipbottom, NJ |
| 18 | Heather McKeown | | 1:36:31 | 44 | Enosburg Falls, VT |
| 19 | Colleen Allen | WMM | 1:36:32 | 30 | Concord, NH |
| 20 | Alice Freid | BRC | 1:36:39 | 36 | Belmont, MA |
| 21 | Johanne DE Boer | | 1:37:11 | 41 | Ayers Cliff, CAN |
| 22 | Vicki Miller | WCRC | 1:37:14 | 44 | Durham, NH |
| 23 | Karen Palmer | NMC | 1:37:17 | 32 | Fitchburg, MA |
| 24 | Amy Pierce-Root | | 1:37:40 | 26 | Peru, MA |
| 25 | Anne Marie Davee | CMeS | 1:37:46 | 41 | Pownal, ME |

## 5-Year Age Groups

| Place | Name | Time | Age | City and State | Category |
|---|---|---|---|---|---|
| 756 | Kathy Fortin | 2:05:15 | 18 | Gorham, NH | Under 20 |
| 327 | Julie Bruno | 1:41:41 | 21 | Topsfield, MA | 20-24 |
| 17 | Cathy O'Brien | 1:12:24 | 29 | Durham, NH | 25-29 |
| 84 | Kerry Arsenault | 1:25:50 | 32 | Guilford, CT | 30-34 |
| 44 | Julie Peterson | 1:20:07 | 37 | Beverly, MA | 35-39 |
| 27 | Joan Benoit-Samuelson | 1:16:03 | 40 | Freeport, ME | 40-44 **AGR** |
| 251 | Dorothy Helling | 1:38:01 | 47 | Montpelier, VT | 45-49 |
| 439 | Faye Gagnon | 1:47:35 | 52 | Minot, ME | 50-54 |
| 400 | Carrie Parsi | 1:45:22 | 58 | Lexington, MA | 55-59 |
| 598 | Barbara Robinson | 1:55:07 | 63 | Franconia, NH | 60-64 |
| 850 | Hildy Fosse | 2:16:38 | 68 | Holderness, NH | 65+ |
| 25 | Seth Williams | 1:15:37 | 19 | Manomet, MA | Under 20 |
| 24 | Andrew Baird | 1:15:22 | 24 | Foster, RI | 20-24 |
| 9 | Craig Widnes | 1:10:24 | 26 | Denver, CO | 25-29 |
| 2 | Eric Morse | 1:05:38 | 32 | Montpelier, VT | 30-34 |
| 1 | Craig Fram | 1:04:48 | 38 | Plaistow, NH | 35-39 |
| 12 | Brian Reinhold | 1:11:44 | 43 | Akersberga, SWE | 40-44 |
| 20 | Keith Woodward | 1:13:55 | 46 | E Corinth, VT | 45-49 |

| Place | Name | Time | Age | City and State | Category |
|---|---|---|---|---|---|
| 35 | Sumner Brown | 1:18:51 | 53 | Belmont, MA | 50-54 |
| 106 | Robert Ludwig | 1:27:36 | 56 | Westford, MA | 55-59 |
| 232 | Gerald Barney | 1:36:44 | 64 | Swanton, VT | 60-64 |
| 370 | Donald Ross | 1:43:51 | 67 | Marblehead, MA | 65-69 |
| 788 | Peter Pantelis | 2:08:16 | 71 | Waterford, CT | 70-74 |
| 738 | Carlton Mendell | 2:03:10 | 75 | Portland, ME | 75+ |

## Top 5 Teams

| Men | | Men 40+ | |
|---|---|---|---|
| 1 CMS | 5:38:52 | 1 Will. AC | 7:06:54 |
| 2 GCS | 6:11:07 | 2 CSU | 7:10:53 |
| 3 Will. AC | 6:42:38 | 3 WCRC | 7:14:07 |
| 4 GLRR | 6:52:12 | 4 NMC | 7:14:33 |
| 5 WCRC | 6:53:03 | 5 GLRR | 7:25:34 |

| Women | | Women 40+ | |
|---|---|---|---|
| 1 BAA | 4:44:26 | 1 WCRC | 5:07:47 |
| 2 WCRC | 4:59:23 | 2 CMeS | 5:15:32 |
| 3 BRC | 5:04:12 | 3 WMM | 5:45:43 |
| 4 NMC | 5:05:53 | 4 AA | 6:10:44 |
| 5 WMM | 5:10:01 | 5 PFIZER | 6:12:14 |

**38th Mt Washington Road Race**

June 20, 1998
Saturday, 10:00 AM
892 Finishers

Favorites heading into the race included two time winner Matt Carpenter, Simon Gutierrez of Albuquerque and 1997's runner-up Eric Morse.  The women's favorite was three time champion J'Ne Day-Lucore and newcomer Magdelena Thorsell.  Thorsell, from Sweden, had been a member of her country's national cross country team and a three-time half marathon champion.  The top runners would be chasing $4850 in prize money and time bonuses in the USATF-sanctioned event.

The weather was mild with temperatures in the 50s and winds of only 5 MPH as the field made its way out from the Route 16 starting line.  Thorsell led the field of 171 women as 14 broke 1:30.  Thorsell finished a record high fifteenth place overall.  She noted in the *Mountain Ear*, "It was fun!  I've never done anything like this before."  She won $750 for placing first and another $1,000 for setting a new course record.

Matt Carpenter ran with Gutierrez and Kenyan runner Levis Anyega (who did not finish) in the early miles.  As Carpenter pulled away to his third victory, Morse began working his way past the

102

early leaders.  Carpenter took top honors in 1:00:23 with Morse second, just over two minutes back.  Gutierrez completed his debut in 1:03:23 for third place.  His time combined with his wife, Magdelena Thorsell, to give them the title of fastest couple ever on Mt Washington.  They ran an amazing combined time of 2:13:32, which was more than 19 minutes faster than the previous best couple.  Steve and Marjorie Podgajny had run 2:32:35 in 1981.  Thomas Borschel ran on pace to break Fred Norris' masters (40+) record of 1:04:57, but ultimately came up short, finishing in sixth overall with a 1:05:42.  A record tying five runners finished under 1:05.  The women narrowed the average finishing time-gap to 8 minutes, with men averaging 1:47:30 to the women's 1:55:41.

Sumner Brown a veteran of 13 Mt Washington races told *New England Runner,* "I ran negative splits.  I've never done that before.  After 13 years of going out hard and dying, I knew I was going to be slow, but at least I could be slow and smart."  Brown was the top 50+ finisher in 1:17:29.

CMS took the team title in a fast 5:28:58; finishing 37 minutes ahead of GCS and 27 other teams.  The CMS team prepared for Mt Washington by taking the first four, and six of the top eight, places at the Pack Monadnock 10 mile race two weeks earlier.  They were led at Pack by Dunham, who was returning from nearly a year off due to a broken bone in his foot.  CSU set a new record for 40+ teams with a close battle with NMC, WCRC, and GSC all finished within three minutes.  The women's team victory went to CMS over CSU by 17 minutes in 4:21:27.  The female 40+ team was also taken by CMS with a 4:56:57, 25 minutes faster than second place WCRC.

For the first time the "Mt Washington Hill Climb" (as it was called in the race information packet) was part of the 12-event Fila Skyrunning circuit.  Also new this year was the "Tuscan bean and pasta soup with fixin's prepared by the Thompson House Eatery in Jackson."  This year also marked the first time that a results book was not printed and sent to all finishers.  Check-in was held at the Eagle Mountain House from 4 – 9:30 PM on Friday and at the base of the Auto Road from 7:30 – 9 AM on race day.

## Top 25 Finishers

| Place  Name | Club | Time | Age | City and State | |
|---|---|---|---|---|---|
| 1 Matt Carpenter | | 1:00:24 | 33 | Manitou Springs, CO | |
| 2 Eric Morse | CMS | 1:02:31 | 33 | Montpelier, VT | |
| 3 Simon Gutierrez | | 1:03:23 | 32 | Albuquerque, NM | FW |
| 4 Dave Dunham | CMS | 1:03:38 | 34 | Bradford, MA | FW |
| 5 Thierry Icart | | 1:04:40 | 29 | Levillaret, FRA | |
| 6 Tom Borschel | GCS | 1:05:42 | 40 | Idaho Falls, ID | |
| 7 Mike Casner | CMS | 1:05:48 | 36 | Keene, NH | |
| 8 Dan Verrington | CMS | 1:07:20 | 35 | Bradford, MA | |
| 9 Jeremy Wright | | 1:07:50 | 24 | Laramie, WY | |
| 10 Spyros Barress | PFIZR | 1:09:17 | 35 | Mystic, CT | |
| 11 Stephen Peterson | CMS | 1:09:41 | 32 | Chelmsford, MA | |

| Place | Name | Club | Time | Age | City and State | |
|-------|------|------|------|-----|----------------|---|
| 12 | Bob Hodge | CMS | 1:09:54 | 42 | Clinton, MA | FW |
| 13 | Tony Bates | | 1:09:59 | 39 | Salisbury, VT | |
| 14 | Seth Williams | | 1:10:02 | 20 | Manoment, MA | |
| **15** | **Magdelena Thorsell** | | **1:10:09** | **33** | **Albuquerque, NM** | Course Record |
| 16 | Adam Hersh | CMS | 1:10:43 | 26 | Hanover, NH | |
| 17 | Fergus Cullen | HTC | 1:10:51 | 26 | W Hartford, CT | |
| 18 | Thomas Murdock III | IATC | 1:11:19 | 34 | Somerville, MA | |
| 19 | Edward Sheldon | GCS | 1:11:50 | 33 | Manchester, NH | |
| 20 | George Adams | CMS | 1:11:55 | 28 | Keene, NH | |
| 21 | Kevin Williams | | 1:12:02 | 40 | Scotia, NY | |
| 22 | Gary Johnson | | 1:12:47 | 47 | Irasburg, VT | FW |
| 23 | Rick Stuart | CMeS | 1:12:55 | 40 | Santa Fe, NM | |
| 24 | Thompson Parker | HS | 1:12:57 | 28 | Bow, NH | |
| 25 | Len Hall | | 1:13:06 | 45 | W Lebanon, NH | |
| 26 | Brian Stevens | GCS | 1:13:30 | 34 | New Boston, NH | |
| 31 | Keith Woodward | GMAA | 1:15:26 | 47 | E. Corinth, VT | FW |
| 109 | John Cederholm | BAA | 1:27:39 | 55 | Boston, MA | FW |

## Top 25 Women

| Place | Name | Club | Time | Age | City and State | |
|-------|------|------|------|-----|----------------|---|
| 1 | Magdelena Thorsell | | 1:10:09 | 33 | Albuquerque, NM | Course Record |
| 2 | J'Ne Day-Lucore | | 1:20:58 | 37 | Denver, CO | FW |
| 3 | Barbara Remmers | | 1:22:16 | 34 | New York, NY | FW |
| 4 | Tonya Dodge | | 1:23:52 | 23 | Alamosa, NY | |
| 5 | Amy Williams | | 1:24:22 | 42 | Denver, CO | |
| 6 | Rebecca Stockdale-Woolley | | 1:24:52 | 47 | Chaplin, CT | |
| 7 | Kerry Arsenault | AF | 1:25:32 | 33 | Guilford, CT | |
| 8 | Karen McGahie | CMS | 1:26:55 | 36 | W Newbury, MA | |
| 9 | Allison Suchenski | AF | 1:27:09 | 36 | Trumbull, CT | |
| 10 | Cathy Lifschultz | BAA | 1:27:49 | 35 | Sudbury, MA | |
| 11 | Ellen McCurtin | MR | 1:28:27 | 31 | New York, NY | |
| 12 | Gail Breslow | CSU | 1:28:48 | 43 | Watertown, MA | |
| 13 | Lori Lambert | GCS | 1:28:54 | 34 | Nashua, NH | |
| 14 | Jacqueline Shakar | CMS | 1:29:40 | 38 | Worcester, MA | |
| 15 | Gillian Fucigna | RIRR | 1:31:21 | 30 | Greenville, RI | |
| 16 | Delwyn Williamson | CSU | 1:33:20 | 36 | Jamaica Plain, MA | |
| 17 | Kim Young | | 1:33:44 | 30 | Jackson, WY | |
| 18 | Karen Tripp | AA | 1:35:06 | 39 | Deerfield, NH | |
| 19 | Celeste St Pierre | | 1:35:46 | 33 | Franconia, NH | |
| 20 | Lauri Harris | | 1:35:59 | 28 | Jackson, WY | |
| 21 | Nixie Raymond | CSU | 1:36:11 | 38 | Roslindale, MA | |
| 22 | Andrea Brayman | | 1:36:16 | 25 | Jamestown, RI | |

| Place | Name | Club | Time | Age | City and State |
|-------|------|------|------|-----|----------------|
| 23 | Deborah Sheedy | BAA | 1:37:16 | 42 | Waltham, MA |
| 24 | Kathleen Newton | HMRR | 1:37:30 | 38 | Bennington, VT |
| 25 | Donna Smyth | CSU | 1:38:00 | 38 | Northfield, MA |

Magdelena Thorsell

## Top 5 Teams

| Men | | | Men 40+ | |
|-----|-----|---|---------|---|
| 1 CMS | 5:28:58 | | 1 CSU | 7:04:28 |
| 2 GCS | 6:05:41 | | 2 NMC | 7:06:44 |
| 3 PFIZER | 6:45:00 | | 3 WCRC | 7:07:34 |
| 4 WCRC | 6:58:24 | | 4 GCS | 7:07:47 |
| 5 NMC | 6:59:28 | | 5 CMeS | 7:18:56 |

| Women | | | Women 40+ | |
|-------|-----|---|-----------|---|
| 1 CMS | 4:21:27 | | 1 CMS | 4:56:57 **CR** |
| 2 CSU | 4:38:19 | | 2 WCRC | 5:19:43 |
| 3 AF | 4:43:26 | | 3 GLRR | 5:28:05 |
| 4 BAA | 4:47:52 | | 4 CMeS | 5:35:46 |
| 5 GCS | 5:01:13 | | 5 WMM | 5:41:21 |

| Place | Name | Time | Age | City and State | Category |
|---|---|---|---|---|---|
| 714 | Jessie Benthien | 2:03:50 | 16 | Goffstown, NH | Under 20 |
| 70 | Tonya Dodge | 1:23:52 | 23 | Alamosa, NY | 20-24 |
| 212 | Lauri Harris | 1:35:59 | 28 | Jackson, WY | 25-29 |
| 15 | Magdelena Thorsell | 1:10:09 | 33 | Albuquerque, NM | 30-34 |
| 56 | J'Ne Day-Lucore | 1:20:58 | 37 | Denver, CO | 35-39 |
| 78 | Amy Williams | 1:24:22 | 42 | Denver, CO | 40-44 |
| 82 | Rebecca Stockdale-Woolley | 1:24:52 | 47 | Chaplin, CT | 45-49 |
| 447 | Faye Gagnon | 1:48:21 | 53 | Minot, ME | 50-54 |
| 448 | Marcia Puryear | 1:48:23 | 55 | Concord, MA | 55-59 |
| 624 | Diana Avery | 1:58:16 | 60 | Concord, NH | 60-64 |
| 793 | Hildy Fosse | 2:13:00 | 69 | Holderness, NH | 65-69 |
| 867 | Nancy Stokes | 2:26:41 | 71 | Kittery Point, ME | 70-71 **AG Record** |
| 879 | Louise Rossetti | 2:33:04 | 76 | Saugus, MA | 75+ |
| | | | | | |
| 191 | Aaron Poulin | 1:34:34 | 16 | Queensbury, NY | Under 20 |
| 9 | Jeremy Wright | 1:07:50 | 24 | Laramie, WY | 20-24 |
| 5 | Thierry Icart | 1:04:40 | 29 | Levillaret, FRA | 25-29 |
| 1 | Matt Carpenter | 1:00:24 | 33 | Manitou Sprgs, CO | 30-34 |
| 7 | Mike Casner | 1:05:48 | 36 | Keene, NH | 35-39 |
| 6 | Tom Borschel | 1:05:42 | 40 | Idaho Falls, ID | 40-44 |
| 22 | Gary Johnson | 1:12:47 | 47 | Irasburg, VT | 45-49 |
| 37 | Sumner Brown | 1:17:29 | 54 | Belmont, MA | 50-54 |
| 109 | John Cederholm | 1:27:39 | 55 | Boston, MA | 55-59 |
| 249 | Fred Zuleger III | 1:37:53 | 60 | Coventry, RI | 60-64 |
| 209 | Gerald Barney | 1:35:56 | 65 | Swanton, VT | 65-69 |
| 548 | Leon Beverly | 1:53:26 | 71 | Stamford, VT | 70-74 **AG Record** |
| 686 | Carlton Mendell | 2:01:52 | 76 | Portland, ME | 75-79 |
| 843 | Phil Campbell | 2:19:48 | 80 | Lynnfield, MA | 80+ **AG Record** |

Jim Laprel longtime Mt Washington runner

**39<sup>th</sup> Mt Washington Road Race**

June 19, 1999
Saturday, 10:00 AM
918 Finishers


Favorites heading in were Tatiana Titova, a Russian marathoner who had recently won the Pittsburgh marathon, J'Ne Day-Lucore from Denver, and many time top-five finisher Julie Peterson.  The men's field looked to be one of the best ever assembled.  Course record holder Daniel Kihara was returning along with defending champion Matt Carpenter.  Others expected to be in the mix included Simon Gutierrez who finished third in 1998, and Scott Elliott, who had won the Pikes Peak ascent six times.  New England favorites included Joe Lemay, who had personal bests of 2:14 and 1:04 for the marathon and half-marathon respectively along with a 28:00 10K personal best.  Eric Morse and Dave Dunham came into the race showing excellent fitness having finished first and second at the USATF 10K championships two weeks prior.  They also battled at the USATF 12K championships and at the New England Mountain circuit races.

The 45-degree temperatures coupled with little wind, 90-mile visibility and 70 degree temperatures at the base set the stage for a fast race.  Gutierrez fronted the lead pack through two miles in 13:59.  Carpenter and Kihara broke the race open after three miles and hit the half together in 28:44.  They continued together with Kihara sitting behind Carpenter most of the way.  They passed 5 miles in 38:00 and six miles in 45:58.  As they surged on each other, Dunham pulled away from the chase pack of Gutierrez, Lemay and Morse, with a strong second half.  Carpenter and Kihara passed 7 miles in 54:00 and Kihara surged with about quarter mile to go.  He held on to win with Carpenter 13 seconds back.  They led a record 20 men under 1:10 and seven men under 1:04.  Carpenter noted in the *Mountain Ear* "He (Kihara) put on such a decisive move on me.  I really didn't have time to react."  Kihara was awarded $750 for winning and another $500 for running under one hour.  Carpenter received $500 for second place and an additional $500 for finishing under one hour.

The women's field was also deep, with a record 17 women finishing under 1:30.  Barbara Remmers led the way taking nine minutes off her time from the year before.  She told Don Allison, in his online account of the race, "I ran on a treadmill at a health club at 11.5% grade."  Remmers turned away the challenge by Titova taking the lead at four miles and continuing on to win by 1:05.  Julie Peterson took third and told the *Mountain Ear,* "I guess I'll have to get the first I've always wanted next year, in the masters."  Titova found mountain running difficult and told the Union Leader, "At four miles I felt like sitting.  This was hard – up, up, up."  The women made up more than 20% of the field, as they came in with a record high 21.24% of finishers.

CMS set yet another team record, putting six runners in the top 16 and combining for a time of 5:20:44.  The average finishing time for a CMS scoring member was 1:04:09.   The team was awarded $500 for a new record. The GLRR finished second in the rare feat of two teams under six hours.  Four of the 40+ teams broke the record, led by WCRC in 6:46:04.  The male seniors (50+) were scored for the first time, with the top five runners times combined for the scoring.

WCRC edged CMeS by nearly ten minutes in 8:18:40.  The CMS women ran a fast 4:18:49 to take the team title as five clubs broke the five-hour mark.  CSU won the woman's team 40+ division (three score) by three and a half minutes combining for a 5:33:00.

Healthsource, Bridgton Academy, and Citizens Bank again sponsored the race.  The race was again part of the Skyrunning circuit, and all finishers within 20% of the winning time qualified for additional Skyrunning events.   The Federation for Sport at Altitude (FSA) offered a $250 prize to the top US male and female finishers.  This year a pasta meal at the Thompson house was added.  Also new this year was a jump in the entry fee to $30 and an expansion of the lottery winners to 1,100.  The prize structure also grew with the purse of $4,850 and added a new $5,000 Course Record bonus along with time incentive bonuses.  A blind auction for 100 spots was added this year.  The top 100 who donated the most to the Special Olympics would be lottery by-pass entries.

Other notes from the race included 77-year-old Carlton Mendell setting a new age group record and then running down the mountain after finishing.  Although not a recognized category, two couples finished in the top 25.   Joe Lemay and Ellen McCurtin had a combined time of 2:31:10 and Russel and Deb Bollig combined for a time of 2:37:05.  Final notes on the race from Matt Carpenter in the *Union Leader* and Dave Dunham in the Boston Globe.  Carpenter on his second place finish "Sometimes it's good to lose.  It makes you better.  I'll just have to train harder next year."  Dunham on the difficultly of the course "The only way to make it worse is to have you climb the radio tower at the end."

**Top 25 Finishers**

| Place  Name | Club | Time | Age | City and State | |
|---|---|---|---|---|---|
| 1 Daniel Kihara | | 0:59:03 | 31 | Royersford, KEN | |
| 2 Matt Carpenter | | 0:59:16 | 34 | Manitou Springs, CO | FW |
| 3 Dave Dunham | CMS | 1:00:37 | 35 | Bradford, MA | FW |
| 4 Eric Morse | CMS | 1:01:09 | 34 | Berlin, VT | |
| 5 Simon Gutierrez | AD | 1:01:38 | 33 | Albuquerque, NM | FW |
| 6 Joseph Lemay | AD | 1:03:04 | 32 | Danbury, CT | |
| 7 Rich Davis | | 1:03:32 | 29 | Ft. Collins, CO | |
| 8 Thomas Anderson | CMS | 1:04:36 | 34 | Keene, NH | |
| 9 Scott Elliott | | 1:05:53 | 35 | Boulder, CO | |
| 10 Richard Bolt | CMS | 1:06:00 | 28 | Pepperell, MA | |
| 11 Fergus Cullen | GLRR | 1:06:22 | 27 | W. Hartford, CT | |
| 12 Thomas Murdock | IATC | 1:06:43 | 35 | Somerville, MA | |
| 13 Edward Sheldon | GCS | 1:07:02 | 34 | Manchester, NH | |
| 14 Stephen Peterson | CMS | 1:08:22 | 33 | Chelmsford, MA | |
| 15 Richard Doubleday | BBRR | 1:09:00 | 37 | Brookline, MA | |
| 16 Mike Casner | CMS | 1:09:26 | 37 | Keene, NH | |
| 17 Peter Hammer | BRC | 1:09:34 | 32 | Brighton, MA | |
| 18 Francis Burdett | GLRR | 1:09:42 | 34 | Worcester, MA | |
| 19 Thompson Parker | HS | 1:09:51 | 29 | Bow, NH | |

| Place | Name | Club | Time | Age | City and State | |
|---|---|---|---|---|---|---|
| 20 | Mark Behan | WC | 1:09:55 | 36 | Newton, NH | |
| 21 | Tony Bates | GLRR | 1:10:50 | 40 | Salisbury, VT | |
| 22 | Andy Macdonald | BRC | 1:11:16 | 39 | Somerville, MA | |
| 23 | Len Hall | | 1:11:40 | 46 | W. Lebanon, NH | |
| 24 | Rick Stuart | CME | 1:11:58 | 41 | Santa Fe, NM | |
| 25 | Russel Bollig | | 1:12:08 | 35 | Boulder, CO | |
| 38 | Keith Woodward | GMAA | 1:16:34 | 48 | E. Corinth, VT | FW |

## Top 25 Women

| Place | Name | Club | Time | Age | City and State | |
|---|---|---|---|---|---|---|
| 1 | Barbara Remmers | | 1:13:52 | 35 | New York, NY | |
| 2 | Tatiana Titova | | 1:14:57 | 33 | Gainesville, FL | |
| 3 | Julie Peterson | | 1:16:36 | 39 | Beverly, MA | |
| 4 | J'Ne Day-Lucore | | 1:20:20 | 38 | Denver, CO | FW |
| 5 | Suzy West | | 1:20:40 | 36 | Putney, VT | |
| 6 | Catherine Lifschultz | BAA | 1:23:22 | 36 | Sudbury, MA | |
| 7 | Rebecca Stockdale-Woolley | CMS | 1:23:54 | 48 | Chaplin, CT | |
| 8 | Karen McGahie | CMS | 1:24:13 | 37 | Boylston, MA | |
| 9 | Deb Bollig | | 1:24:57 | 35 | Boulder, CO | |
| 10 | Donna Smyers | CVT | 1:25:12 | 41 | Montpelier, VT | |
| 11 | Kerry Arsenault | HITK | 1:26:42 | 34 | Guilford, CT | |
| 12 | Magdalena Boudreau | | 1:27:26 | 37 | Fall River, MA | |
| 13 | Gail Breslow | CSU | 1:27:26 | 44 | Watertown, MA | |
| 14 | Ellen McCurtin | | 1:28:06 | 32 | New York, NY | |
| 15 | Kiersten Lippmann | | 1:28:42 | 18 | Colchester, VT | |
| 16 | Cheryl Theodore | GNBTC | 1:28:59 | 39 | Dartmouth, MA | |
| 17 | Sue Long | | 1:29:30 | 39 | Rumford, ME | |
| 18 | Johanne De Boer | | 1:30:16 | 43 | Ayers Cliff, CAN | |
| 19 | Jacqueline Shakar | CMS | 1:30:42 | 39 | Worcester, MA | |
| 20 | Karen Tripp | AA | 1:30:47 | 40 | Deerfield, NH | |
| 21 | Swenja Surminski | | 1:30:55 | 23 | Durham, NH | |
| 22 | Brenda Baxter | GCS | 1:31:38 | 36 | Groton, MA | |
| 23 | Lori Lambert | GCS | 1:31:52 | 35 | Nashua, NH | |
| 24 | Donna Smyth | CSU | 1:32:49 | 39 | Northfield, MA | |
| 25 | Andrea Leonard | MVS | 1:32:52 | 21 | N. Andover, MA | |

## 5-Year Age Groups

| Place | Name | Time | Age | City and State | Category | |
|---|---|---|---|---|---|---|
| 152 | Kiersten Lippmann | 1:28:42 | 18 | Colchester, VT | Under 20 | AGR |
| 186 | Swenja Surminski | 1:30:55 | 23 | Durham, NH | 20-24 | |
| 224 | Wendy Hagan | 1:33:03 | 29 | Cambridge, MA | 25-29 | |
| 33 | Tatiana Titova | 1:14:57 | 33 | Gainesville, FL | 30-34 | |

| Place | Name | Time | Age | City and State | Category |
|---|---|---|---|---|---|
| 39 | Julie Peterson | 1:16:36 | 39 | Beverly, MA | 35-39 |
| 103 | Donna Smyers | 1:25:12 | 41 | Montpelier, VT | 40-44 |
| 87 | Rebecca Stockdale-Woolley | 1:23:54 | 48 | Chaplin, CT | 45-49 |
| 469 | Marjorie Kos | 1:44:42 | 54 | City Island, NY | 50-54 |
| 497 | Louisa Dunlap | 1:46:13 | 58 | Belfast, ME | 55-59 |
| 385 | Carrie Parsi | 1:41:16 | 60 | Lexington, MA | 60-64 **AGR** |
| 490 | Barbara Robinson | 1:46:03 | 65 | Franconia, NH | 65-69 |
| 853 | Hildy Fosse | 2:14:02 | 70 | Holderness, NH | 70-74 **AGR** |
| 911 | Louise Rossetti | 2:38:13 | 77 | Saugus, MA | 75+ |
| | | | | | |
| 119 | Robert Hopkinson | 1:26:51 | 16 | Middlebury, VT | Under 20 |
| 59 | Jonathan Williams | 1:20:25 | 20 | W. Hartford, CT | 20-24 |
| 7 | Rich Davis | 1:03:32 | 29 | Ft. Collins, CO | 25-29 |
| 1 | Daniel Kihara | 0:59:03 | 31 | Royersford, KEN | 30-34 |
| 3 | Dave Dunham | 1:00:37 | 35 | Bradford, MA | 35-39 **AGR** |
| 21 | Tony Bates | 1:10:50 | 40 | Salisbury, VT | 40-44 |
| 23 | Len Hall | 1:11:40 | 46 | W. Lebanon, NH | 45-49 |
| 40 | James Imprescia | 1:16:38 | 50 | Leominster, MA | 50-54 |
| 47 | Sumner Brown | 1:17:59 | 55 | Belmont, MA | 55-59 |
| 95 | John Pelton | 1:24:32 | 60 | W. Rupert, VT | 60-64 **AGR** |
| 248 | Gerald Barney | 1:34:59 | 66 | Swanton, VT | 65-69 |
| 698 | Leon Beverly | 1:57:40 | 72 | Stamford, VT | 70-74 |
| 763 | Carlton Mendell | 2:03:12 | 77 | Portland, ME | 75-79 |
| 908 | Phil Campbell | 2:36:47 | 81 | Lynnfield, MA | 80+ |

## Top 5 Teams

| Men | | Men 40+ | | Men 50+ | |
|---|---|---|---|---|---|
| 1 CMS | 5:20:44 **CR** | 1 WCRC | 6:46:04 **CR** | 1 WCRC | 8:18:40 **CR** |
| 2 GLRR | 5:56:09 | 2 CSU | 6:52:56 | 2 CMeS | 8:28:01 |
| 3 GCS | 6:19:31 | 3 GLRR | 6:59:22 | 3 WAC | 8:41:19 |
| 4 WCRC | 6:23:05 | 4 CMeS | 7:02:50 | 4 GLRR | 8:41:50 |
| 5 CSU | 6:39:39 | 5 GMAA | 7:17:22 | 5 MVS | 8:43:23 |

| Women | | Women 40+ | | Women 50+ | |
|---|---|---|---|---|---|
| 1 CMS | 4:18:49 | 1 CSU | 4:37:51 **CR** | 1 LAC | 5:33:00 **CR** |
| 2 CSU | 4:34:37 | 2 CMS | 4:41:23 | | |
| 3 GCS | 4:43:14 | 3 WCRC | 5:09:42 | | |
| 4 NMC | 4:44:42 | 4 MVS | 5:16:05 | | |
| 5 BAA | 4:55:23 | 5 LAC | 5:33:00 | | |

**40<sup>th</sup> Mt Washington Road Race**

June 17, 2000
Saturday, 10:00 AM
891 Finishers


Favorites for the 40<sup>th</sup> anniversary of the race looked to be Kenyan runners.  Daniel Kihara, the three-time champion, was scheduled to return as was his sometimes-training partner Joseph Kibor.  Simon Karori was expected to take a run at the masters (40+) record.  He had never raced Mt Washington before, but his credentials included winning the Falmouth Road Race three times.  Mark Donahue, who among his many accomplishments was the 1986 New England Cross Country champion, was tearing up the local racing scene including an overall win at the USATF New England 10K championships the week before Mt Washington.  He was expected to give Karori a chase in the master's category.  Local favorites included Eric Morse, Craig Fram, and Dave Dunham, who had been tuning up for the race by running up mountains on most weekends during the spring.  At Mt Kearsarge they went 1, 2, and 3 with Fram destroying the master's record.  At Wachusett Mountain Morse and Dunham went 1, 2, and followed that with a 1, 2 finish at Pack Monadnock.  Women's favorites included Alice Muriithi, a Kenyan living in Pennsylvania, former champion Jacqueline Gareau, and top local runner Julie Peterson.

Kihara flew in from Kenya earlier in the week and may have been tired from the 17-hour flight.  He ran with Kibor for most of the race and made a decisive move in the last mile to take a 40-second victory in 59:24.  Kibor missed an additional $500 time bonus by four seconds, just missing the one-hour mark.  CMS runners dominated the top ten, placing third through sixth and eighth and tenth.  Fergus Cullen in seventh place was the only non-Kenyan and non-CMS runner in the top ten.  Karori defeated Robert Ratcliffe by three minutes to take the master's victory however; he came up six minutes shy of the course record.  This was only the second time in a decade that less than ten men finished under 1:10.  The average finishing time for men hit a high of 1:56:31, nearly seven minutes slower than the past high.  The gap between men's and women's average finishing time narrowed to just over four minutes, the closest to date.

Alice Muriithi took the lead early on and was never challenged for the ladies' crown.  Jacqueline Gareau took second and was on pace for the master's mark, and the $4,000 bonus, through the half but faded in the second half.  Both women finished in the top 25 overall.  Former champion Barbara Remmers told *New England Runner* "It was a lot different for me this year, but I love that race.  I'll run it every year the rest of my life."  Gareau also chimed in, "I love this race.  I've run this course four times and I still can't tell where the finish is.  Can you believe that?"

CMS led the charge in the team category with a one hour and 13 minute victory over the WCRC in 5:35:47.  The WCRC took the win in the 40+ team finishing 2:49 ahead of CSU and 5 minutes ahead of GMAA.  CSU turned the tables, taking first in the 50+ category. CMS won the women's team title by 12 minutes over CSU in 4:34:13.  CMS also won the 40+ category, their time of 4:44:46 would have been fast enough to rank second among open women's teams and beat the CSU masters team by nearly 20 minutes.

*New England Runner* presented the story of the CMS fifth man with a colorful account of his "Annual peristalsis that CMS Steve Peterson experiences at the summit of Mt Washington was evidence of the uniqueness of the race. Peterson pleaded 'I don't know what it is, I only throw up at this race'."

Streaker (continuous finishes at Mt Washington) Ron Johnston told *New England Runner,* "This race is what keeps me going. I can't miss a year because I've run 20 straight." Johnston is in rare company as only twenty runners have completed 20 or more in a row. Leo Tomasetti along with teammates Anthony Zablocki and Lou Lapirviere carried the race number of fellow Rhode Island Road Runner Jerry Musco who had died six days earlier. Former club president Fred Zuleger told *New England runner,* "Jerry was such an optimist he'd signed up for Mt Washington even though he was battling cancer."

The race packet called the event the "40<sup>th</sup> Run to the Clouds." Healthsource, Bridgton Academy, and Citizens Bank sponsored the race. Number pickup had to be completed prior to 9:00 AM on race day. New features this year were Shaklee performance drinks at the half, along with Polar water at the aid stations. A "Rides" area was available in the tent at the base where runners and drivers could meet to arrange rides down from the summit after the race as no formal transportation is provided. *New England Runner* sponsored a $4,000 bonus for the first runner to break the 40+ age group record. USATF membership cards and a Direct Payment license were required for money prizewinners. The prize purse was $4,850 plus time bonuses. Medals were presented to the top two in five year age groups, the top ten overall, the first five open teams, the top three WAVA master's, the top three master teams, the top 50+ team, and the top two Clydesdales and top Filly. The traditional Crossan cup was awarded to the top NH finisher.

## Top 25 Finishers

| Place | Name | Club | Time | Age | City & State | |
|---|---|---|---|---|---|---|
| 1 | Daniel Kihara | | 0:59:24 | 32 | KEN | |
| 2 | Joseph Kibor | | 1:00:04 | 27 | Concord, MA (KEN) | |
| 3 | Dave Dunham | CMS | 1:02:48 | 36 | Bradford, MA | **FW** |
| 4 | Eric Morse | CMS | 1:04:54 | 35 | Berlin, VT | |
| 5 | Dan Verrington | CMS | 1:07:50 | 37 | Bradford, MA | |
| 6 | Mike Casner | CMS | 1:09:30 | 38 | Keene, NH | |
| 7 | Fergus Cullen | GLRR | 1:09:58 | 28 | W Hartford, CT | |
| 8 | Richard Bolt | CMS | 1:10:45 | 29 | Manchester, NH | |
| 9 | Simon Karori | | 1:11:25 | 40 | Concord, MA (KEN) | |
| 10 | Stephen Peterson | CMS | 1:13:35 | 34 | Chelmsford, MA | |
| 11 | Robert Ratcliffe | | 1:14:49 | 42 | Lincoln, MA | |
| 12 | Michael Kinter | Reeb | 1:15:22 | 35 | Morro Bay, CA | |
| 13 | Mark Behan | WCRC | 1:15:27 | 37 | Newton, NH | |
| 14 | Mark Donahue | CMS | 1:15:39 | 41 | Newport, RI | |
| 15 | Francis Burdett | GLRR | 1:15:40 | 35 | Worcester, MA | |
| 16 | Michael Danahy | | 1:16:00 | 21 | Lewiston, ME | |

| Place | Name | Club | Time | Age | City & State | |
|---|---|---|---|---|---|---|
| 17 | Ernest Brake | GSRT | 1:16:14 | 38 | Warner, NH | |
| 18 | Stephen Marsalese | NYH | 1:17:03 | 34 | New York, NY | |
| 19 | Tony Bates | GLRR | 1:17:07 | 41 | Salisbury, VT | |
| **20** | **Alice Muriithi** | | **1:17:26** | **26** | **Westchester NY (KEN)** | |
| 21 | Edward Sheldon | GCS | 1:17:49 | 35 | Hooksett, NH | |
| 22 | Sumner Brown | CSU | 1:18:33 | 56 | Belmont, MA | |
| **23** | **Jacqueline Gareau** | | **1:18:43** | **47** | **Boulder, CO** | **FW** |
| 24 | Tek Kilgore | | 1:19:50 | 46 | Park City, UT | |
| 25 | Thompson Parker | CIGN | 1:20:00 | 30 | Bow, NH | |
| 26 | Keith Woodward | GMAA | 1:20:10 | 49 | E Corinth, VT | |
| 27 | Rod Viens | | 1:20:22 | 32 | Sunapee, NH | |
| 128 | John Cederholm | BAA | 1:32:14 | 57 | Marion, MA | FW |

## Top 25 Women

| Place | Name | Club | Time | Age | City & State | |
|---|---|---|---|---|---|---|
| 1 | Alice Muriithi | | 1:17:26 | 26 | Westchester, NY (KEN) | |
| 2 | Jacqueline Gareau | | 1:18:43 | 47 | Boulder, CO | FW |
| 3 | Julie Peterson | SAUC | 1:23:00 | 40 | Beverly, MA | |
| 4 | Suzy West | CSU | 1:24:20 | 37 | Putney, VT | |
| 5 | Colleen Allen | GSRT | 1:24:49 | 33 | Newport Center, VT | |
| 6 | Kerry Arsenault | HITK | 1:27:00 | 35 | Clinton, CT | |
| 7 | Catherine Lifschultz | BAA | 1:27:17 | 37 | Sudbury, MA | |
| 8 | Nikki Kimball | | 1:28:11 | 29 | Elizabethtown, NY | |
| 9 | Donna Smyers | CVT | 1:29:27 | 42 | Montpelier, VT | |
| 10 | Karen McGahie | CMS | 1:29:28 | 38 | Boylston, MA | |
| 11 | Rebecca Stockdale-Woolley | CMS | 1:29:37 | 49 | Chaplin, CT | |
| 12 | Julie Denney | CPTC | 1:32:53 | 32 | New York, NY | |
| 13 | Sue Long | | 1:33:03 | 40 | Gorham, NH | |
| 14 | Lynn Achee | BKVR | 1:33:30 | 44 | Manchester Center, VT | |
| 15 | Amy Ireland | GSRT | 1:34:21 | 34 | Concord, NH | |
| 16 | Barbara Remmers | | 1:35:02 | 36 | New York, NY | FW |
| 17 | Jacqueline Shakar | CMS | 1:35:08 | 40 | Worcester, MA | |
| 18 | Ann Remmers | | 1:36:01 | 38 | Ann Arbor, MI | |
| 19 | Maureen Sullivan | GLRR | 1:36:32 | 43 | Concord, MA | |
| 20 | Lorrie Marnell | | 1:38:23 | 39 | Locke, NY | |
| 21 | Eileen Greeley | CAA | 1:38:48 | 35 | Portsmouth, NH | |
| 22 | Shawna Walega | WCRC | 1:39:02 | 39 | Manchester NH | |
| 23 | Jennifer Blastow | | 1:39:11 | 28 | Otisfield, ME | |
| 24 | Jodi-Lyn Couture | NMC | 1:39:27 | 40 | Fitchburg, MA | |
| 25 | Paulette Bolton | | 1:39:38 | 40 | Danielson, CT | |

## 5-Year Age groups

| Place | Name | Time | Age | City and State | Category |
| --- | --- | --- | --- | --- | --- |
| 232 | Kiersten Lippmann | 1:39:46 | 19 | Wayland MA | Under 20 |
| 310 | Andrea Leonard | 1:44:45 | 22 | N Andover MA | 20-24 |
| 20 | Alice Muriithi | 1:17:26 | 26 | Westchester, NY | 25-29 |
| 47 | Colleen Allen | 1:24:49 | 33 | Newport Ctr., VT | 30-34 |
| 45 | Suzy West | 1:24:20 | 37 | Putney, VT | 35-39 |
| 40 | Julie Peterson | 1:23:00 | 40 | Beverly, MA | 40-44 |
| 23 | Jacqueline Gareau | 1:18:43 | 47 | Boulder, CO | 45-49 |
| 341 | Dorothy Helling | 1:46:41 | 50 | Montpelier, VT | 50-54 |
| 381 | Faye Gagnon | 1:49:24 | 55 | Minot, ME | 55-59 |
| 748 | Diana Avery | 2:12:59 | 62 | Loudon, NH | 60-64 |
| 716 | Maggie Solomon | 2:09:17 | 66 | Glen, NH | 65-69 |
| 839 | Hildy Fosse | 2:25:47 | 71 | Holderness, NH | 70-74 |
| 889 | Louise Rossetti | 2:54:12 | 78 | Saugus, MA | 75+ |
| 77 | Joshua Dixson | 1:35:17 | 19 | Rockport, ME | Under 20 |
| 16 | Michael Danahy | 1:16:00 | 21 | Lewiston, ME | 20-24 |
| 2 | Joseph Kibor | 1:00:04 | 27 | Concord, MA | 25-29 |
| 1 | Daniel Kihara | 0:59:24 | 32 | KEN | 30-34 |
| 3 | Dave Dunham | 1:02:48 | 36 | Bradford, MA | 35-39 |
| 9 | Simon Karori | 1:11:25 | 40 | Concord, MA | 40-44 |
| 24 | Tek Kilgore | 1:19:50 | 46 | Park City, UT | 45-49 |
| 53 | Tom Maynard | 1:25:18 | 53 | Durango, CO | 50-54 |
| 22 | Sumner Brown | 1:18:33 | 56 | Belmont, MA | 55-59 |
| 97 | John Pelton | 1:29:43 | 61 | W Rupert, VT | 60-64 |
| 289 | Gerald Barney | 1:43:21 | 67 | Swanton, VT | 65-69 |
| 572 | Robert Hall | 1:59:37 | 71 | Sudbury, MA | 70-74 |
| 784 | Carlton Mendell | 2:15:31 | 78 | Portland, ME | 75+ |

Alice Muriithi

Top 5 Teams

| Men | | Men 40+ | | Men 50+ | |
|---|---|---|---|---|---|
| 1 CMS | 5:35:47 | 1 WCRC | 7:11:34 | 1 CSU | 8:27:28 |
| 2 WCRC | 6:49:10 | 2 CSU | 7:14:23 | 2 RIRR | 8:51:13 |
| 3 GLRR | 6:59:42 | 3 GMAA | 7:17:19 | 3 WCRC | 9:07:45 |
| 4 GCS | 7:00:26 | 4 CMeS | 7:42:53 | 4 CMeS | 9:20:05 |
| 5 CSU | 7:14:23 | 5 NMC | 7:45:17 | 5 GCS | 9:41:49 |

| Women | | Women 40+ | |
|---|---|---|---|
| 1 CMS | 4:34:13 | 1 CMS | 4:44:46 |
| 2 CSU | 4:46:01 | 2 CSU | 5:04:32 |
| 3 GSRT | 4:47:02 | 3 CVTRC | 5:10:18 |
| 4 WCRC | 5:08:29 | 4 GCS | 5:26:50 |
| 5 CVTRC | 5:10:18 | 5 WCRC | 5:29:03 |

Top ten finisher Stephen Peterson

June 16, 2001
Saturday 10:00 AM
897 Finishers

The favorites heading into this edition of the race included course record holder Daniel Kihara and Janko Bensa, a 2:14 marathoner who finished third at the Litchfield Hills 7.1 mile race the previous week.  Others considered possible contenders were New Englanders Craig Fram, Eric Morse, Dave Dunham, and Mike Casner.  They took the top four spots at the Pack Monadnock 10 mile race earlier in the month.  Morse and Dunham had a final tune-up the week before when they tied in a course record 56:26 at the Whiteface Mountain 8 mile.

Favorites among the women included Anna Pichrtova and Joan Samuelson.  Others in contention were Rene Frazee, a US Mountain team member and perennial top finisher Julie Peterson from Beverly MA.  Pichrtova had finished in the top ten at the World Mountain running Trophy and was a top marathoner in her home country of the Czech Republic.

Bob Fitzgerald of *New England Runner* recounts seeing Dunham the day before the race.  "You might as well write the check out now, Fram Loves the heat.  The record is gonna go."  Dunham was referring to the new bonus of $4,100 that New England Runner was offering for a master's record.

Temperatures on race day set the tone as it was in the 80s at the base and the summit reached 56 degrees.  Winds on the top were 50 mph and at times the visibility was down to thirty feet.  Mike Casner was seen soaking in the Peabody River just before the start.  He noted in the *Union Leader,* "I've had a great race one year and come back the following edition thinking I had it all figured out and of course I ran horribly."

Kihara told the *Union Leader,* "I am terribly tired" after his seventeen-hour flight from Kenya.  He also told *New England Runner* that it was "too hot".  This did not stop Bensa and Colombian Mountain expert German Fernandez from blasting out a first mile in 6:02.  Fernandez was the first off the back, paying for the early pace with a 34ᵗʰ place finish.  Bensa and Kihara strode past two miles side by side in 13:52.  In the next mile Kihara forged a 25-second lead as Bensa passed in 22:25.  Soon after Bensa flagged down a passing press van and climbed in, his race over.  The New England trio of Fram, Dunham and Morse reached the half together, spanning the road 1:19 after Kihara passed alone in first in 29:25.  Kihara continued to pull away as he passed six miles in 46:42.  The record was out of reach but breaking an hour was still possible.  He missed the additional $1,000 for a sub 60-minute finish with his fourth win in 1:00:06.  Dunham and Fram charged up the final hill four minutes later with Dunham taking second place and Fram taking third in a new masters (40+) record of 1:04:20.  Fram collapsed after finishing and told *New England Runner,* "In all the races I've run that's the first time my legs wouldn't support me through the finish chute."  Fram won $4,100 for the masters record, $300 for finishing third overall, $250 for winning the age graded (WAVA) competition, and $100 for being the top New Hampshire finisher.  The weather conditions proved to be a deterrent in running fast as only five men finished in under 1:10, the fewest since 1976.

Anna Pichrtova passed the three-mile mark in 25:58 with Joan Samuelson just over one minute back.  Pichrtova expanded her lead and took a three-minute victory over Samuelson.  She also finished an incredible thirteenth place overall.  In *New England Runner* Pichrtova said, "Never again."  Samuelson's time was just 44 seconds shy of her own master's record.  She told the *Hartford Courant*, "It was survival.  It was steeper than I recalled."  Samuelson was awarded $500 for her second place finish and an additional $250 for topping the age graded (WAVA) competition.  The *Hartford Courant* also caught up with Fram and Dunham at the finish line and related the following "Craig you're the man! Dunham yelled. Woooo!  I haven't run this enough to know what the splits are said Fram.  By about six or seven miles I knew I had a shot.  I knew he had it Dunham said.  It hurt though Fram noted.  I've never heard anyone groan so much said Dunham."  The women's field made up over 25% of the field, coming in at 25.31%.  The average women's finishing time was an all time high of 2:02:17.

CMS won the team title for the tenth straight year with a one-hour and sixteen-minute victory over the Whirlaway Racing Team in 5:39:58.  The WCRC earned the 40+ title with a 15 minute win over the NMC in 7:11:29.  The 50+ was also won by the WCRC with an 8:53:16 to defeat CSU by 11 minutes.  The women's title went to CMS finishing a little over four minutes ahead of CSU in 4:32:53.  CMS also beat CSU in the 40+ category 4:42:47 to 4:54:14.  The GCS took the win in the women's 50+ team by 15 minutes over the MVS 6:15:45 to 6:30:27.

Mark Behan, of Newton, NH, a sub 1:10 Mt Washington runner and a writer for the *Eagle-Tribune* talked about his post race run.  "I joined Dunham and Verrington for the run down the mountain which was much more enjoyable than the ascent.  The view of the presidential range was spectacular and the sheer beauty of the mountain is not appreciated while staring down at ones knees on the run up."  Dan Verrington, a top local runner, told the *Eagle-Tribune*, "I've always walked a little.  If you do it at strategic points, it sometimes feels better."  His plan worked well as he finished fifth and doubled up with a second place finish the following day at the Whirlaway 10K race.  Final word on the race came from Simon Karori, one of the top 40+ racers, as he told Vin Sylvia of the Union Leader, "It was very tough – the record, this course, the weather."

<u>Top 25 Finishers</u>

| Place | Name | Club | Time | Age | City and State | |
|---|---|---|---|---|---|---|
| 1 | Daniel Kihara | | 1:00:06 | 33 | KEN | |
| 2 | Dave Dunham | CMS | 1:04:20 | 37 | Bradford, MA | FW |
| 3 | Craig Fram | Whirl | 1:04:29 | 42 | Plaistow, NH | FW |
| 4 | Eric Morse | CMS | 1:05:00 | 36 | Berlin, VT | |
| 5 | Dan Verrington | CMS | 1:08:42 | 38 | Bradford, MA | |
| 6 | Larry Sayers | CMS | 1:10:43 | 41 | Bellows Falls, VT | |
| 7 | Mike Casner | CMS | 1:11:13 | 39 | Keene, NH | |
| 8 | Nick Conway | Willow | 1:11:15 | 26 | Alpaus, NY | |

| Place | Name | Club | Time | Age | City and State | |
|---|---|---|---|---|---|---|
| 9 | Fergus Cullen | CMS | 1:11:21 | 29 | Laconia, NH | |
| 10 | Michael Woodman | | 1:12:07 | 35 | Timonium, MD | |
| 11 | Jeff Day | | 1:12:22 | 30 | Berea, OH | |
| 12 | Steve Peterson | CMS | 1:12:33 | 35 | Chelmsford, MA | |
| **13** | **Anna Pichrtova** | | **1:13:48** | **27** | **Waynesboro, VA (CZE)** | |
| 14 | David Herr | | 1:14:23 | 36 | Canaan, VT | |
| 15 | Thomas Murdock III | AE | 1:15:11 | 37 | Somerville, MA | |
| 16 | Rick Copley | WMM | 1:15:25 | 28 | Conway, NH | |
| 17 | Joel St Louis | | 1:15:54 | 39 | Fleurimont, CAN | |
| 18 | Ernest Brake | GSRT | 1:15:57 | 39 | N Sutton, NH | |
| 19 | Matthew Curran | | 1:16:20 | 44 | Gloucester, MA | |
| 20 | Andrew Baird | | 1:16:20 | 28 | Fairlee, VT | |
| 21 | Mark Berman | CAA | 1:16:33 | 43 | Eliot, ME | |
| **22** | **Joan Samuelson** | **Nike** | **1:16:47** | **44** | **Freeport, ME** | |
| 23 | Charlie Casey | Willow | 1:17:30 | 38 | Alpaus, NY | |
| 24 | Sproule Love | | 1:17:48 | 29 | Brooklyn, NY | |
| 25 | Francis Burdett | GLRR | 1:17:59 | 36 | Worcester, MA | |
| 26 | Stephen Marsalese | NYH | 1:18:09 | 35 | New York, NY | |
| 27 | Peter Lopriore | | 1:18:40 | 35 | Somerset, MA | |
| 28 | Keith Woodward | GMAC | 1:18:52 | 50 | E Corinth, VT | FW |
| 37 | Bob Hodge | | 1:20:21 | 45 | Clinton, MA | FW |
| 106 | John Cederholm | BAA | 1:30:12 | 58 | Marion, MA | FW |

## Top 25 Women

| Place | Name | Club | Time | Age | City and State | |
|---|---|---|---|---|---|---|
| 1 | Anna Pichrtova | | 1:13:48 | 27 | CZE | |
| 2 | Joan Samuelson | Nike | 1:16:47 | 44 | Freeport, ME | |
| 3 | Cathy Pearce | | 1:20:02 | 38 | Socorro, NM | |
| 4 | Nikki Kimball | WMAC | 1:20:11 | 30 | Elizabethtown, NY | |
| 5 | Suzy West | CSU | 1:24:20 | 38 | Putney, VT | |
| 6 | Rene Frazee | | 1:25:01 | 34 | Salida, CO | |
| 7 | Marjorie Shearer | | 1:25:16 | 30 | Northampton, MA | |
| 8 | Colleen Allen | GSRT | 1:25:22 | 34 | Newport Center, VT | |
| 9 | J'Ne Day-Lucore | | 1:29:18 | 40 | Denver, CO | FW |
| 10 | Kerry Arsenault | Hitek | 1:29:59 | 36 | Clinton, CT | |
| 11 | Jacqueline Shakar | CMS | 1:30:08 | 41 | Worcester, MA | |
| 12 | Rebecca Stockdale-Woolley | CMS | 1:30:27 | 50 | Chaplin, CT | |
| 13 | Joselle Germano | | 1:30:41 | 27 | Dover, NH | |
| 14 | Donna Smyers | CVRC | 1:31:53 | 43 | Montpelier, VT | |
| 15 | Barbara McManus | CMS | 1:32:18 | 33 | Worcester, MA | |
| 16 | Ellen McCurtin | Millrs | 1:32:40 | 34 | Danbury, CT | |
| 17 | Leslie Krichko | CSU | 1:32:56 | 42 | Ridgefield, CT | |
| 18 | Kara Molloy | GLRR | 1:33:16 | 30 | Westford, MA | |

| Place | Name | Club | Time | Age | City and State | |
|---|---|---|---|---|---|---|
| 19 | Jennifer Rappaport | BAA | 1:33:18 | 37 | Melrose, MA | |
| 20 | Lesley Keene | NMC | 1:33:22 | 43 | Fall River, MA | |
| 21 | Kristin White | | 1:33:58 | 29 | Fayetteville, NY | |
| 22 | Jessica Blake | GBTC | 1:34:35 | 23 | N Attleboro, MA | |
| 23 | Catherine Lifschultz | BAA | 1:34:59 | 38 | Sudbury, MA | |
| 24 | Deborah Schieffer | Horst | 1:36:13 | 26 | Vernon, CT | |
| 25 | Christine Pratt-Gorrill | CCAC | 1:36:44 | 38 | Centerville, MA | |
| 31 | Barbara Remmers | | 1:41:33 | 37 | New York, NY | FW |

## 5-Year Age Groups

| Place | Name | Time | Age | City and State | Category |
|---|---|---|---|---|---|
| 380 | Elizabeth Boucher | 1:50:02 | 14 | Groton, CT | Under 20 |
| 149 | Jessica Blake | 1:34:35 | 23 | N Attleboro, MA | 20-24 |
| 13 | Anna Pichrtova | 1:13:48 | 27 | Waynesboro (CZE) | 25-29 |
| 35 | Nikki Kimball | 1:20:11 | 30 | Elizabethtown, NY | 30-34 |
| 33 | Cathy Pearce | 1:20:02 | 38 | Socorro, NM | 35-39 |
| 22 | Joan Samuelson | 1:16:47 | 44 | Freeport, ME | 40-44 |
| 250 | Pam Hall | 1:42:18 | 47 | Litchfield, NH | 45-49 |
| 107 | Rebecca Stockdale-Woolley | 1:30:27 | 50 | Chaplin, CT | 50-54 **AGR** |
| 512 | Jane Levesque | 1:57:18 | 59 | Nashua, NH | 55-59 |
| 691 | Diana Avery | 2:10:12 | 63 | Loudon, NH | 60-64 |
| 749 | Maggie Solomon | 2:16:45 | 67 | Glen, NH | 65-69 |
| 839 | Hildy Fosse | 2:33:34 | 72 | Holderness, NH | 70+ |
| | | | | | |
| 65 | Brian Oliver | 1:25:57 | 16 | Belmont, NH | Under 20 |
| 75 | Angus McCusker | 1:26:58 | 20 | Buckland, MA | 20-24 |
| 8 | Nick Conway | 1:11:15 | 26 | Alpaus, NY | 25-29 |
| 1 | Daniel Kihara | 1:00:06 | 33 | KEN | 30-34 |
| 2 | Dave Dunham | 1:04:20 | 37 | Bradford, MA | 35-39 |
| 3 | Craig Fram | 1:04:29 | 42 | Plaistow, NH | 40-44 **AGR** |
| 31 | Bob Johnson | 1:19:14 | 45 | Leominster, MA | 45-49 |
| 28 | Keith Woodward | 1:18:52 | 50 | E Corinth, VT | 50-54 |
| 90 | Jonathan Stableford | 1:28:29 | 56 | Andover, MA | 55-59 |
| 145 | John Pelton | 1:34:19 | 62 | W Rupert, VT | 60-64 |
| 503 | George Bisson | 1:56:50 | 65 | Hooksett, NH | 65-69 |
| 464 | Geoffrey Etherington | 1:55:02 | 72 | Jupiter, FL | 70-74 |
| 829 | Peter Pantelis | 2:31:07 | 75 | Waterford, CT | 75-79 |
| 894 | Phil Campbell | 3:07:41 | 83 | Lynnfield, MA | 70-84 |
| 897 | Howard Kellogg | 3:11:57 | 85 | Gwynedd, PA | 85+ |

Top 5 Teams

| Men | | Men 40+ | | Men 50+ | |
| --- | --- | --- | --- | --- | --- |
| 1 CMS | 5:39:58 | 1 WCRC | 7:11:29 | 1 WCRC | 8:53:16 |
| 2 WHIRL | 6:55:04 | 2 NMC | 7:26:17 | 2 CSU | 9:04:50 |
| 3 WCRC | 6:58:55 | 3 CSU | 7:53:08 | 3 NMC | 9:21:55 |
| 4 BAA | 7:16:50 | 4 CMeS | 8:17:12 | 4 WMM | 9:41:22 |
| 5 HTC | 7:18:42 | 5 GSRT | 8:26:37 | 5 CR | 9:44:22 |

| Women | | Women 40+ | | Women 50+ | |
| --- | --- | --- | --- | --- | --- |
| 1 CMS | 4:32:53 | 1 CMS | 4:42:47 | 1 GCS | 6:15:45 |
| 2 CSU | 4:37:17 | 2 CSU | 4:54:44 | 2 MVS | 6:30:27 |
| 3 BAA | 4:51:13 | 3 WCRC | 5:27:43 | | |
| 4 NMC | 4:55:42 | 4 GCS | 5:30:16 | | |
| 5 GSRT | 5:08:18 | 5 WMM | 5:32:16 | | |

Fram setting a new 40+ age group record

42nd Mt Washington Road Race

June 15, 2002
Saturday, 10:00AM
878 Finishers


The favorites heading into the 42nd running appeared to be Daniel Kihara, a four-time winner and Anna Pichrtova, who had won in 2001.  Pichrtova came in looking strong having placed second at the Wheeling 20K two weeks earlier.  The others who looked to challenge included Kenyan Alice Muriithi, who won in 2000, and Anita Ortiz, a top US mountain runner from Colorado.  The men's field featured Kenyan Zablon Mokaya, who was victorious the week before in the James Joyce 10k running a 29:29, and Simon Wangai who ran 45:12 for 10 miles the month before.  Craig Fram looked to have competition in the master's race with US mountain team member Richard Shelley making his debut at Mt Washington.  Other hopefuls for the title included Simon Gutierrez with a 1:01 personal best and the New England favorites.  New Englanders Fram, Eric Morse, Paul Low, Mike Casner, and Dave Dunham showed promise by taking the top five spots at the Pack Monadnock 10 mile race on June 2.

Newspaper headlines told the major story for the 2002 race.  "Summit Canceled" announced the *Union Leader.* "The Mountain pulls rank for us mortals." and "Unsafe conditions on unforgiving peak." were also headlines in New Hampshire sports pages.  For the first time in race history it was deemed unsafe to have runners complete the entire 7.6 mile distance.  Winds over 50 miles per hour with freezing rain and a wind chill in the teens forced the Auto Road to ban vehicles from the road.  With no transportation for runners to get down safely from the summit, the decision was made to end the race at just short of the halfway mark.   Runners were required to walk or run down to the base from the halfway point.   Howie Wemyss, the general manager of the Auto Road told *the Union Leader,* "Our first concern was for cars on the auto road.  In a couple of hours the road may be freezing.  I kind of like the idea of runners challenging themselves under the conditions, but it was too unsafe for everybody else."

During the event a larger than "normal" group of a dozen runners passed through the mile in just over six minutes.  During the second mile Fram, Morse and Gutierrez gapped the chase group, as the leading Kenyans Mokaya, and Kihara fell back.  In the third mile Gutierrez established a lead that would not be narrowed.  He crossed the hastily created new finish line in 28:02, ten seconds ahead of Morse.  Morse took exception to a reporter asking him "What happened?" telling the reporter, "I got *#!@*ing second place, what do you mean what happened?"  Morse followed up the Mt Washington race with a victory and course record at Mt Ascutney the following week.

Pichrtova, a 2:33 marathoner, showed her speed as she dominated the women's race.  She assumed the lead at the start and was never challenged, crossing the line in 32:32.  Anita Ortiz, a top mountain runner who had recently won at the Pikes Peak ascent and the Wolverine mountain race in Alaska, finished over one minute back in 34:10.

CMS won the team title in 2:26:23, or an average of 29:17 per person, finishing 28 minutes ahead of the WCRC.  The WCRC took the top spot in the 40+ competition in 3:01:57 over nine minutes up on CSU.  CSU reversed the result with an eight minute victory over WCRC in the 50+ category.  The women's team victory went to CMS in 1:53:24, six minutes ahead of CSU.  CSU took the 40+ win by four minutes over WMM in 2:12:20.  The WCRC won the 50+ in 2:33:46, just over a minute ahead of the WMM.

## Top 25 Finishers

| Place Name | Club | Time | Age | City and State | |
|---|---|---|---|---|---|
| 1 Simon Gutierrez | ADD | 28:02 | 36 | Albuquerque, NM | |
| 2 Eric Morse | CMS | 28:12 | 37 | Berlin, VT | |
| 3 Craig Fram | Whirl | 28:28 | 43 | Plaistow, NH | FW |
| 4 Paul Low | CMS | 28:46 | 28 | Amherst, MA | |
| 5 Dave Dunham | CMS | 28:58 | 38 | Bradford, MA | FW |
| 6 Daniel Kihara | | 29:06 | 34 | KEN | FW |
| 7 Nephat Kinyanjui | | 29:38 | 24 | KEN | |
| 8 Richard Shelley | | 29:48 | 40 | Albuquerque, NM | |
| 9 Richard Bolt | CMS | 29:52 | 31 | Manchester, NH | |
| 10 Sean Livingston | | 30:07 | 33 | Barrington, RI | |
| 11 Kevin Tilton | WMM | 30:19 | 20 | Center Conway, NH | |
| 12 David Hackworth | | 30:26 | 33 | Oakmont, PA | |
| 13 Scott Elliott | | 30:31 | 38 | Boulder, CO | |
| 14 Daniel Verrington | CMS | 30:35 | 39 | Bradford, MA | |
| 15 Scott Creel | Hgel | 30:49 | 39 | Bozeman, MT | |
| 16 Nick Conway | GUTS | 30:50 | 26 | Alpaus, NY | |
| 17 Simon Wangai | | 30:54 | 23 | KEN | |
| 18 Benjamin Nephew | | 31:05 | 26 | Canton, MA | |
| 19 William Fanselow | | 31:28 | 35 | Golden, CO | |
| 20 Matt VonThun | | 31:42 | 36 | Colorado Springs, CO | |
| 21 Sean Hanley | | 31:49 | 41 | Attleboro, MA | |
| 22 David Herr | | 31:51 | 37 | Canaan, VT | |
| 23 Bruce Bridgham | | 31:54 | 41 | Jonesboro, ME | |
| 24 Mark Behan | WCRC | 32:07 | 39 | Newton, NH | |
| 25 Casey Carroll | | 32:13 | 30 | Dover, NH | |
| 36 Keith Woodward | | 32:51 | 51 | E. Corinth, VT | FW |
| 170 John Cederholm | BAA | 40:35 | 59 | Marion, MA | FW |

## Top 25 Women

| Place Name | Club | Time | Age | City and State | |
|---|---|---|---|---|---|
| 1 Anna Pichrtova | | 32:32 | 28 | CZE | |
| 2 Anita Ortiz | | 34:10 | 38 | Eagle, CO | |
| 3 Julie Ann White | | 35:05 | 40 | Vista, CA | |
| 4 Alice Muriithi | | 35:31 | 28 | KEN | FW |
| 5 Julie Bryan | | 35:34 | 33 | Jackson, WY | |

| Place | Name | Club | Time | | Age | City and State |
|---|---|---|---|---|---|---|
| 6 | Nikki Kimball | CMS | 36:02 | | 31 | Elizabethtown, NY |
| 7 | Cathy Pearce | Whirl | 36:49 | | 39 | Chelmsford, MA |
| 8 | Inge Aiken | | 36:58 | | 40 | E Greenbush, NY |
| 9 | Suzy West | CSU | 37:46 | | 39 | Putney, VT |
| 10 | Barbara McManus | CMS | 37:57 | | 34 | Worcester, MA |
| 11 | Ellen McCurtin | | 38:51 | | 35 | Danbury, CT |
| 12 | Kiersten Lippmann | | 39:02 | | 22 | Anchorage, AK |
| 13 | Bonnie Wheeler | | 39:12 | | 29 | Littleton, NH |
| 14 | Jacqueline Shakar | CMS | 39:25 | | 42 | Worcester, MA |
| 15 | Amy Bourgault | GSRT | 39:31 | | 36 | Concord, NH |
| 16 | Deborah Livingston | | 39:52 | | 27 | Vernon, CT |
| 17 | Elizabeth Doubleday | | 40:32 | | 28 | Quincy, MA |
| 18 | Sue Long | WMM | 40:40 | | 42 | Gorham, NH |
| 19 | Cathy Lifschultz | | 40:47 | | 39 | Sudbury, MA |
| 20 | Patricia Dalconzo | NMC | 40:47 | | 39 | Lancaster, MA |
| 21 | Sherry Sikora | | 40:51 | | 21 | Succasunna, NJ |
| 22 | Lori Lambert | GCS | 41:00 | | 37 | Nashua, NH |
| 23 | Rebecca Stockdale-Woolley | CMS | 41:01 | | 51 | Chaplin, CT |
| 24 | Antonia Rosavargas | | 41:02 | | 27 | Santos Domingo |
| 25 | Tara Cardi | | 41:39 | | 33 | E Greenwich, RI |

## 5-Year age groups

| Place | Name | Time | Age | City and State | Category |
|---|---|---|---|---|---|
| 262 | Jennifer Goransson | 43:00 | 19 | Eliot, ME | Under 20 |
| 127 | Kiersten Lippmann | 39:02 | 22 | Anchorage, AK | 20-24 |
| 30 | Anna Pichrtova | 32:32 | 28 | CZE | 25-29 |
| 62 | Julie Bryan | 35:34 | 33 | Jackson, WY | 30-34 |
| 50 | Anita Ortiz | 34:10 | 38 | Eagle, CO | 35-39 |
| 55 | Julie Ann White | 35:05 | 40 | Vista, CA | 40-44 |
| 323 | Anne Marie Davee | 44:41 | 46 | Pownal, ME | 45-49 |
| 190 | Rebecca Stockdale-Woolley | 41:01 | 51 | Chaplin, CT | 50-54 |
| 458 | Marjorie Kos | 48:26 | 57 | City Island, NY | 55-59 |
| 594 | Louisa Dunlap | 52:06 | 61 | Belfast, ME | 60-64 |
| 505 | Barbara Robinson | 49:31 | 68 | Franconia, NH | 65-69 |
| 873 | Louise Rossetti | 1:15:29 | 80 | Saugus, MA | 80+ |
| 131 | Nick Soule | 39:07 | 16 | Manchester, NH | Under 20 |
| 7 | Nephat Kinyanjui | 29:38 | 24 | KEN | 20-24 |
| 4 | Paul Low | 28:46 | 28 | Amherst, MA | 25-29 |
| 6 | Daniel Kihara | 29:06 | 34 | KEN | 30-34 |
| 1 | Simon Gutierrez | 28:02 | 36 | Albuquerque, NM | 35-39 |
| 3 | Craig Fram | 28:28 | 43 | Plaistow, NH | 40-44 |
| 43 | Matthew Curran | 33:25 | 45 | Gloucester, MA | 45-49 |

| Place | Name | Time | Age | City and State | Category |
|---|---|---|---|---|---|
| 36 | Keith Woodward | 32:51 | 51 | E Corinth, VT | 50-54 |
| 76 | Sumner Brown | 36:38 | 58 | Belmont, MA | 55-59 |
| 160 | John Pelton | 40:22 | 63 | W Rupert, VT | 60-64 |
| 295 | Wally Kurz | 43:55 | 65 | Salem, MA | 65-69 |
| 533 | Don Ross | 50:32 | 72 | Marblehead, MA | 70-74 |
| 754 | Leon Beverly | 56:54 | 75 | Stamford, VT | 75-79 |
| 859 | Carlton Mendell | 1:05:34 | 80 | Portland, ME | 80+ |

## Top 5 Teams

| Men | | Men 40+ | | Men 50+ | |
|---|---|---|---|---|---|
| 1 CMS | 2:26:23 | 1 WCRC | 3:01:57 | 1 CSU | 3:13:17 |
| 2 WCRC | 2:54:58 | 2 CSU | 3:10:21 | 2 WCRC | 3:21:21 |
| 3 GCS | 2:59:50 | 3 GSRT | 3:13:21 | 3 WMM | 3:59:35 |
| 4 GUTS | 3:00:17 | 4 NMC | 3:14:04 | 4 GCS | 4:04:31 |
| 5 WMM | 3:04:15 | 5 CMeS | 3:29:02 | 5 RIRR | 4:11:07 |

| Women | | Women 40+ | | Women 50+ | |
|---|---|---|---|---|---|
| 1 CMS | 1:53:24 | 1 CSU | 2:12:29 | 1 WCRC | 2:33:46 |
| 2 CSU | 2:03:48 | 2 WMM | 2:16:16 | 2 WMM | 2:34:56 |
| 3 GSRT | 2:06:11 | 3 WCRC | 2:22:05 | | |
| 4 NMC | 2:08:26 | 4 NMC | 2:26:10 | | |
| 5 WMM | 2:09:26 | 5 GCS | 2:31:42 | | |

Morse, Fram, and Gutierrez (left to right)

**43<sup>rd</sup> Mt Washington Road Race**

June 22, 2003
Saturday, 10:00 AM
863 Finishers


Favorites this year included Simon Gutierrez and Craig Fram, who had finished first and third in the rain-shortened 2002 race.  Others expected to be in the mix were New Englander's Dave Dunham and Richard Bolt and Kenyan Andrew Masai.  Anna Pichrtova appeared to be a distinct favorite on the women's side.  Others expected to be in the mix included Nikki Kimball, a US Mountain team and US 100K team member, and Kelli Lusk, a national class mountain bike racer.  Suzy West and Julie Anne White were predicted to be among the top master's.

Gutierrez went out strong, stringing the field out behind him in the early going.  Craig Fram and Andrew Masai were the only ones to stay with Gutierrez.  The trio passed the mile in 6:03 and three miles in 22:10.  Masai surged just before the half and gapped the 2002 winner (Gutierrez) and the top master (Fram).  Fram told *New England Runner* that he didn't lose hope as "too many times I've seen a guy go out great and just stop."  Masai began to fade after five miles and was passed by Gutierrez just before six miles and Fram soon after.  Gutierrez proceeded to win in 1:02:54, just over thirty seconds ahead of Fram.  Fram took over a minute off of his master's record and was awarded $2,000 for his efforts along with $500 for finishing second overall, and $250 for topping the age graded (WAVA) competition.  Masai would alternate jogging and walking and finished in tenth place.  Masai told press liaison John Stifler "At four miles I thought I would win.  At five I was completely dead."  The average finishing time for men dipped back under 1:50 as they averaged 1:49:06.

Anna Pichrtova stormed across the line in sixteenth place overall, just ahead of junior record holder Sean Livingston and longtime top ten finisher Mike Casner.  Pichrtova won by nearly five minutes over Elizabethtown New York's Nikki Kimball.

CMS won the team competition with the slowest winning time in a decade with a 30-minute victory over the MM& M in 5:51:44.  CMS was feeling the effects of longtime top finisher Eric Morse missing the race because of injury.  Team Gloucester took a narrow victory in the 40+ team category edging Coastal Athletic Association by three minutes with a 6:48:07.  The Cambridge Sports Union was victorious in the 50+ team category in 7:39:51.  The CMS women won the team title finishing ten minutes ahead of CSU.  CSU rebounded with a victory in the women's 40+ category with a 26 minute victory over NMC in 4:30:23.  The WCRC won the women's 50+ team category with a 5:22:18.


<u>Top 25</u>

| Place  Name | Club | Time | Age | City and State | |
|---|---|---|---|---|---|
| 1 Simon Gutierrez | | 1:02:54 | 37 | Alamosa, CO | |
| 2 Craig Fram | WRT | 1:03:27 | 44 | Plaistow, NH | FW |
| 3 Dave Dunham | CMS | 1:06:19 | 39 | Bradford, MA | FW |

| Place | Name | Club | Time | Age | City and State | |
|-------|------|------|------|-----|----------------|---|
| 4 | Richard Bolt | CMS | 1:06:58 | 32 | Manchester, NH | |
| 5 | Michael Danahy | | 1:07:52 | 24 | Princeton, NJ | |
| 6 | Jeff Day | | 1:08:16 | 32 | Berea, OH | |
| 7 | Bruce Bridgham | | 1:08:29 | 42 | Jonesboro, ME | |
| 8 | Daniel Verrington | CMS | 1:09:14 | 40 | Bradford, MA | |
| 9 | Scott Elliott | | 1:09:35 | 39 | Boulder, CO | |
| 10 | Andrew Masai | | 1:10:31 | 43 | Albuquerque, NM | |
| 11 | Robert Ratcliffe | | 1:10:37 | 45 | Cambridge, MA | |
| 12 | David Herr | MMM | 1:10:56 | 38 | Canaan, VT | |
| 13 | Michael Woodman | | 1:11:09 | 37 | Timonium, MD | |
| 14 | Ernest Brake | GSRT | 1:11:52 | 41 | N Sutton, NH | |
| 15 | Joel St Louis | | 1:12:45 | 41 | Fleurimont, CAN | |
| **16** | **Anna Pichrtova** | | **1:12:50** | **30** | **Waynesboro, VA** | |
| 17 | Sean Livingston | BAA | 1:13:06 | 34 | Barrington, RI | |
| 18 | Mike Casner | GSRT | 1:13:32 | 41 | Keene, NH | |
| 19 | Mark Pitts | MMM | 1:13:40 | 40 | North Woodstock, NH | |
| 20 | Stephen Peterson | CMS | 1:14:07 | 37 | Chelmsford, MA | |
| 21 | John Barbour | TG | 1:14:29 | 49 | Gloucester, MA | |
| 22 | Fergus Cullen | CMS | 1:15:06 | 31 | Wolfeboro, NH | |
| 23 | Keith Woodward | | 1:15:08 | 52 | E Corinth, VT | FW |
| 24 | Evan Pilachowski | MMM | 1:15:16 | 22 | Bennington, VT | |
| 25 | Bob Johnson | NMC | 1:15:18 | 47 | Leominster, MA | |
| 26 | Francis Burdett | GLRR | 1:15:34 | 38 | Worcester, MA | |

## Top 25 Women

| Place | Name | Club | Time | Age | City and State |
|-------|------|------|------|-----|----------------|
| 1 | Anna Pichrtova | | 1:12:50 | 30 | Waynesboro, VA |
| 2 | Nikki Kimball | CMS | 1:17:34 | 32 | Elizabethtown, NY |
| 3 | Kelli Lusk | PWBR | 1:19:40 | 33 | Manitou Springs, CO |
| 4 | Suzy West | CSU | 1:20:18 | 40 | Putney, VT |
| 5 | Julie Anne White | | 1:21:35 | 41 | San Jacinto, CA |
| 6 | Barbara McManus | CMS | 1:24:01 | 35 | Worcester, MA |
| 7 | Julie Bryan | | 1:25:33 | 35 | Jackson, WY |
| 8 | Inge Aiken | | 1:26:10 | 41 | East Greenbush, NY |
| 9 | Jennifer Sacheck | | 1:26:38 | 30 | Cambridge, MA |
| 10 | Evelyn Dong | CSU | 1:26:51 | 18 | Wayland, MA |
| 11 | Bonnie Wheeler | | 1:26:55 | 30 | Littleton, NH |
| 12 | Ellen McCurtin | MAA | 1:27:46 | 36 | Danbury, CT |
| 13 | Donna Smyers | CVT | 1:28:32 | 45 | Montpelier, VT |
| 14 | Pamela Alexander | NMC | 1:28:53 | 44 | Harvard, MA |
| 15 | Jacqueline Shakar | CMS | 1:29:20 | 43 | Worcester, MA |
| 16 | Catherine Lifschultz | BAA | 1:29:57 | 40 | Sudbury, MA |
| 17 | Raelyn Crowell | GCS | 1:30:21 | 32 | Hudson, NH |

| Place | Name | Club | Time | Age | City and State |
|---|---|---|---|---|---|
| 18 | Vanessa McGowan | | 1:30:44 | 26 | Portland, ME |
| 19 | Kara Haas (Molloy) | GLRR | 1:31:51 | 31 | Burlington, MA |
| 20 | Kiersten Lippmann | | 1:33:10 | 23 | Anchorage, AK |
| 21 | Sue Wemyss | WMM | 1:33:16 | 43 | Gorham, NH |
| 22 | Leslie Krichko | CSU | 1:33:58 | 44 | Ridgefield, CT |
| 23 | Kelly Robison | | 1:34:04 | 34 | Webster, MA |
| 24 | Sarah Peters | | 1:34:29 | 26 | Ottawa, CAN |
| 25 | Fran O'Donoghue | HTC | 1:35:22 | 40 | Wallingford, CT |

## 5-Year Age Groups

| Place | Name | Time | Age | City & State | Category |
|---|---|---|---|---|---|
| 91 | Evelyn Dong | 1:26:51 | 18 | Wayland, MA | Under 20 **AGR** |
| 161 | Kiersten Lippmann | 1:33:10 | 23 | Anchorage, AK | 20-24 |
| 137 | Vanessa McGowan | 1:30:44 | 26 | Portland, ME | 25-29 |
| 16 | Anna Pichrtova | 1:12:50 | 30 | Waynesboro, VA | 30-34 |
| 68 | Barbara McManus | 1:24:01 | 35 | Worcester, MA | 35-39 |
| 48 | Suzy West | 1:20:18 | 40 | Putney, VT | 40-44 |
| 106 | Donna Smyers | 1:28:32 | 45 | Montpelier, VT | 45-49 |
| 310 | Vicki Miller | 1:42:50 | 50 | Durham, NH | 50-54 |
| 409 | Marcia Masland | 1:49:20 | 58 | Lebanon, NH | 55-59 |
| 591 | Sally Swenson | 2:00:25 | 60 | N Conway, NH | 60-64 |
| 610 | Barbara Robinson | 2:01:43 | 69 | Franconia, NH | 65-69 |
| 805 | Hildy Fosse | 2:22:27 | 74 | Holderness, NH | 70-74 |
| 855 | Louise Rossetti | 2:48:52 | 81 | Saugus, MA | 80+ **AGR** |
| 79 | Jacob Edwards | 1:25:37 | 16 | N. Stonington, CT | Under 20 |
| 5 | Michael Danahy | 1:07:52 | 24 | Princeton, NJ | 20-24 |
| 30 | Jason Burke | 1:16:26 | 25 | Allston, MA | 25-29 |
| 4 | Richard Bolt | 1:06:58 | 32 | Manchester, NH | 30-34 |
| 1 | Simon Gutierrez | 1:02:54 | 37 | Alamosa, CO | 35-39 |
| 2 | Craig Fram | 1:03:27 | 44 | Plaistow, NH | 40-44 **AGR** |
| 11 | Robert Ratcliffe | 1:10:37 | 45 | Cambridge, MA | 45-49 |
| 23 | Keith Woodward | 1:15:08 | 52 | E Corinth, VT | 50-54 |
| 70 | Sumner Brown | 1:24:07 | 59 | Belmont, MA | 55-59 |
| 142 | John Cederholm | 1:31:07 | 60 | Marion, MA | 60-64 |
| 353 | Wally Kurz | 1:46:03 | 66 | Salem, MA | 65-69 |
| 514 | Don Ross | 1:56:01 | 73 | Marblehead, MA | 70-74 |
| 812 | Peter Pantelis | 2:24:30 | 77 | Waterford, CT | 75-79 |
| 831 | Carlton Mendell | 2:31:31 | 81 | Portland, ME | 80-84 |
| 861 | Philip Campbell | 3:03:18 | 85 | Scarborough, ME | 85+ |

Top 5 Teams

| Men | | Men 40+ | | Men 50+ | |
| --- | --- | --- | --- | --- | --- |
| 1 CMS | 5:51:44 | 1 TG | 6:48:07 | 1 CSU | 7:39:51 **CR** |
| 2 MM&M | 6:22:16 | 2 CAA | 6:51:43 | 2 WCRC | 7:47:38 |
| 3 GSRT | 6:36:25 | 3 GSRT | 6:55:05 | 3 RIRR | 8:24:25 |
| 4 WMM | 6:46:36 | 4 CSU | 7:11:22 | 4 WMM | 8:32:41 |
| 5 TG | 6:48:07 | 5 WCRC | 7:13:34 | 5 NMC | 8:33:21 |

| Women | | Women 40+ | | Women 50+ | |
| --- | --- | --- | --- | --- | --- |
| 1 CMS | 4:10:55 | 1 CSU | 4:30:23 **CR** | 1 WCRC | 5:22:18 **CR** |
| 2 CSU | 4:21:07 | 2 NMC | 4:56:11 | 2 WMM | 5:49:21 |
| 3 WMM | 4:52:56 | 3 CVTR | 4:57:10 | 3 AR | 6:54:28 |
| 4 NMC | 4:56:11 | 4 WMM | 5:02:43 | | |
| 5 CVTR | 4:57:10 | 5 WCRC | 5:18:14 | | |

Anna Pichrtova and Stephen Peterson at an early waterstop

**44<sup>th</sup> Mt Washington Road Race**

June 19, 2004
Saturday, 10:00 AM
931 Finishers

The 44<sup>th</sup> edition of the 7.6 mile run to the summit of Mt Washington looked to be fast as the race was named the US National Championship.  It would also serve as a selection race for the US team to participate in the World Mountain Running Trophy (World championship) later that year.  Top runners included last year's champion Simon Gutierrez, Paul Low the 2002 and 2003 US Mountain runner of the year; and sub-2:22 marathoner Eric Blake.  Blake tuned up for Mt Washington with a victory at the Whiteface Mountain race earlier in June.  A major favorite was Jonathan Wyatt from Wellington, New Zealand.  Wyatt was not only an excellent road runner with personal bests of 2:13 for the marathon and 28:00 for 10k, but also a mountain expert.  Wyatt had won the World Mountain trophy multiple times along with victories and course records in numerous mountain races around the world.  Anna Pichrtova the three-time female winner appeared to be an overwhelming favorite.  Top US runners included Erica Larson, Laura Haefeli, and Kelli Lusk.  Masters favorites were Cathy Pearce and former US mountain team member Kari Distefano.

Wyatt set the tone before the race even started: as he did a practice run up the mountain earlier in the week and ran easily in 1:06.  Race day featured high humidity and scattered downpours at the base and strong winds and fog on the summit.  Gutierrez led the way for the first flat section.  Wyatt assumed the lead at the base of the hill and by the mile was nearly 30 seconds up on the chase pack.  Wyatt's time at the mile was an unbelievably fast 5:47.  Wyatt passed through three miles in 20:05, and halfway in 26:48.  He continued on to smash the course record by over one and a half minutes and earned a $5,000 prize for doing so and $1,000 for finishing first.  Paul Low won the national championship breaking away from Gutierrez and Blake in the second half.  A large group followed with fifth through tenth place all within a minute.  The average age for male finishers topped 45 with 45.34.  Over the previous ten years the average age for men went up five years, whereas women stayed steady.  The women's average in 1995 was 40.08 and in 2004 it was 41.97.

Pichrtova led from the firing of the start cannon, running much of the race with CMS stalwart Steve Peterson.  She ran her fastest time in a record four consecutive victories, beating Erica Larson by nearly two minutes.  Larson, who was a four-time winner of the Pike's Peak marathon, won the national championship with a 1:14:17, leading Laura Haefeli, and top master Cathy Pearce to sub 1:20 efforts.  A record 24 women broke 1:30 and a record tying four broke 1:20.  The women's field made up a record 25.56% of finishers.

CMS led the way in the team category with another sub-5:30 effort, defeating MM&M by 35 minutes.  Coastal AA finished third overall with a team that also won the 40+ category in a record 6:15:37 besting the MM&M (who also ran under the previous record) by just under 14 minutes.  Guy Stearns, who had run a 28:31 10k and 47:06 10 mile in his prime, led the Coastal team posting a new age group record time in the 45-49 category.  MM&M won the 50+ category over CSU by about 3 minutes in 7:25:00.  The CMS ladies took the team title in an excellent 4:07:23, beating the BAA by 15 minutes.  CSU won the 40+ team competition and the WCRC was the only team to finish in the 50+ group.

Streaker (consecutive Mt Washington finishes) Dean Rasmussen ran his twenty-second straight Mt Washington race, sandwiching it between a trip to Italy and Alaska.

## Top 25 Finishers

| Place Name | Team | Time | Age | City and State | |
|---|---|---|---|---|---|
| 1 Jonathan Wyatt | | 0:56:41 | 31 | Wellington, NZL | Course Record |
| 2 Paul Low | CMS | 1:03:12 | 30 | Amherst, MA | |
| 3 Simon Gutierrez | Teva | 1:04:17 | 38 | Taos, NM | FW |
| 4 Eric Blake | CMS | 1:04:30 | 25 | Plattsburgh, NY | |
| 5 Mark Werner | | 1:06:02 | 32 | Rochester, NY | |
| 6 Andy Ames | | 1:06:10 | 41 | Boulder, CO | |
| 7 Joshua Ferenc | | 1:06:21 | 22 | Westmoreland, NH | |
| 8 Eric Morse | CMS | 1:06:46 | 39 | Berlin, VT | |
| 9 Bill Raitter | | 1:06:56 | 34 | Bend, OR | |
| 10 Kevin Tilton | CMS | 1:07:10 | 22 | Conway, NH | |
| 11 Philippe Rolly | WSCR | 1:07:49 | 31 | Tuckahoe, NY | |
| 12 Richard Bolt | CMS | 1:08:15 | 33 | Manchester, NH | |
| 13 Michael Wardian | | 1:08:46 | 30 | Arlington, VA | |
| 14 Bob Sweeney | | 1:09:03 | 37 | Rye Brook, NY | |
| 15 Ben Nephew | CMS | 1:09:09 | 28 | Foxboro, MA | |
| 16 Keiron Tumbleton | | 1:09:24 | 38 | Hopkinton, MA | |
| 17 Joel St-Louis | | 1:10:15 | 42 | Cookshire, CAN | |
| 18 Sean Livingston | BAA | 1:10:22 | 35 | Barrington, RI | |
| 19 Guy Stearns | Cstal | 1:10:29 | 45 | New Castle, NH | |
| 20 Bruce Bridgham | MMM | 1:10:39 | 43 | Jonesboro, ME | |
| 21 Matt Ebiner | | 1:10:44 | 43 | Covina, CA | |
| 22 Daniel Verrington | CMS | 1:10:56 | 41 | Bradford, MA | |
| 23 David Herr | MMM | 1:11:05 | 39 | Canaan, VT | |
| 24 Bernie Boettcher | | 1:11:30 | 41 | Silt, CO | |
| 25 Bob Winn | | 1:12:03 | 45 | Ogunquit, ME | |
| 46 Keith Woodward | MMM | 1:17:17 | 53 | E. Corinth, VT | FW |
| 142 John Cederholm | BAA | 1:31:07 | 60 | Marion, MA | FW |

## Top 25 Women

| Place Name | Team | Time | Age | City and State |
|---|---|---|---|---|
| 1 Anna Pichrtova | | 1:12:19 | 31 | CZE |
| 2 Erica Larson | | 1:14:17 | 32 | Los Alamos, NM |
| 3 Laura Haefeli | | 1:17:42 | 36 | Del Norte, CO |
| 4 Cathy Pearce | | 1:18:54 | 41 | Chelmsford, MA |
| 5 Kelli Lusk | CMS | 1:21:41 | 34 | Amherst, MA |

| Place Name | Team | Time | Age | City and State | |
|---|---|---|---|---|---|
| 6 Nikki Kimball | CMS | 1:22:07 | 33 | Elizabethtown, NY | |
| 7 Kari Distefano | | 1:23:05 | 45 | Telluride, CO | |
| 8 Lisa Goldsmith | LSpor | 1:23:13 | 39 | Nederland, CO | |
| 9 Cathy O'Brien | | 1:23:29 | 36 | Durham, NH | FW |
| 10 Barbara McManus | CMS | 1:23:35 | 36 | Worcester, MA | |
| 11 Julie Peterson | BAA | 1:24:39 | 44 | Beverly, MA | |
| 12 Beth Darnall | | 1:24:54 | 33 | Catonsville, MD | |
| 13 Suzy West | CSU | 1:26:01 | 41 | Putney, VT | |
| 14 Jacqueline Shakar | CMS | 1:26:40 | 44 | Worcester, MA | |
| 15 Inge Aiken | | 1:26:52 | 42 | East Greenbush, NY | |
| 16 Bonnie Ritchotte | MMM | 1:26:58 | 31 | Littleton, NH | |
| 17 Sarah Raitter | | 1:27:37 | 31 | Bend, OR | |
| 18 Jennifer Sacheck | | 1:27:59 | 31 | Arlington, MA | |
| 19 Cathi Campbell | BAA | 1:28:37 | 36 | Allston, MA | |
| 20 Donna Smyers | CVT | 1:29:02 | 46 | Montpelier, VT | |
| 21 Ellen McCurtin | Mlrse | 1:29:18 | 37 | Danbury, CT | |
| 22 Catherine Lifschultz | BAA | 1:29:20 | 41 | Sudbury, MA | |
| 23 Sue Wemyss | WMM | 1:29:39 | 44 | Gorham, NH | |
| 24 Jennifer Lassen | TG | 1:30:14 | 25 | Gloucester, MA | |
| 25 Kara Haas | GLRR | 1:31:01 | 33 | Burlington, MA | |
| 68 Barbara Remmers | | 1:46:34 | 40 | Blacksburg, VA | FW |

Jonathan Wyatt on his way to a new record

## 5-Year Age Groups

| Place | Name | Time | Age | City and State | Category | |
|---|---|---|---|---|---|---|
| 785 | Jennifer Paradis | 2:13:10 | 12 | Rochester, NH | Under 20 | |
| 368 | Michelle Boudreau | 1:43:49 | 23 | Lincoln, RI | 20-24 | |
| 156 | Jennifer Lassen | 1:30:14 | 25 | Gloucester, MA | 25-29 | |
| 27 | Anna Pichrtova | 1:12:19 | 31 | CZE | 30-34 | |
| 49 | Laura Haefeli | 1:17:42 | 36 | Del Norte, CO | 35-39 | |
| 54 | Cathy Pearce | 1:18:54 | 41 | Chelmsford, MA | 40-44 | |
| 81 | Kari Distefano | 1:23:05 | 45 | Telluride, CO | 45-49 | |
| 170 | Rebecca Stockdale-Woolley | 1:31:18 | 53 | Chaplin, CT | 50-54 | |
| 601 | Marjorie Kos | 1:58:07 | 59 | City Island, NY | 55-59 | |
| 647 | Louisa Dunlap | 2:01:54 | 63 | Belfast, ME | 60-64 | |
| 497 | Carrie Parsi | 1:52:14 | 65 | Gloucester, MA | 65-69 | |
| 632 | Barbara Robinson | 2:00:42 | 70 | Franconia, NH | 70-74 | **AGR** |
| 875 | Hildy Fosse | 2:24:43 | 75 | Holderness, NH | 75-79 | |
| 929 | Louise Rossetti | 3:00:52 | 82 | Saugus, MA | 80+ | |
| 34 | Zach Emerson | 1:13:57 | 19 | Hillsboro, NH | Under 20 | |
| 7 | Joshua Ferenc | 1:06:21 | 22 | Westmoreland, NH | 20-24 | |
| 4 | Eric Blake | 1:04:30 | 25 | Plattsburgh, NY | 25-29 | |
| 1 | Jonathan Wyatt | 0:56:41 | 31 | Wellington, NZL | 30-34 | **AGR & CR** |
| 3 | Simon Gutierrez | 1:04:17 | 38 | Taos, NM | 35-39 | |
| 6 | Andy Ames | 1:06:10 | 41 | Boulder, CO | 40-44 | |
| 19 | Guy Stearns | 1:10:29 | 45 | New Castle, NH | 45-49 | |
| 45 | John Barbour | 1:16:46 | 50 | Gloucester, MA | 50-54 | |
| 143 | Jonathan Stableford | 1:29:10 | 59 | Andover, MA | 55-59 | |
| 98 | Sumner Brown | 1:24:34 | 60 | Belmont, MA | 60-64 | |
| 413 | Bob Coughlin | 1:46:47 | 65 | Cape Elizabeth, ME | 65-69 | |
| 634 | Richard Fedion | 2:00:53 | 70 | N Conway, NH | 70-74 | |
| 709 | Robert Hall | 2:06:06 | 75 | Sudbury, MA | 75-79 | |
| 923 | Carlton Mendell | 2:47:58 | 82 | Portland, ME | 80+ | |

| Top 5 Teams Men | | Men 40+ | | Men 50+ | |
|---|---|---|---|---|---|
| 1 CMS | 5:29:53 | 1 CAA | 6:15:37 **CR** | 1 MM&M | 7:25:00 **CR** |
| 2 MM&M | 6:05:27 | 2 MM&M | 6:29:02 | 2 CSU | 7:27:54 |
| 3 CAA | 6:15:37 | 3 TG | 6:52:30 | 3 WCRC | 7:50:02 |
| 4 TG | 6:52:30 | 4 CSU | 7:13:10 | 4 NMC | 8:30:03 |
| 5 WMM | 6:58:54 | 5 NMC | 7:19:49 | 5 RIRR | 8:36:32 |

| Women | | Women 40+ | | Women 50+ | |
|---|---|---|---|---|---|
| 1 CMS | 4:07:23 | 1 CSU | 4:38:40 | 1 WCRC | 5:43:37 |
| 2 BAA | 4:22:36 | 2 WMM | 4:52:25 | 2 WMM | 6:22:30 |
| 3 CSU | 4:37:25 | 3 CVTRC | 5:02:02 | 3 FLRC | 7:12:05 |
| 4 MM&M | 4:44:12 | 4 MM&M | 5:02:11 | 4 GCS | 7:18:46 |
| 5 WMM | 4:46:27 | 5 NMC | 5:30:08 | | |

45th Mt Washington Road Race

June 18, 2005
Saturday, 10:00 AM
811 Finishers

Leading up to the 45th edition of the classic New England mountain race a great field was being assembled.  On the women's side Anna Pichrtova of the Czech Republic was the favorite based on her four prior wins.  Melissa Moon of Wellington, New Zealand looked to unseat the reigning champion.  Moon had twice won the Mountain running World Trophy (in 2001 and 2003), and was rumored to be in excellent form.  She had an impressive seven national cross-country titles to go with her many accomplishments.  Moon and Pichrtova dueled two weeks before at the USATF trail running championships in Vail Colorado.  They exchanged leads throughout with Pichrtova taking the win by twenty seconds.

On the men's side there would be no repeat champion as Jonathon Wyatt chose not to return.  The men's field looked to be strong, with many top runners returning.  Those expected to challenge for the win included Simon Gutierrez who had won in 2002 and 2003, Paul Low the 2004 runner-up, and Eric Blake who finished fourth in 2004.

Local favorites included Kelli Lusk who had finished third in 2003 and fifth in 2004.  Top ten finisher Kevin Tilton of Conway NH was running well on the USATF New England mountain circuit, including a win at the Mt Kearsarge race.  Tristan Colangelo was also a potential frontrunner, based on his personal bests of 4:09 for the mile and 14:06 for 5K.

The 40+ age group competition looked to be one of the better races within the race as Matt Carpenter and Eric Morse were returning.  Morse has the most top five finishes without a victory, and Carpenter has run a 59:16 in his last Mt Washington appearance when he won in 1999.  Both runners would be aiming for Craig Fram's course record of 1:03:27, and the $2,000 bonus for bettering it.  The duo were also considered to be in the hunt for the overall victory, as Carpenter had won the USATF trail running championships two weeks prior and Morse had placed a close second to Low at the Mt Ascutney run on June 13.  Local runners Suzy West and Cathy Pearce figured to be the top women in the 40+ category.  Former champions Peg Donovan (1987) and Jacqueline Gareau (1989, 1994, and 1996) would be racing in the 50+ age group.

Conditions on race day pointed toward fast times, and the top runners were quick to take advantage.  Moon and Pichrtova ran side by side in the mist and light rain on the lower slopes of the mountain.  Moon called it "cat and mouse the whole way".  As they battled back and forth, Gutierrez led the men's pack. He drew Carpenter, Blake, and Low away from the rest of the field.  After passing the half way mark, Low slid off the back.  Blake and Gutierrez continued side by side.  As they pressed the pace, Carpenter was dropped.  Gutierrez pulled away from Blake in the last half mile to record a personal best 1:00:54.  Blake crossed the line thirteen seconds later and noted "Simon is very savvy; he knows what he is doing".  Gutierrez proved him right as he now owns two of the three closest victories ever recorded.  In 2002 he won over

Low by ten seconds in the weather shortened version, this trails only the 1989 two second margin of victory between Dave Dunham and Bob Hodge.

The women's race proved to be just as exciting as the men's. Pichrtova and Moon ran together until the last 200 meters. Moon pulled ahead just before the final steep pitch and took the victory by fifteen seconds. This was the second closest finish, behind only the thirteen second gap when Jacqueline Gareau won in 1989. Moon missed the course record by two seconds. Pichrtova stated "I think she could have broken the record if the course wasn't muddy". She was alluding to a short steep section of the road just after five miles. It was muddy and rutted as a race vehicle tore up some of the surface when it became stuck earlier in the morning.

Matt Carpenter was overtaken by Low in the closing stages of the race. He finished fourth overall lowering Fram's 40+ record by 1:25, thus earning a $2,000 bonus.

In the team competition the CMS streak of victories continued. CMS broke the team record of 5:20:44, which they had set in 1999, running 5:17:59. The average time for the five scoring members was and impressive 1:03:35. The CMS men's 40+ team also broke the team record, taking sixteen minutes off of the Coastal AC's 2004 time of 6:15:27. The 5:59:04 by CMS was the first time a 40+ team broke six hours. In the 45 years the race has been held the six hour mark has only been broken 30 times. CMS leads the way with fourteen of those times, followed by GLRR with six, BAA with five, and GBTC with two. The remaining sub-six times were run once by Marathon Tours, US Biathlon team, and North Country AC. The CMS 40+ time was fast enough that it would have placed second in the open standings, behind only CMS. The Moose Milers and Marathoners and Coastal placed a close second and third in the 40+. MM&M also took a close victory in the 50+, defeating CMS by twenty-three seconds. Their times were the fourth and fifth best for a 50+ team. In an unusual quirk of the team scoring CMS would have won had the top 50+ woman Rebecca Stockdale-Woolley scored for the men's team.

The MM&M women took home the open team win with the sixth fastest time. They also took the 40+ category in a course record time of 4:26:43. They knocked nearly four minutes off of the course record set by CSU in 2003. CSU finished in second, running the third fastest team time. The Gate City Striders were victorious in the 50+ class, with an eighteen minute cushion over the Athletic Alliance and the Winners Circle Running Club. The top three teams all finished with top ten (all time) times.

The speedy conditions were apparent as state records were set for Alaska, Arizona, Indiana, Kansas, Mississippi, Montana, Nebraska, North Carolina, New York, Ohio, Rhode Island, and Washington. Records were also set for the Czech Republic and New Zealand. Sixteen single age record were also set. Fred Ross continued his longest recorded streak, finishing in his twenty-eighth consecutive race. Anna Pichrtova moved into a tie for seventh on the all time money maker list with Jacqueline Gareau. Each has earned $4,350. Craig Fram tops the list having earned just under ten thousand dollars in six Mt Washington races.

<u>Top 25 Finishers</u>

| Place Name | Team | Time | Age | City and State | |
|---|---|---|---|---|---|
| 1 Simon Gutierrez | TEVA | 1:00:54 | 39 | Alamosa, CO | |
| 2 Eric Blake | CMS | 1:01:07 | 26 | Plattsburgh, NY | |
| 3 Paul Low | CMS | 1:02:01 | 31 | Amherst, MA | |
| 4 Matt Carpenter | | 1:02:12 | 40 | Manitou Springs, CO | FW |
| 5 Kevin Tilton | CMS | 1:03:42 | 23 | Conway, NH | |
| 6 Eric Morse | CMS | 1:05:26 | 40 | Berlin, VT | |
| 7 Peter Maksimow | CMS | 1:05:43 | 26 | Springfield, MA | |
| 8 Chad Newton | | 1:06:38 | 35 | Pisgah Forest, NC | |
| 9 Sean Livingston | BAA | 1:07:13 | 36 | Barrington, RI | |
| 10 Richard Bolt | CMS | 1:07:30 | 34 | Nashua, NH | |
| 11 Josh Ferenc | BAA | 1:08:07 | 23 | Westmoreland, NH | |
| 12 Dan Verrington | CMS | 1:09:23 | 42 | Bradford, MA | |
| 13 Tim Livingston | WMM | 1:09:29 | 31 | Conway, NH | |
| 14 Gregory Colburn | MMM | 1:09:40 | 27 | Arlington, MA | |
| **15 Melissa Moon** | | **1:10:11** | **35** | **Wellington, NZL** | |
| 16 David Herr | MMM | 1:10:14 | 40 | Canaan, VT | |
| **17 Anna Pichrtova** | | **1:10:26** | **32** | **Boulder, CO (CZE)** | **FW** |
| 18 Dave Dunham | CMS | 1:10:37 | 41 | Bradford, MA | FW |
| 19 Ben Nephew | CMS | 1:11:03 | 29 | Foxboro, MA | |
| 20 David Hannon | NEW | 1:11:56 | 34 | Newton, MA | |
| 21 Joseph McVeigh | NYAC | 1:12:39 | 41 | Convent Station, NJ | |
| 22 Matt Mallet | SRT | 1:12:52 | 30 | Saratoga Spring, NY | |
| 23 Michael Woodman | CMS | 1:13:17 | 39 | Timonium, MD | |
| 24 Stephen Peterson | CMS | 1:13:33 | 39 | Chelmsford, MA | |
| 25 Kevin Walsh | | 1:13:37 | 41 | Dayton, OH | |
| 26 John Friedman | BAA | 1:14:22 | 24 | Cambridge, MA | |
| 27 Brad Lebo | CAA | 1:14:43 | 48 | Portsmouth, NH | |
| 61 Keith Woodward | MMM | 1:20:54 | 54 | E. Corinth, VT | FW |
| 179 John Cederholm | BAA | 1:33:50 | 62 | Marion, MA | FW |


<u>Top 25 Women</u>

| Place Name | Team | Time | Age | City and State | |
|---|---|---|---|---|---|
| 1 Melissa Moon | | 1:10:11 | 35 | Wellington, NZL | |
| 2 Anna Pichrtova | | 1:10:26 | 32 | Boulder, CO (CZE) | FW |
| 3 Liza Grudzinski | | 1:19:32 | 25 | Harriman, NY | |
| 4 Julia Stamps | | 1:19:43 | 26 | New York, NY | |
| 5 Cathy Pearce | WRT | 1:20:15 | 42 | Chelmsford, MA | |
| 6 Suzy West | CSU | 1:21:24 | 42 | Putney, VT | |
| 7 Raelyn Crowell | MMM | 1:23:12 | 34 | Amherst, NH | |
| 8 Chari Walsh | | 1:23:23 | 41 | Dayton, OH | |
| 9 Kathy Maddock | MMM | 1:25:51 | 40 | Wilton, NH | |

| Place | Name | | Time | Age | City and State | Category |
|---|---|---|---|---|---|---|
| 10 | Jacqueline Gareau | | 1:27:08 | 52 | St-Bruno, PQ | FW |
| 11 | Bonnie Ritchotte | MMM | 1:27:37 | 32 | Littleton, NH | |
| 12 | Kimberly Saddic | | 1:27:49 | 35 | West Chester, PA | |
| 13 | Donna Smyers | CTVT | 1:27:53 | 47 | Adamant, VT | |
| 14 | Ann Rasmussen | MMM | 1:29:55 | 41 | Plymouth, NH | |
| 15 | Sue Wemyss | WMM | 1:30:18 | 45 | Gorham, NH | |
| 16 | Maggie Ramos | MMM | 1:30:57 | 43 | Peterborough, NH | |
| 17 | Jacqueline Shakar | CMS | 1:31:23 | 45 | Sutton, MA | |
| 18 | Adrienne Cyrulik | MVS | 1:31:46 | 31 | Andover, MA | |
| 19 | Katie Schroth | | 1:31:58 | 26 | Chelmsford, MA | |
| 20 | Katja Fox | WMM | 1:32:06 | 39 | Wolfeboro, NH | |
| 21 | Laura Harding | RR | 1:32:59 | 38 | Durham, NH | |
| 22 | Rebecca Stockdale-Woolley | | 1:33:13 | 54 | Chaplin, CT | |
| 23 | Annie Ericson | | 1:34:13 | 25 | Northampton, MA | |
| 24 | Layce Alves | TG | 1:34:27 | 25 | Gloucester, MA | |
| 25 | Donna Smyth | CSU | 1:34:33 | 45 | Vernon, VT | |
| 42 | Peg Donovan | | 1:42:59 | 50 | Auburn, NH | FW |

## 5-Year Age Groups

| Place | Name | Time | Age | City and State | Category |
|---|---|---|---|---|---|
| 175 | Marie-Michelle Tessier | 2:11:42 | 18 | Sherbrooke, PQ | Under 20 |
| 86 | Kate Nydam | 1:52:31 | 23 | Plainville, CT | 20-24 |
| 3 | Liza Grudzinski | 1:19:32 | 25 | Harriman, NY | 25-29 |
| 2 | Anna Pichrtova | 1:10:26 | 32 | Boulder, CO | 30-34 |
| 1 | Melissa Moon | 1:10:11 | 35 | Wellington, NZ | 35-39 **AGR** |
| 5 | Cathy Pearce | 1:20:15 | 42 | Chelmsford, MA | 40-44 |
| 13 | Donna Smyers | 1:27:53 | 47 | Adamant, VT | 45-49 |
| 17 | Jacqueline Gareau | 1:27:08 | 52 | St-Bruno, PQ | 50-54 **AGR** |
| 84 | Jeannie Weber | 1:52:15 | 56 | Lewiston, ME | 55-59 |
| 65 | Marjorie Kos | 1:49:50 | 60 | City Island, NY | 60-64 |
| 73 | Carrie Parsi | 1:50:36 | 66 | Gloucester, MA | 65-69 |
| 138 | Barbara Robinson | 2:01:34 | 71 | Franconia, NH | 70-74 |
| 210 | Hildy Fosse | 2:39:06 | 76 | Holderness, NH | 75-79 |
| 72 | David Hunt | 1:22:03 | 19 | Fryeburg, ME | Under 20 |
| 5 | Kevin Tilton | 1:03:42 | 23 | Conway, NH | 20-24 |
| 2 | Eric Blake | 1:01:07 | 26 | Plattsburgh, NY | 25-29 |
| 3 | Paul Low | 1:02:01 | 31 | Amherst, MA | 30-34 |
| 1 | Simon Gutierrez | 1:00:54 | 39 | Alamosa, CO | 35-39 |
| 4 | Matt Carpenter | 1:02:12 | 40 | Manitou Springs, CO | 40-44 **AGR** |
| 27 | Brad Lebo | 1:14:43 | 48 | Portsmouth, NH | 45-49 |
| 43 | Buzz Burrell | 1:17:20 | 53 | Boulder, CO | 50-54 |
| 105 | Jerry Learned | 1:27:11 | 56 | Hopkinton, MA | 55-59 |

| Place | Name | Time | Age | City and State | Category |
|---|---|---|---|---|---|
| 84 | Jerry Rosa | 1:24:54 | 61 | Hampton, NH | 60-64 |
| 267 | John Pelton | 1:40:23 | 66 | West Rupert, VT | 65-69 |
| 528 | John Howe | 1:56:35 | 70 | Waterford, ME | 70-74 |
| 674 | Robert Hall | 2:09:22 | 76 | Sudbury, MA | 75-79 |
| 805 | Carlton Mendell | 2:49:19 | 83 | Windham, ME | 80-84 |
| 784 | George Etzweiler | 2:33:20 | 85 | State College, PA | 85-89 |

## Top 5 Teams

| Men's | | Men 40+ | | Men 50+ | |
|---|---|---|---|---|---|
| 1 CMS | 5:17:59 **CR** | 1 CMS | 5:59:04 **CR** | 1 MM&M | 7:33:07 |
| 2 MM&M | 6:07:54 | 2 MM&M | 6:33:03 | 2 CMS | 7:33:30 |
| 3 BAA | 6:34:00 | 3 CAA | 6:37:31 | 3 WCRC | 8:07:10 |
| 4 CAA | 6:37:31 | 4 NMC | 7:09:01 | 4 RIRR | 8:37:21 |
| 5 WMM | 6:46:47 | 5 WCRC | 7:19:17 | 5 CSU | 8:51:48 |

| Women | | Women 40+ | | Women 50+ | |
|---|---|---|---|---|---|
| 1 MM&M | 4:16:40 | 1 MM&M | 4:26:43 | 1 GCS | 6:04:01 |
| 2 CSU | 4:31:24 | 2 CSU | 4:31:24 | 2 AA | 6:22:02 |
| 3 WMM | 4:42:06 | 3 WMM | 4:58:58 | 3 WCRC | 6:23:01 |
| 4 CMS | 4:44:31 | 4 NMC | 5:23:13 | | |
| 5 TG | 5:07:48 | 5 GCS | 5:25:05 | | |

Mt Washington Medal

## 1988

I'm not sure why I decided to run Mt Washington that first time. I'm guessing it had something to do with my teammate Bob Hodge. We were doing a lot of racing together and even some track workouts. The Greater Lowell Road Runners were trying to build a strong road racing team around Hodgie and me.

Racing had gone pretty well in '88 I had raced a total of 32 times which is pretty low for me. Heading into Mt Washington I had done three races in May. I was fourth in the NEAC (New England Athletic Congress) Grand Prix 10K in Nashua NH in 29:17. I also traveled out to Boulder CO for the Bolder Boulder 10K race and ran 32:04, which was pretty disappointing as time bonus money ended at 32:00. Training was going well leading up to the race. The week of the Mt Washington I had 99 miles and 80 miles of biking despite the 100-degree heat (Wednesday).

I drove up to the White Mountains on Friday night and did 5 miles on route 16 at 10:00 PM. On the morning of the race Petey (Steve Peterson) and I did a three-mile warmup and some strides to get ready. George Davis, who was our college coach and team coach for the GLRR, had predicted that we would walk and that Petey would walk before half way. Neither of us walked.

I remember that the conditions were very good and the view was great. I kept expecting the course to level out at every turn and was really disappointed when it didn't. Once I moved into the lead, I just enjoyed the run. I recall not being sure where to go when I got into the lower parking lot near the summit and remarking after the race that the only way they could make it tougher would be to have the runners climb up the radio tower.

Petey and I ran back down to the base in 65 minutes. I was given $1,100 total for the win, course record, and leading at half way. After the race I had a long chat with Jay Johnson. He seemed like a nice guy, but I had a hard time believing some of his tales of mountain racing in Europe. I just couldn't believe that someone would pay to have me come over to Europe to run up mountains. It would be a few years before I took the plunge and headed over to Europe to run the circuit of races over there.

The next day I did a seven-mile run to my parents' house in Billerica at 4 AM and played a round of golf with my Dad. After the game I ran seven miles back to Lowell. The week after the race I covered 103 miles with one day off and biked 90 miles. I also won the Cappy's Copper Kettle race in Lowell that week with a 25:03 and got $500 for the effort.

Splits = 1 mile 06:05. 2 mile 13:42. Half 29:02. 5 mile 38:21. 1:00:50 Finish. Second half 31:48.

## 1989

My training was focused on getting ready for the Boston Marathon, which was to be my debut at that distance. Training was geared to race at 5:10 pace and I did tempo runs up to 13 miles at that pace. I didn't race as much in '89 because of my marathon plans, and leading into Mt

Washington I had only raced six times.  I had trouble recovering from Boston where I ran 2:22 (17th place), but was on 2:14 pace at 20 miles.

I felt that I was in good form as I had weeks of 100, 85 (with a day off), 95, and 99 miles leading up to Mt Washington.  I had also done some solid workouts including a four mile tempo run of 20:35, a six mile tempo in 29:45 and two times two miles on the track in 9:28 and 9:27.  The week before Mt Washington I raced the Nipmuck half marathon, which is a tough trail race, and set a course record.

On Friday morning I ran eight miles then took the day off from work and went to the Eagle Mountain House where I stayed courtesy of race director Bob Teschek.  I ran an easy four miles in the afternoon and got to bed early.

On race day I felt lousy.  I ran with my Greater Lowell Road Runners teammate Bob Hodge (Hodgie) from the gun and at half way I was ready to drop out despite being just over course record pace. I stuck it out and stayed with Bob through seven miles.  We ran side-by-side, neither of us tucking in.  It was windy and very foggy at the summit.   Conditions for the lower half of the race were moderate with temperatures in the low 70s.  Once we got higher up, the 50 mph winds and 40-degree temperatures slowed the pace.  At seven miles I asked Bob if he wanted to tie and he said something like "The sponsors paid for a race."  I hung with him until the final brutal climb and launched into a kick.  I nipped him by a little over one second in the closest finish to date.  I garnered $600 for the win.

Hodgie and I lead GLRR to its second consecutive win in 5:50:24.  Petey, Tom Carroll and I ran down to the base in a quick (for us) 59:47.

I stayed at the Eagle Mountain House that night and ran 12 miles the next day to complete the week with 97 miles.  The following weekend, Bob and I duked it out at the NEAC 5K championships.  I got him on a kick 14:23 to 14:26 as we repeated our finish order.

Splits = 1 mile 6:05.  2 mile 13:46.  3 mile 21:55.  Half 29:12.  4 mile 30:00.  6 mile 47:54.  Finish 1:02:59.  Second Half 33:47.

## 1990

My preparation for this year's run was not my best.  I had weeks of 87, 102, and 100 miles leading up to and including the week of the race.  I had been racing sparingly, having completed only nine races leading up to the Mountain.  Earlier in the year I ran my first race outside the USA, the Omhe 30K in Japan.  The trip included two runs in the same day more than 24 hours apart (thanks to the International Date Line).  I had a good run at New Bedford for the NEAC half-marathon finishing eighteenth in 1:05:27 and then placed fourteenth at the Boston Milk Run (29:52 10K) where I met a very cute Uta Pippig just beginning to make her mark in the States.  In May I ran the Worcester 10 mile, which was also the NEAC Champs, in 49:58 to take third.  My last two races leading up to the Mountain were the Pepsi Police chase in Nashua and the NEAC 10k in Attleboro.  Times of 30:06 and 30:38 and places of second and eight respectively, didn't bode well for being in my best form.  I did have a good workout the week prior which bolstered my confidence running a 4:38 mile, 9:27 two-mile, and 4:38 mile on the track in Derry.

I took off work on Friday and ran seven miles in the morning before driving up North.  I ran another three miles in the afternoon to stay loose after the long drive.  On race day I felt sick and had stomach cramps.  I ran with Petey for a three-mile warmup.  I heard that Derek Froude was the guy to beat although some other names were being thrown.  Froude had some fast personal bests but you can never be sure how that will translate to mountain running.

I didn't like the warm temperatures in the early going, but tried to go with Froude.  He was tough and just floated away.  I settled in to second place and aimed for a respectable time.  One of the reasons I felt lousy was the early pace, which was fast.  We hit the mile in 6:00, which is pretty darn quick on this course, despite the flat running in the first minute and the fact that the mile post is actually .9 miles.  This opening mile still remains my fastest start.

I was pretty happy with my time.  Scott Elliott, the third place finisher, was quoted in one of the papers saying something like "If it had been a mile longer I would have gotten second."  That quote got a lot of mileage among my teammates and me.  At races and workouts we'd claim, "If it had been ten miles longer I would have won." or "If it were 100 yards I would have won."  It was one of the many bizarre quotes from Mt Washington competitors.  My team (GLRR) took the win in a fast time.  It was cool to be on a team that was focused on a race that I really liked doing.

Petey and I did the run down to the base in 1:02 and the next day I did an 11-mile run from the Eagle Mountain House.  I stayed there for three extra days as a mini-vacation.

Splits = 1 mile 6:00.  2 mile 13:37.  3 mile 21:36.  Half 29:02.  4 mile 29:49.  5 mile 38:33.  6 mile 47:06.  7 mile 55:49.
Finish 1:01:37.  Second half 32:35.

## 1991

I came into the race in pretty decent shape this year.  I had run the Nipmuck trail marathon the first week in June and set a course record.  I followed that with a third place at the USATF New England 10K championships in Winthrop with a 30:50.  Hodgie finished a couple of seconds behind me at the 10K.  Leading up to the race I had weeks of 97, 80, and 80.  I took Friday off from work and ran five miles in the morning then drove up to the Eagle Mountain house.  I ran a tough loop that is part of the Jackson 10K and was sacked out by 9:00 PM.

On race day I was up at 7:00 AM and felt lousy.  I did a three-mile warmup but still felt beat so I didn't do much in the way of strides.  I just focused on staying relaxed.  I liked the conditions a bit better this year.  It was rainy and cold in the second half and the wind was pretty tough.  I went out conservatively, not wanting to run "the other guy's" race.  I was in fifth place at the mile and passed Hodgie to get into second a little after two miles.  Froude moved out early and was almost a minute ahead by the half.  I felt crappy in the first half, but after the four-mile turn I felt a lot better and settled in.  With Hodgie pretty far back and Derek just as far in front, the race was pretty much over for me by the half way mark.  At the summit I continued through the chute and ran to the top of the rock pile, becoming the first runner that day to actual summit.  Petey and I ran down to the base in a slow 1:10.

GLRR took the team champs with the second fastest team time only two minutes behind the record.  I ran 11 miles in the morning the next day and played a mosquito-enshrouded golf game at the Eagle Mountain course before heading home.

Splits = 1 mile 6:14.  2 mile 13:59.  3 mile 21:55.  Half 29:20.  4 mile 30:08.  5 mile 38:44.  6 mile 47:41.  7 mile 56:28.
Finish 1:02:07.  Second Half 32:47.


## 1992

This was a big year of racing for me; I did 47 races through the year.  I was pretty happy with my fitness leading into the race as I had run a 2:21 at the Olympic trials marathon and followed that with a 29:26 10K.  The final tune-ups prior to Mt Washington were the NEAC 10K championship where I ran 30:12 and the Litchfield hills 7.1m where I finished fifth in 34:59, which was 34 seconds behind Froude's winning time.  This was my first year running for the Central MA striders (CMS) and we took the team title.

In the weeks leading up to the race I logged miles of 94, 94, 100, and 94 miles.  On Friday I ran in the morning and then completed another three miles in the afternoon.  On race day I found it to be very humid.  I did an easy three-mile warmup with Petey.

Carpenter and Froude pushed each other until three miles when Carpenter pulled ahead.  I was off of the back early on.  They passed the half in 29:00 and 29:30 with me just under 30 minutes.  Froude slowed to a walk at one point but kept going.  I caught him at five miles but he regrouped and pulled away.

Post race, Petey and I ran down to the base in 1:10.  On Sunday I ran eight miles in the morning then went to an Orienteering meet in the afternoon.  Later in the summer I went to Europe with Jay Johnson, although still having a hard time believing that someone would pay to bring me over to race.  We ran the Challenge Stellina and followed that up with the World Mountain Trophy race in Italy where I finished ninth.

Splits = 1 mile 6:14.  2 mile 14:06.  3 mile 22:20.  Half 29:55.  4 mile 30:44.  5 mile 39:43.  6 mile 48:34.  7 mile 57:28.
Finish 1:03:18.  Second half 33:23.

## 1993

My training was going well, although not my best heading into the race. I had run the Dipsea race in Mill Valley CA a couple of weeks prior to Mt Washington, which was a new experience. The Dipsea is one of the oldest continuous races in the country and also one of the most unusual. Start times are adjusted based on age and sex. As a "scratch" runner I started last and had to pass the 500+ runners who had already started. The course was a mix of narrow trail, major climbs/descents, and over 500 stairs. I ended up finishing sixth despite running the fastest time of the day. My final tune-up was the NEAC 8K race where I ran a 23:59 for third place. I had weeks of 74, 83, 82, 84 and 87 miles leading up to the race.

On Friday I ran in the morning and then drove to the Eagle Mountain House where I ran another three miles. It was warm and muggy during the three-mile warmup with Hodge, Eric Morse, and Dan Verrington. I felt tired and lousy. I didn't feel much better in the race as Matt Carpenter broke away after the mile and I stayed about 15 seconds back. I lost him in the fog after five miles. It was very wet and muddy over the last three miles. I ran my best time, but as Eric Morse was quick to point out "you are the first loser." I did the run down with Hodgie in about 1:10. The next day I did nine miles in the morning before heading home.

Splits = 1 mile 6:13. 2 mile 13:43. 3 mile 21:27. Half 28:38. 4 mile 29:23. 5 mile 37:57. 6 mile 46:39. 7 mile 55:17.
Finish 1:00:44. Second half 32:06.

## 1994

I was doing decent mileage leading up to this year's race and was feeling pretty good. I had weekly mileage of 90, 79, 80, and 116 miles prior to the race. Racing was going well with a win at the USATF 12K in 36:59, and a 24:19 8K in Manchester NH. Petey and I went to the Dipsea race again. This time I finished fourth overall despite running the fastest time (it is a handicap race). Petey and I took off for Yosemite right after the race and did 16 miles at 8,000' the day after the race. We followed that up with a run from the valley floor to Glacier point, a 5,000' climb with spectacular views. We flew home overnight and I then headed up to Mt Washington.

It was very hot when race day dawned. A big group of us (CMS runners and CMS wannabees) did a two-mile warmup and tried to hydrate properly for this extremely warm day. I felt okay as I eased out in sixth place at the mile, 30 seconds behind the leader. I caught Morse at two miles and took the lead just before three miles. I felt in control in the second half and was surprised that no one went with me. In an unusual turn, I took a ride down for a rare time and did two miles warm down with Petey and Spinney at the base. Spinney's wife had the quote of the day yelling to Keith, as she drove to the summit, "Don't embarrass me!" We stayed over night and went to Bretton Woods on Sunday for a Summer Biathlon (run and shoot). My wife, Cathy, turned out to be the best shooter in the group. I ended up with the second fastest time, behind Keith Woodward.

Splits = 1 mile 06:23. 2 mile 14:14. 3 mile 22:33. Half 30:14. 4 mile 31:00. 5 mile 40:14. 6 mile 49:04. 7 mile 57:42. Finish 1:03:22. Second half 33:08.

**1995**

My training was going pretty well leading up to the Mountain.  I had weeks of 94, 100, 82, and 80 miles prior to the race.  Warmup races included the Wachusett mountain race where I set a course record, winning in 24:31 on the 4.3m 900' climb road race.  I also returned to California for the Dipsea race (90th running of the race).  I ended up in second place, despite running the fastest time.  Such is the outcome when running a handicap race.  Friday before Mt Washington I did four miles in the early morning, three miles at lunch, and then drove up the Thornhill Inn.  A few of us went out for a three-mile run to loosen up. Caz (Mike Casner), Jim Garcia, and Craig Fram were in the group.  On race day I did a three-mile warmup with Petey, Fram, and Byrne Decker and felt pretty decent.  I started out feeling good, running with Fram and Eddy Hellebuyck.  By the time we hit the mile the Kenyan runner was way out in front.  Once we got above treeline it got very windy.   Hellebuyck noted, "This sucks." and I replied, "No, actually this blows."  Soon after our exchange he dropped off and Craig and I were on our own in second/third.  At seven miles we decided it would be best to tie as we were teammates and really had nothing to gain by fighting it out.  Eric Morse had moved into fourth but was far enough back that he wouldn't catch us.

I started the run down alone and when I reached the three-mile post a car pulled along side me.  Petey, Hodgie, and Byrne were in the vehicle.  Byrne opened the door and said, "You **ARE** getting in."  This was one of the rare times I didn't run down the entire way; I completed 4.6 miles in 33:59.

Splits = 1 mile 6:11.  2 mile 13:53.  3 mile 22:00.  Half 29:30.  4 mile 30:17.  5 mile 39:10.  6 mile 48:41.  7 mile 57:52.
Finish 1:03:20.  Second half 33:50.

**1996**

This year I felt that things were going really well leading up to the race.  I ran a course record at the Kearsarge Mountain race in Warner, NH, covering the 8.5m course in 51:23.  I followed that up with decent runs at Agawam (5 miles), Wachusett Mountain (just missing my course record), and Pack Monadnock.  Kearsarge, Wachusett, and Pack were the races in the newly formed USATF New England Mountain circuit.  They worked well as a build-up to the big race.  My final tune-up was the Litchfield 7.1 mile race where I placed seventh in 35:41.  Some of the top guys would also be at Mt Washington including Gideon Mutisya (second – 34:02) and Daniel Kihara (third – 34:41).

On Friday I ran three miles at 4:30 AM then went to work.  I did another three miles at lunch and then motored up to Attitash after work.  Dan Verrington and Craig Fram joined me for a three-mile run.  I felt lousy and tired.

On race day I felt okay, which in and of itself is unusual.  I had an interview with New Hampshire Cross Roads, a local PBS show that was doing a feature on the race.  They wanted me to run with a microphone so they could get the "sounds of the race."  I agreed, although I was a little nervous about the battery pack and transmitter that I had to wear around my waist.

A big group of CMS guys and other friends did a three-mile warmup.  It was warm and muggy and I felt a bit tired.  After the gun sounded Craig and some of the other guys were giving me grief, so that it would be picked up on the mike.  I put in a sprint and took the lead before we even got to the tollbooth.  The lead was very short lived as I slowed to "normal" pace and Daniel Kihara stormed past.  Craig and I ran together through three miles then I pulled ahead.  At the half, I couldn't see Kihara ahead of me and Eric Morse had moved into third about 20 seconds behind me.  I gained a bit more on Eric in the second half but Kihara was in his own world.

The run down was fun, with great views; Petey and I ran comfortably in 1:06:44.  After the race I went to the Eagle Mountain House and played the buggiest round of golf ever.  The black flies were brutal and I was happy with a 60 for nine holes.  Obviously golf is not my strong suit.

Splits = 1 mile 6:18.  2 mile 14:06.  3 mile 22:15.  Half 29:42.  4 mile 30:30.  5 mile 39:19.  6 mile 48:08.  7 mile 56:48.
Finish 1:02:24.  Second half 32:42.

**1997**  I spent the good part of the year in a walking cast.  What was thought to be a stress fracture turned out to be a non-union fracture.  I ended up having a screw put into my foot and didn't run for almost six months.  I stayed away from the race, as I couldn't bear to watch it while injured.

**1998**
I returned to running in December of 1997 and started the long buildup back.  I was in pretty good shape by the time the race rolled around, but nowhere near what I hoped for.  I had weeks of 84, 80, 80, and 80 miles heading into the race.  I also had a Cortisone shot in my ankle a few days before to the race.  As was the case in 1996 I prepared for the big race by running the USATF Mountain circuit races.  I fared well, but was considerably slower than in years past.  My speed wasn't quite what I had hoped as I finished the Market Square 10K in 31:33 the week before Mt Washington.

On Friday I headed up to Attitash, where Bob Teschek had set up a place for me and some of my teammates, and did an eight-mile run with Mike Casner, Dan Verrington, Bob Hodge, George Adams and Thierry Icart.  Thierry came over from France and was staying with Caz.  He was among the favorites for the race.  I had a lousy night sleep and woke up feeling terrible.  A huge group of CMS and CMS-wannabees (including Francis Burdett one of the group favorites despite his predilection for racing for the Greater Lowell Road Runners) did a two-mile warmup.  We cut our normal warmup to just two miles, as it was very warm and humid.  I went out conservatively and moved through the pack throughout the race.  I had hoped to run under 1:08 and was quite pleased with breaking 1:04.  I thought I had a shot at Simon Gutierrez, but he maintained his distance in the second half.

It was in the 50s and calm on top, which made for a nice run down with Eric Morse in 1:03:48.  I put in 11 miles the next day with a big group.  Most of our group also traveled to Stratton Mountain the following week for the USATF NE mountain championships.  It was a pretty cool race and a fun weekend.  The quote of the weekend was from a guide who was talking me through my first attempt at rock climbing.  He said, "Stick your hand in the crack and make a fist."  Needless to say the gang I was with got a good laugh from that for a long time.

Splits = 1 mile 6:33.  2 mile 14:26.  3 mile 22:45.  Half 30:21.  4 mile 31:10.  5 mile 40:15.  6 mile 49:09.  7 mile 57:55.  Finish 1:03:38.  Second half 33:17.

## 1999

I was finally feeling like I was over my 1997 injury.  I ran a 2:21 in Pittsburgh at the USATF National championships to qualify for the Olympic trials and followed that with a record run up Mt Kearsarge six days later.  I ran decent times at Wachusett and Pack Monadnock and ran 30:31 at the USATF NE 10K championships.  With weeks of 83, 86, 90, 85, and 72 miles I felt my chances were good for a respectable run.

On Friday I got up at 4:30 AM and ran an easy five miles, then worked for a half day.  I went up to Attitash and ran five miles on the trails along the river, which was nice and relaxing but buggy.  On race day I did a warmup with a big group of guys and felt lousy and sluggish.

I felt good during the race and went out strong, running with Eric Morse for the first two miles.  Around 2.5 miles I passed Joe Lemay and then went by Simon Gutierrez at around three miles.  Soon after that I was able to pull away from Eric.  I didn't gain anything on Kihara and Carpenter who were long gone and basically just held a 20 second lead over Eric to the finish.  Conditions were very good and CMS set a new team record.

The run down was a lot of fun with incredible views thanks to the 90 miles of visibility.   I ran down to the base in 1:10:42 with Eric, Petey, and Richard Bolt.

Splits = 1 mile 6:14.  3 mile 21:49.  Half 29:07.  4 mile 29:54.  5 mile 38:30.  6 mile 46:54.  7 mile 55:14.  Finish 1:00:37.   Second half 31:30.

## 2000

This year I was running some decent mileage leading up to the race but wasn't feeling fit.  I had weeks of 100, 96, and 100 miles the three weeks leading up to the race.  I had raced up Wachusett at the end of May and my time wasn't great.  I followed up with a 30:57 at Portsmouth and raced at Pack Monadnock the next day.

On Friday I took the day off from work and did eight miles with Dan and then drove up to Attitash.  I ran another easy three miles once I got up there.  On race day I did about two miles on the Glen trails and felt pretty good.

I felt okay early on as the two Kenyans took off.  I settled in with teammates Eric Morse and Mark Donahue.  At about 1.5 miles Donahue was off the back.  Morse fell off at 2.5 and I was on my own in third place.  I looked back at five miles and figured I had about a minute on Eric and finished with a sub 1:03.

145

The run down with Eric Morse, Mark Donahue, Dan Verrington and Mark Behan was the fastest I had ever done. We had a good time zipping down the hill in 58:33.

Splits = 1 mile 6:20. 2 mile 14:09. 3 mile 22:13. Half 29:38. 4 mile 30:26. 5 mile 39:11. 6 mile 47:59. 7 mile 57:00. Finish 1:02:48. Second half 33:10.

## 2001

Injuries this year left me hoping for a good run but not really sure of my fitness. I did have a good month leading up to the race with weeks of 109, 90, 80, 80, but only had 51 miles the week of the race as I missed three days. Racing leading up to the big one included a five-mile version of the Mt Kearsarge race, which really wasn't a mountain race as it ended at the entrance to the park due to snow on the road. Dan Verrington and I tied at the USATF NE Mountain championships that I also directed at the Windblown ski area. We tied because we thought Eric Morse had won the race going away, only to find out that he went off course. Other races included the Wachusett mountain race where I ran 25:01, Pack Monadnock where I ran 59:41, and Whiteface Mountain where Eric and I tied for first in a course record.

On Friday I ran five miles in the morning with Hungarian au pair Robert Molnar, who was training with me in Bradford. We drove up to Attitash and did another five miles on the trails. Race day dawned very warm. I warmed up with a big CMS group but only did about 12 minutes of running then just sat in the shade since the temperature was already in the 80s and the summit was up to 60 degrees.

Kihara took off from the start and the race was on for second place. I ran with Eric Morse and Craig Fram. We were dead even through the half, then Eric fell back a bit. Craig almost ran into the press van with his head down. I called out at the last moment and he dodged the van. I was aiming for second, but also keeping my eye on the watch, I wanted Craig to break the master's record. I broke away from him in the last ½ mile to take second.

I ran down in 1:03:53 and did ten miles on Sunday morning on the trails around Attitash.

Splits = 1 mile 6:29. 2 mile 14:32. 3 mile 22:56. Half 30:43. 4 mile 31:34. 5 mile 40:42. 6 mile 49:42. 7 mile 58:36.
Finish 1:04:20. Second half 33:37.

## 2002

My form was definitely not good, as I had been injured off and on for a good portion of the previous year. Mileage was not very good with weeks of 59, 70, and 73 miles leading up to the race. I had pretty good runs at Mt Kearsarge (53:33), Wachusett (24:59), and Pack Monadnock (1:04:51). I went out to Alaska and ran the Wolverine Peak race, which was a qualifier for the US Mountain team and finished second to Eric Morse.

On Thursday I headed up to Attitash and Friday did an easy eight miles in the morning.  In the afternoon my wife, Cathy, and my college roommate Mike Woodman and I went out and played miniature golf.  After the game I ran five miles with Woody and called it a day.  Race day was gloomy and raining.  I couldn't believe it when I was told the race was shortened to halfway, for me that would be a "sprint."  This was not exactly my strength.  It was taking me a few miles just to get loose in a race, probably from the Ultra (longer than marathon) racing I'd been doing.

I went out with a big CMS group for a warmup on the trails and did about two miles then an additional mile on my own.  Just before the start Anna Pichrtova, one of the favorites, pulled my tail and gave me a big smile.  Boy, talk about losing your concentration right before the start!  It was amazing how fast everyone started out.  I was about thirtieth at the base of the hill at only a minute into the race.  By the mile, which was not much faster than a typical first mile on the mountain, I had moved up to the top twenty.  It was definitely a record for the number of people in the lead group at that point.  Typically, the field is strung out by a half mile into the race, this was not typical.  I moved up to tenth by two miles and started reeling in some of the fast starters and in the last mile passed Kihara to take fifth.  I ran down with a big group, as everyone had to run down since cars were not allowed up.  We reached the bottom in 31:00 and then went out on the trails for additional mileage.  On Sunday I did eight miles before heading home.

Splits = 1 mile 6:15.  2 mile 14:12.  3 mile 22:28.  Finish 28:57.

## 2003

This was another year of not being quite ready for the race.  This time I had spent a good portion of the second half of 2002 in and out of various hospitals.   After a bunch of years struggling with Anorexia I got drastically worse and spent a fair amount of time getting back to the point where I could run consistently.  I did learn an important lesson; you can't run or race without being properly fueled.   I had weeks of 76, 73, 75, 88 and 91 miles leading up to Mt Washington.  In a new twist this year Eric Morse, Rich Bolt and I went out to Prospect Mountain in NY to test ourselves on that course.  It was a great race, and a nice view from the top.  We took the top three spots, with Eric setting a course record ahead of Rich.  I had a lousy run at Wachusett finishing seventh and a decent run at Kearsarge getting fourth.  I tried a different tactic at Kearsarge, running the first five less than all-out and then hammering the final 3.5 mountain section.  I got fifth at Pack Monadnock and sixth at a new race that I directed at Northfield Mountain.  This was a new version of the USATF NE mountain championships on trails around the Northfield Mountain recreation area in Western Mass.  It seemed like a decent lead-in for Mt Washington.

I headed up to Attitash on Thursday and had a good time relaxing around the "cottage".  On Friday I went seven miles in the morning and another four in the afternoon.  Our big CMS group went over to the Eagle Mountain House and picked up our numbers.  I also gave a speech describing different parts of the race and tactics for getting through it.

On race day I got up with a terrible headache and dead legs.  I did a two-mile warmup with Craig Fram, Dan Verrington, Steve Peterson, and Mike Woodman.  Conditions looked to be pretty good and the field actually looked to be a bit weak, especially with Eric Morse pulling out with an injury.  It was warm at the start and clear and sunny at the top.  I ran with Rich Bolt from the mile and lost him when I moved into fourth around 2.5 miles.  I caught the early leading Kenyan at seven miles and he was moving very slowly.  I was pleased with the run all things considered.

I had a fun run down with Eric who had gone to the top to watch and Mike Woodman who raced.  We ran down in 1:09:53 and I got in a nice 10 mile run the next day at Attitash.

Splits = 1 mile 6:36.  2 mile 14:56.  3 mile 23:37.  Half 31:34.  4 mile 32:26.  5 mile 41:51.  6 mile 51:08.  7 mile 1:00:17.
Finish 1:06:18.  Second half 34:44.

## 2004
I partially tore my Achilles tendon in late May which left me on the sidelines for the race.  I went up to support CMS and to assist Rich Bolt in a speech on Mountain running.  I also joined teammate Alan Bernier in the lead press vehicle to do the commentary on the race.  It was a lot of fun but was difficult to watch my favorite race without being really part of it.

In August I went up to Mt Washington on the day of the annual bicycle hill climb.  Rich Bolt and Kevin Tilton joined me for a jog to the summit.  We ran evenly despite a strong wind, fog, and rain above treeline.  We completed the run in 1:29 and got to watch the top riders come in.  Our run back down was a different experience as we went through the huge packs of riders.  I was truly surprised to see a tandem bike competing; I can only imagine how tough that would be.

## 2005
Once again I was recovering from extended injuries leading up to Mt Washington.  This time I tore a hip muscle while competing in a 33 mile trail race in December of 2004.  Leading up to the race I had weeks around 70 miles.  Training included a run with Team Gloucester on their Mt Washington prep day.  We did an interesting mix of trail and road running, repeat hills, and a 30' jump into a very cold quarry.  I was not very confident of my ability to run well at Mt Washington based on poor showings at Mt Kearsarge, Wachusett, and Pack Monadnock.  The week prior to Mt Washington I ran 33:39 at Mt Ascutney which is very similar to a half-way run up Washington.  I figured, based on that result, that a sub 1:15 was a reasonable goal.

I went up to Attitash on Thursday and had a relaxing run with Cathy.  On Friday Rich Bolt and I did the dog & pony show at the Eagle Mountain house.  It seemed to go over well.  We had dinner at the traditional spot, the spaghetti shed, and a late bed time of 11:30 PM.  Race day dawned drizzly and cool, which was a major relief after the hot weather of the past few weeks.  The CMS group plus various other runners (including Anna Pichrtova) did an easy three miles of running on the Great Glen trails.

I started out slowly in the race, with a goal of running with teammate Steve Peterson.  It seemed to me that a lot of people went out too fast as I was passing many in the first few miles.  At two miles I caught Petey and we could see Anna and Melissa Moon a few seconds ahead.  At around three miles we caught Tristan Colangelo who had gone fast, but was now walking.  I motioned for him to tuck in with us and told him "Find a rhythm".  He replied "I had a rhythm", meaning that walking was the way to go for him.  Soon after this I pulled ahead on my own.  Just before halfway, Sean Livingston passed me and said "Stay with me, I'm going to run a fast second half".  I tried, but his pace was a little quick for me.  He went on to finish in the top ten.  I hovered about 10-20 seconds behind the lead women and got a great view of an epic battle.  Moon stayed just off of Pichrtova's shoulder and covered every move she made.  At five miles I heard a runner catching me, at this point the only person to pass me was Livingston, and I was surprised as I was maintaining an even pace.   Tim Livingston, Sean's brother, stormed by on his way to a personal best.  They were the only two to pass me during the race.

At seven miles the ladies threw it into another gear and I slogged on to the finish.  It was exciting to watch their race come down to the final steep pitch.  I beat my goal of 1:15, but my stretch goal of sub-1:10 was just out of reach.   I was happy to finish in the top twenty and be part of the CMS 40+ team which broke the team record.   I made a quick trot to the actual summit then headed down.  Teammates Petey, Mike Woodman, Eric Morse, Larry Sayers and I did a leisurely run down the mountain in 1:12.

Splits: 1 mile 7:09, 2 miles 15:59, 3 miles 25:04, halfway 33:24, 4 miles 34:17, 5 miles 44:21, 6 miles 54:13, 7 miles 1:04:05.
Finish 1:10:37.  Second half 37:13.

**Youngsters on the Mountain – Fred Ross IV and Chris Ross from 1992.**

<u>Exceptional Individuals</u>

The following chart gives the percent of runners under a certain time, thus giving some perspective to the accomplishments listed.

Sub 1:10 men = Top 1.75% (152 men have broken 1:10 of the 19,615 men who have raced)
Sub 1:05 men = Top .41% (32 men have broken 1:05 of the 19,615 men who have raced)
Sub 1:00 men = Top .04% (4 men have broken 1:00 of the 19,615 men who have raced)

Sub 1:30 women = Top 6.36% (122 women have broken 1:30 of the 3,819 women who have raced)
Sub 1:20 women = Top  1.13% (25 women have broken 1:20 of the 3,819 women who have raced)
Sub 1:15 women = Top    .47% (12 women have broken 1:15 of the 3,819 women who have raced)

Bob Teschek – Race director from 1982 to present.  Bob also ran the race five times between 1966 and 1982 with a personal best of 1:15:52 in 1977.

Jock (John) Semple – Many time race director, he resurrected the race in 1961.  He finished in the top ten in his two finishes.  His tenth place finish in 1937, running a 1:24:45 was his personal best.  His top place was eighth in 1937.

Kerry Arsenault – Finished in the top ten six times over a span of seven years from 1994 - 2001.  All of her times were between 1:25:32 and 1:28:44.  She finished seven times under 1:30.

Joan Benoit-Samuelson – Set the Maine state record of 1:16:03 in 1997, and the 40+ age group record.  Joan has the age 40 and age 44 single age records running 1:16:03 and 1:16:47.

Leon Beverly – Has four times that make it into the top ten in various age groups.  He set an age group record in 1990 with his 1:34:26 to top the 60+ age group.  His other times are in the 70+ age group, including the age group record of 1:53:26 set in 1998.  Leon has the single age record for age 64 and age 71 running 1:36:15 and 1:53:26.  He finished thirteen times from 1983 – 2002.

Sumner Brown – Has six times that make it into the top ten in various age groups.  He set an age group record in 1994 when he placed 18 overall in 1:12:27 which topped the 50+ age group.  He has four other times in the top ten for the 50+ age group and in 2004 broke into the 60+ age group with the second fastest time.  Sumner has run the race eighteen times between the years 1984 - 2004.  He currently holds the single age records for age 47, 49, 50, 51, 54, 55, 56, and 59.

Matt Carpenter – Colorado state record of 59:16 in 1999.  Matt has three wins, one second, and fourth in five attempts.  He is one of only two runners with multiple times under one hour, with two.  Matt set the new standard for 40+ runners with his 1:02:12 in 2005, he also has the single age record for age 34 with his 59:16.

Mike Casner – Has finished fourteen times in the top ten from 1984 – 2001.  Mike has the most top ten finishes without a victory.  His personal best is 1:05:48 which he ran in 1998, with his best place being fourth in 84, 91, and 94.  He has fourteen times under 1:10 averaging 1:07:49 and has run the race twenty-one times.

John Cederholm – Won the race in 1973 in his first attempt, and went on to finish five times in the top ten between 1973 and 1978.  At age 60 he set a top ten age group time of 1:31:07.  He has run four times under 1:10.  John has run the race twenty-six times.

Gary Crossan – Has four wins among his six top ten finishes from 1980 - 1986.  He set the course record of 1:01:13 in 1984 and won the race in 1981, 82, 84, and 86.  He has run six times under 1:10 averaging 1:03:01.  Gary has the single age record for age 26 with his 1:01:13 from 1984.

Matt Cull – Has finished nine times in the top ten from 1983-95.  He finished second twice (1983/84).  Matt has a personal best of 1:03:41 and has run under 1:10 eight times averaging 1:06:35.

J'Ne Day-Lucore – Set the Colorado state record in 1992 running 1:11:45.  She is a three-time winner (1992, 93, and 95) and finished six times in the top ten including a fourth place finish at age 40.  She has run three times under 1:20.  J'Ne set the course record in 1992 with a 1:11:45 and ran six times under 1:30.  She has the age 31 record with her 1:11:45 run in 1992.

Peg Donovan – Won the race in 1987 and finished five times in the top ten all five times sub 1:30 averaging 1:19:24.  Peg has the single age record for age 34 with a 1:13:26 run in 1989.  She raced five times from 1986 – 1995 and returned in 2005.

Dave Dunham – Set the Massachusetts state record in 1999 (1:00:37) and the New Hampshire state record in 1993 (1:00:44).  He set the course record in 1988 and won in the closest finish (1.5 seconds) in 1989.  He won the race three times and has fifteen finishes in the top ten (all in the top five).  He ran sub 1:10 fourteen times averaging 1:02:44.  Dave has the single age record for age 24, 25, 29, 35, and 36.  Dave raced sixteen times from 1988 – 2005, missing only 1997 and 2004.

Louisa Dunlap – Set age group records in 1991, 1992, and 1993 in winning the 50+ age group.  She also placed in the top ten in the 60+ age group in 2004.  Louisa has the single age record for age 52 running a 1:40:46 in 1993.  She has finished the race fifteen consecutive times from 1991 – 2005.

Rudy Fahl – Oldest finisher (88) at Mt Washington with his 3:18:12 in 1986.  He set the record for 85+ in consecutive years from 1983-1985 with his top time being 3:09:51 Rudy has the single age records for age 86, 87, and 88.

Hildy Fosse – Set an age group record in 1990 at age 61 with a 1:59:45, breaking her own 1989 record.  In 1999 at age 70 she again set an age group record running 2:14:02.  She has six times in top ten age group listings.  She set the 50+ age group record in 1987.  Hildy has run the race twenty-one times from 1985 - 2005.  She has the single age records for age 67, 68, 71, 74, and 75.

Craig Fram – Won the race in 1997.  He set the course record for 40+ in 2001 and again in 2003.  He has finished six times in the top ten; his worst finish is fourth place in 1996.  He has won more money than any other runner, taking home just under $10,000 racing up Mt Washington.  He has run five times under 1:10 averaging 1:04:05.  Craig ties Keith Woodward as the oldest runner to break 1:10 when he ran 1:03:27 in 2003 at age 44.  His 2001 40+ age group record broke Fred Norris's longstanding time from 1962 of 1:04:57.  Craig has the single age records for age 42 and age 44.

Derek Froude – Two-time winner, first runner to break one hour.  He set the course record in 1990 with his 59:17.  Derek raced three times from 1990-1992 and his only defeat was a second place finish in 1992.

Mike Gallagher – Four consecutive wins from 1968 to 1971.  Mike ran a personal best of 1:06:13.

Jacqueline Gareau – Won the race three times, and was a runner-up at age 47.  She set the 40+ record in 1994 with a 1:16:15.  She has five times that rank in the top ten for various age groups and has the Canadian record of 1:13:13.  Jacqueline finished in the top 10 six times including three wins, two of which were after age 40.  She was the overall champion in 1989, 94, and 1996.  She set a course record in 1989 in the closest women's victory (13 seconds).   She has run six times under 1:30 averaging 1:17:35.  She set a new standard for the 50+ age group running a 1:27:53 in 2005.  Jacqueline has the single age records for age 36, 41, 43, 47, and 52.

Simon Gutierrez – Set the New Mexico state record in 1999 running 1:01:38.  Simon has six top ten finishes including three wins in 2002, 2003, and 2005.  Simon has five times under 1:10 averaging 1:03:03.  He has the single age record for age 38 with his 1:04:17.

Bob Hodge – Seven-time winner of the race.  He has the second fastest time for a runner under the age of 20 with his 1:10 from 1975.  His other top ten age group time was run in 1998 when he ran 1:09:54 at age 42.  Has finished thirteen times in the top ten from 1975 – 1993.  Bob finished second (1:03:01) in 1989 in the narrowest margin, losing by one second.  He set the course record in 1977, 78, 79, and tied it in 1987.  Bob has run thirteen times under 1:10.  His age group record for under age 20 lasted for 12 years.  He has run the race twenty times from 1974 - 2001.  He holds the single age record for age 19, 20, 22, and 23.

Kathy Hodgdon – Three consecutive wins from 1980 to 1982.  All three times were under 1:30 averaging 1:24:07.  Kathy holds the single age record for ages 22 and 23 with her 1:22:57 and 1:22:41 in 1981/82.

Kathy Kanes – Has the S. Carolina state record in 1:19:46, which is 26 minutes faster than the men's record.

Frances Kellogg – Has run four times that rank in the top ten 70+ age group.  She set the age group record with a 3:00:50 in 1989 then lowered it the next two years to finish with a 2:29:49 at age 72 in 1991.  Frances has the single age record for age 73 with a 2:36:42 run in 1993.

Howard Kellogg – Has three age group top ten times.  He set an age group record in 1988 at age 72 with a 1:59:29.  Howard set another age group record in 1996 at age 80 running a 2:36:23.  He has the single age record for age 75 and 79, with times of 2:01:51 and 2:27:17.

Daniel Kihara – Four wins in five attempts from 1996 to 2002.  His only loss was a sixth place finish in the weather-shortened race in 2002.  All of his times were between 58:21 and 1:00:06.  Daniel has the single age records for age 28, 32, and 33.  He is the only runner in the history of the race with three sub-one hour finishes.

Catherine Lifschultz – Seven times finishing in the top ten including a fourth in 1992 running 1:21:03.  Ran eleven times under 1:30.  Catherine has run the race thirteen times from 1990 - 2004.

Kiersten Lippmann – Has the state record for Alaska.  Set the under age twenty record in 1999 running a 1:28:42.  She has finished the race five times from 1999 – 2003.

Sean Livingston – Ran two of the fastest times by a runner under the age of 20.  Set the age group record in 1987 placing thirteenth overall in 1:09:14.  Set the state record for Rhode Island in 2005 running a 1:07:13.  Sean has run the race eleven times from 1986 - 2005.  He has the single age record for age 18.

Chris Maisto – Has three wins and a second in four attempts, all of which were under 1:20.  Won in 1985, 86, and 91.  Set a course record in 1985 and 1991, and has a personal best of 1:12:15.  Chris has the single age record for age 25.

Carlton Mendell – Has four top ten age group times.  He ran an age group record in 1992 at age 70, running a 1:54:42.   Carlton had top ten times in the 80+ age group in 2003, 2004, and 2005.  He has a consecutive streak of finishing for 24 years from 1982 through 2005.  He set a 60+ age group record in 1992 that was not beaten until 2000.  His 70+ record in 1992 was not broken until 1998.   Carlton has the single age records for age 70, 76, 77, 78, 81, and age 82.

Ellenora Mendonca – Three consecutive wins from 1976-1978.  She set the course record twice with her 1:30:05 in 1977 and her 1:28:39 in 1978.

Eric Morse – Set the Vermont state record in 1999 running a 1:01:09.   He has finished in the top ten twelve times from 1993 to 2005. He has more top five finishes than anyone without winning (nine).  Eric has finished in second place three times and run under 1:10 eleven times averaging 1:04:26.  Eric has finished twelve times from 1993 – 2005, missing only 2003.  In 2005 he ran the fifth fastest time ever for a 40+ runner with his sixth place overall 1:05:26.

Carrie Parsi – Has run seven times that place in the top ten in various age groups.  She set the age group record in 1996 at age 60 running a 1:41:16.  Her time at age sixty ranks in the top ten for 50+ age group.  Carrie has the single age records for age 54, 55, 56, 57, 58, 59, and 60.  She has finished the race eleven times from 1991 – 2005.

Julie Peterson – Has two times in the top ten for the 40+ age group.  She finished third overall at age forty.  Julie set the Massachusetts state record in 1991 with a 1:14:19.  She has finished seven times in the top ten including three seconds and four thirds.  All of her eight finishes were with times under 1:30.  She has more finishes in the top ten (eight) without a win than anyone.  Julie has the single age record for age 37 and 39.

Stephen Peterson – Ran eight times under 1:10 for an average of 1:09:03 and has a personal best of 1:08:01.  He has finished three times in the top ten.  Steve once ran out of his shoes and finished the race with just socks on his feet.  He has eighteen  consecutive finishes from 1988 – 2005.

Anna Pichrtova – Had four wins in four consecutive attempts (2001-2004), all winning times between 1:12:19 and 1:13:48.  In 2005 she set a single age record (32) and the third fastest time ever run with her second place finish of 1:10:26.

Bill & Sarah Raitter – The only married couple to hold the men's and women's state records (Oregon).  They also have one of the top times ever run by a married couple, combining for a 2:34:33.  They ran 1:06:56 and 1:27:37 respectively in 2004.

Barbara Remmers – Has the New York state record set in 1999 with a 1:13:52, and the Virginia state record in 2004 with a 1:46:34.  She won the race in 1999 after training on a treadmill at 11.5%.  Barbara has the single age record for age 35 with a 1:35:52 run in 1999.  She has finished the race five times from 1998 – 2004.

Barbara Robinson – Has five times in the top ten for the 60+ and 70+ age group.  Set the age group record with a 2:00:42 at age 70.  Her time at age 70 ranks in the top ten for 60+ age group.  Barbara has the single age records for age 65, 69, 70, and 71.

Martha Rockwell – Martha is a former winner (1979) and set age group record at age 50 in 1994.  She set the Vermont state record of 1:19:14 in 1979 winning the race in a course record time.  She has run three sub 1:30's.  Set the 40+ age group record in 1986 and 1987 (1:28:39/1:25:57), which was not broken until 1994.

Don Ross – Has five times in the top ten for the 60+ and 70+ age group.  Don has the single age records for age 62, 63, 68, 69, and age 73.  He has thirteen finishes from 1991 – 2004.

Fred Ross – Tied with Keith Woodward for the most finishes at Mt Washington, with 29 confirmed finishes between 1976 and 2005.

**Fred Ross from 1979**

Louise Rossetti – Has six times in the top ten for the 70+ and 80+ age groups.  She set the age group record with a 2:48:52 at age 81 in 2003.  Her times at age 81 and 82 rank in the top 10 for 70+ age group.  Louise has the single age records for age 76, 77, 78, 79, 81, and age 82.

**Louise Rossetti from 2003**

Donna Smyers – Seven times in the top ten including two fifths.  She has run ten times under 1:30.  Donna has eleven finishes from 1993 – 2005, and also holds one of the top ten times for the 40+ age group.

Rebecca Stockdale-Woolley – Has five times in the top ten for the 40+ and 50+ age groups.  She set the 50+ age group record when she finished in twelfth place with a 1:30:27 in 2001.  She has run three times under 1:30 and is the oldest sub 1:30 runner with a 1:29:37 in 2000 at age 49.  Rebecca has the single age records for age 48, 49, 50, 53, and age 54.

Leslie Thompson – Has finished in the top ten four times, including a second place finish in 1986.  She finished in fifth place at age 16.  Leslie has run three times under 1:30 and set a course record for the under 20 age group that lasted for 19 years.  Leslie has the single age record for age 16 with her 1:29:57 run in 1980, as well as the single age record for age 19 and 20.

Dan Verrington – Has finished seven times in the top ten and has one age group top ten with his 1:09:14 at age 40.  He has a personal best of 1:05:43 set in 1996 and his best finish was fourth in 1997.  Dan has run nine times under 1:10 for an average of 1:08:02.  Dan has thirteen finishes from 1988 – 2005.

**Dan Verrington on the final climb**

Keith Woodward – Won the race in 1983, with a 1:06:38.  He has seven times in the top ten for the 40+ and 50+ age group.   His 1:15:08 run in 2003 is the second fastest for the 50+ age group.  He finished fifteen times in the top ten overall from 1973 through 1991.  Keith ties Craig Fram as the oldest runner to run under 1:10 with his 1:09:05 in 1995.   He has run the race 29 times between 1973 and 2005 tying Fred Ross with the most finishes.  Keith has the single age records for age 39, 43, 48, 52, and age 53.  His personal best was a 1:03:06 in 1985 when he finished second.

**Boston Athletic Association (BAA)** – Topped the Open team category in 1961, 62, 66, 67, 68, 70, 81, 82, and 1983. Had the lowest score for five finishers with 17 points (1,2,3,5,6 places). Set the course record in 1961 that stood for 16 years then set it again in 1981 with a record that lasted another 12 years. They have three times under six hours (average per person under 1:12). The BAA women won the team title in 1992 and 1997.

**Cambridge Sports Union (CSU)** – Women's team won the title in 1978, 79, 84, 86, 94, 95, 96. They set the course record in 1978. The CSU women's 40+ team won the title in 1999, and 2003. The win in 1999 was a course record. The CSU men's 50+ team set a course record in winning the title in 2003.

**Central Massachusetts Striders (CMS)** – First place in the Open team title from 1992 through 2005. The teams fourteen wins are the most any team has won. They set the course record in 1995, 1996, 1999, and 2005. CMS has the top seven times run, and twelve of the top sixteen times. The CMS women won the team title in 1993, 98, 99, 00, 01, 02, 03, 04 and have six of the top ten times. The CMS women's 40+ won the team title in 1998 in a course record. The men's 40+ team set a new course record in 2005 with the first ever sub six hour effort.

**Granite State Racing Team (GSRT)** – Won the women's team title in 1986 and 1987. The course record set in 1987 is still standing.

**Greater Lowell Road Runners (GLRR)** – Won the Open team title in 1988, 89, 90, and 1991. They have six times under six hours. The GLRR women's teams were the champions in 1989 and 1990.

**North Country Athletic Club (NCAC)** – Won the Open team title in 1976, 77, and 1978. Set the course record in 1977.

**Winners Circle Running Club (WCRC)** – The women's 40+ team won in 1995 in a course record, and won again in 1996. The women's 50+ team won in 2003 in a course record. The men's 40+ team won in a course record in 1995 and won again in 1996 and 1999. The men's 50+ team won in a course record in 1999.

## Fast Married couples (running in the same year)

Magdalena Thorsell and Simon Gutierrez ran 1:10:09/1:03:23 in 1998 for a time of 2:13:32.
Joe Lemay and Ellen McCurtin ran 1:03:04 and 1:28:06 in 1999 to combine for a time of 2:31:10.
Kathy and Steve Podgajny ran 1:22:57 and 1:08:52 in 1981 to combine for a time of 2:31:49.
Bill and Sarah Raitter ran 1:06:56 and 1:27:37 in 2004 to combine for a time of 2:34:33.
Deb and Russell Bollig ran 1:24:57 and 1:12:08 in 1999 to combine for a time of 2:37:05.
Mike and Cathy O'Brien ran 1:13:54 and 1:23:29 in 2004 to combine for a time of 2:37:23.
Terrance and Sue McNatt ran 1:11:51 and 1:30:16 in 1995 to combine for a time of 2:42:07.

# Mt Washington Winners 1936 to 2005

| Race | Year | Winner | Age | State | Time | |
|---|---|---|---|---|---|---|
| 1 | 1936 | Francis Darrah | | NH | 1:15:57 | CR |
| 2 | 1937 | Paul Donato | 21 | MA | 1:16:25 | |
| 3 | 1938 | Francis Darrah | | NH | 1:15:28 | CR |
| 4 | 1961 | John J Kelley | 30 | CT | 1:08:54 | CR |
| 5 | 1962 | Fred Norris | 40 | MA | 1:04:57 | CR |
| 6 | 1966 | Leo Carroll | | ENG | 1:07:31 | |
| 7 | 1967 | Angus Wooten | 32 | CT | 1:12:43 | |
| 8 | 1968 | Mike Gallagher | 26 | VT | 1:06:03 | |
| 9 | 1969 | Mike Gallagher | 27 | VT | 1:06:44 | |
| 10 | 1970 | Mike Gallagher | 28 | VT | 1:09:06 | |
| 11 | 1971 | Mike Gallagher | 29 | VT | 1:07:27 | |
| 12 | 1972 | Roland Cormier | 32 | MA | 1:09:16 | |
| | | Charlotte Lettis | 21 | | 1:40:08 | CR |
| 13 | 1973 | John Cederholm | 30 | MA | 1:08:26 | |
| | | Lise Demers | | CAN | 1:51:51 | |
| 14 | 1974 | James Capezzuto | 20 | MA | 1:07:58 | |
| 15 | 1975 | Gary Johnson | 24 | VT | 1:06:01 | |
| | | Hester Sargent | | MA | 1:31:13 | CR |
| 16 | 1976 | Bob Hodge | 20 | MA | 1:05:31 | |
| | | Ellenora Mendonca | 28 | MA | 1:35:05 | |
| 17 | 1977 | Bob Hodge | 21 | MA | 1:04:44 | CR |
| | | Ellen Mendonca | 29 | MA | 1:30:05 | CR |
| 18 | 1978 | Bob Hodge | 22 | MA | 1:04:13 | CR |
| | | Ellen Mendonca | 30 | MA | 1:28:39 | CR |
| 19 | 1979 | Bob Hodge | 23 | MA | 1:02:08 | CR |
| | | Martha Rockwell | 35 | VT | 1:19:14 | CR |
| 20 | 1980 | Bob Hodge | 24 | MA | 1:04:29 | |
| | | Cathy Hodgdon | 21 | NH | 1:26:44 | |
| 21 | 1981 | Gary Crossan | 23 | NH | 1:02:51 | |
| | | Cathy Hodgdon | 22 | NH | 1:22:57 | |
| 22 | 1982 | Gary Crossan | 24 | NH | 1:01:41 | CR |
| | | Cathy Hodgdon | 23 | NH | 1:22:41 | |
| 23 | 1983 | Keith Woodward | 32 | VT | 1:06:39 | |
| | | Anna Sonnerup | 21 | NH | 1:22:19 | |
| 24 | 1984 | Gary Crossan | 26 | NH | 1:01:14 | CR |
| | | Betsey Haydock | 28 | MA | 1:20:46 | |
| 25 | 1985 | Bob Hodge | 29 | MA | 1:01:32 | |
| | | Chris Maisto | 25 | NJ | 1:14:45 | CR |

| Race | Year | Winner | Age | State | Time | |
|---|---|---|---|---|---|---|
| 26 | 1986 | Gary Crossan | 28 | NH | 1:02:10 | |
| | | Chris Maisto | 26 | NJ | 1:19:26 | |
| 27 | 1987 | Bob Hodge | 31 | MA | 1:01:14 | |
| | | Peg Donovan | 32 | NH | 1:15:05 | |
| 28 | 1988 | Dave Dunham | 24 | NH | 1:00:50 | CR |
| | | Janine Aiello | 28 | CA | 1:20:48 | |
| 29 | 1989 | Dave Dunham | 25 | NH | 1:02:10 | |
| | | Jacqueline Gareau | 36 | CAN | 1:13:14 | CR |
| 30 | 1990 | Derek Froude | 31 | NZL | 59:17.0 | CR |
| | | Lynn Brown | 29 | CO | 1:19:57 | |
| 31 | 1991 | Derek Froude | 32 | NZL | 1:00:36 | |
| | | Chris Maisto | 31 | NJ | 1:12:15 | CR |
| 32 | 1992 | Matt Carpenter | 27 | CO | 1:00:43 | |
| | | J'ne Day-Lucore | 31 | CO | 1:11:46 | CR |
| 33 | 1993 | Matt Carpenter | 28 | CO | 59:49.1 | |
| | | J'ne Day-Lucore | 32 | CO | 1:13:00 | |
| 34 | 1994 | Dave Dunham | 30 | NH | 1:03:22 | |
| | | Jacqueline Gareau | 41 | CAN | 1:16:16 | |
| 35 | 1995 | Gideon Mutisya | 28 | KEN | 1:01:42 | |
| | | J'ne Day-Lucore | 34 | CO | 1:17:29 | |
| 36 | 1996 | Daniel Kihara | 28 | KEN | 0:58:21 | CR |
| | | Jacqueline Gareau | 43 | CAN | 1:17:14 | |
| 37 | 1997 | Craig Fram | 38 | NH | 1:04:48 | |
| | | Cathy O'Brien | 29 | NH | 1:12:24 | |
| 38 | 1998 | Matt Carpenter | 33 | CO | 1:00:24 | |
| | | Magdalena Thorsell | 33 | NM | 1:10:09 | CR |
| 39 | 1999 | Daniel Kihara | 31 | KEN | 0:59:03 | |
| | | Barbara Remmers | 35 | NY | 1:13:52 | |
| 40 | 2000 | Daniel Kihara | 32 | KEN | 0:59:24 | |
| | | Alice Muriithi | 26 | KEN | 1:17:26 | |
| 41 | 2001 | Daniel Kihara | 33 | KEN | 1:00:06 | |
| | | Anna Pichrtova | 27 | CZE | 1:13:48 | |
| 42 | 2002 | Simon Gutierrez | 36 | NM | 0:28:02 | |
| | | Anna Pichrtova | 28 | CZE | 0:32:32 | |
| 43 | 2003 | Simon Gutierrez | 37 | NM | 1:02:54 | |
| | | Anna Pichrtova | 29 | CZE | 1:12:50 | |
| 44 | 2004 | Jonathan Wyatt | 31 | NZL | 0:56:41 | CR |
| | | Anna Pichrtova | 30 | CZE | 1:12:19 | |
| 45 | 2005 | Simon Gutierrez | 39 | NM | 1:00:54 | |
| | | Melissa Moon | 35 | NZL | 1:10:11 | |

## Course record progression:

### Men

| Year | Name | Age | State | Time |
|------|------|-----|-------|------|
| 1936 | Francis Darrah | | NH | 1:15:57 |
| 1938 | Francis Darrah | | NH | 1:15:28 |
| 1961 | John J Kelley | 30 | CT | 1:08:54 |
| 1962 | Fred Norris | 40 | MA | 1:04:57 |
| 1977 | Bob Hodge | 21 | MA | 1:04:44 |
| 1978 | Bob Hodge | 22 | MA | 1:04:13 |
| 1979 | Bob Hodge | 23 | MA | 1:02:08 |
| 1982 | Gary Crossan | 24 | NH | 1:01:41 |
| 1984 | Gary Crossan | 26 | NH | 1:01:14 |
| 1988 | Dave Dunham | 24 | NH | 1:00:50 |
| 1990 | Derek Froude | 31 | NZL | 59:17.0 |
| 1996 | Daniel Kihara | 28 | KEN | 0:58:21 |
| 2004 | Jonathan Wyatt | 31 | NZL | 0:56:41 |

### Women

| Year | Name | Age | State | Time |
|------|------|-----|-------|------|
| 1972 | Charlotte Lettis | 21 | | 1:40:08 |
| 1975 | Hester Sargent | | MA | 1:31:13 |
| 1977 | Ellen Mendonca | 29 | MA | 1:30:05 |
| 1978 | Ellen Mendonca | 30 | MA | 1:28:39 |
| 1979 | Martha Rockwell | 35 | VT | 1:19:14 |
| 1985 | Chris Maisto | 25 | NJ | 1:14:45 |
| 1989 | Jacqueline Gareau | 36 | CAN | 1:13:14 |
| 1991 | Chris Maisto | 31 | NJ | 1:12:15 |
| 1992 | J'ne Day-Lucore | 31 | CO | 1:11:46 |
| 1998 | Magdalena Thorsell | 33 | NM | 1:10:09 |

Josh Ferenc collapses at the finish in 2004

Team record progression:

| Category | Year | Club | Time |
|---|---|---|---|
| Male Open | | | |
| 1961 | BAA | 6:02:47 | |
| 1977 | NCAC | 5:59:28 | |
| 1979 | GBTC | 5:35:50 | |
| 1981 | BAA | 5:31:07 | |
| 1993 | CMS | 5:30:34 | |
| 1995 | CMS | 5:25:57 | |
| 1996 | CMS | 5:24:15 | |
| 1999 | CMS | 5:20:44 | |
| 2005 | CMS | 5:17:59 | |
| | | | |
| Male 40+ | | | |
| 1995 | WCRC | 6:59:35 | |
| 1996 | WCRC | 6:47:01 | |
| 1999 | WCRC | 6:46:04 | |
| 2004 | Coastal | 6:15:27 | |
| 2005 | CMS | 5:59:04 | |
| | | | |
| Male 50+ | | | |
| 1999 | WCRC | 8:18:40 | |
| 2003 | CSU | 7:39:51 | |
| 2004 | MMM | 7:25:00 | |
| | | | |
| Women Open | | | |
| 1977 | Seacoast | 5:26:16 | |
| 1978 | CSU | 4:54:21 | |
| 1983 | DOC | 4:23:00 | |
| 1987 | GSRT | 4:00:33 | |
| | | | |
| Women 40+ | | | |
| 1992 | MTC | 5:22:21 | |
| 1993 | WMM | 5:17:27 | |
| 1995 | WCRC | 5:07:22 | |
| 1996 | WCRC | 5:03:39 | |
| 1998 | CMS | 4:56:57 | |
| 1999 | CSU | 4:37:51 | |
| 2003 | CSU | 4:30:23 | |
| 2005 | MMM | 4:26:43 | |
| | | | |
| Women 50+ | | | |
| 1999 | LAC | 5:33:00 | |
| 2003 | WCRC | 5:22:18 | |

161

<u>State and Country Records</u>

| State | Men Name | Year | Time | Women Name | Year | Time |
|---|---|---|---|---|---|---|
| AK | Don Zimmerman | 2005 | 1:29:41 | Kiersten Lippmann | 2003 | 1:33:10 |
| AL | Stanley Bramlett | 1997 | 1:48:13 | None | | |
| AR | None | | | Laura Reardon | 2005 | 2:01:49 |
| AZ | Rick Stuart | 1993 | 1:09:14 | Jean Watson | 2001 | 1:43:29 |
| CA | Matt Ebiner | 1987 | 1:05:03 | Janine Aiello | 1988 | 1:20:48 |
| CO | Matt Carpenter | 1999 | :59:16 | J'ne Day-Lucore | 1992 | 1:11:45 |
| CT | Joe Lemay | 1999 | 1:03:04 | Donna Smyers | 1993 | 1:22:37 |
| DE | William Kauffman | 2000 | 1:26:13 | None | | |
| FL | Moises Sztylerman | 1990 | 1:24:55 | Tatiana Titova | 1999 | 1:14:57 |
| GA | Harold Lambert | 1997 | 1:21:39 | None | | |
| HI | Gary Theriault | 1995 | 1:33:46 | None | | |
| IA | None | | | Tracy Codel | 2005 | 1:42:48 |
| ID | Tom Borschel | 1998 | 1:05:42 | Gail Eberle | 1996 | 1:30:00 |
| IL | Robert Becker | 1986 | 1:29:48 | Lucy Whittaker | 2004 | 1:37:26 |
| IN | John Fiola | 1985 | 1:12:18 | None | | |
| IO | None | | | None | | |
| KS | Michael Mayernik | 1993 | 1:50:06 | Dee Landau | 2005 | 2:09:59 |
| KY | Jerry Bricking | 2000 | 1:26:54 | None | | |
| LA | Dana Melvin | 2001 | 1:49:06 | None | | |
| MA | Dave Dunham | 1999 | 1:00:37 | Julie Peterson | 1991 | 1:14:19 |
| MD | Joseph Daly | 1990 | 1:10:37 | Beth Darnall | 2004 | 1:24:54 |
| ME | Robert Pierce | 1995 | 1:06:44 | Joan Benoit-Samuelson | 1997 | 1:16:03 |
| MI | Mark Werner | 2004 | 1:06:02 | Ann Remmers | 2000 | 1:36:01 |
| MN | Jay Smith | 1986 | 1:09:34 | Amber Hofstad | 1999 | 1:36:39 |
| MO | John Douglass | 1991 | 1:24:01 | Tanya Schwindt | 1998 | 1:52:23 |
| MS | David Seiler | 2005 | 2:18:27 | None | | |
| MT | Kyle Klicker | 1997 | 1:23:17 | Laura Andersen | 2005 | 1:51:14 |
| NB | Christopher Breen | 2005 | 1:46:56 | None | | |
| NC | Chad Newton | 2005 | 1:06:38 | Linda Roper | 1991 | 1:40:16 |
| ND | None | | ND | None | | |
| NH | Dave Dunham | 1993 | 1:00:44 | Cathy O'Brien | 1997 | 1:12:24 |
| NJ | Michael Danahy | 2003 | 1:07:52 | Chris Maisto | 1991 | 1:12:15 |
| NM | Simon Gutierrez | 1999 | 1:01:38 | Magdalena Thorsell | 1998 | 1:10:09 |
| NV | Eward Klotz | 1992 | 1:37:25 | None | | |
| NY | Eric Blake | 2005 | 1:01:07 | Barbara Remmers | 1999 | 1:13:52 |
| OH | Jeff Day | 2003 | 1:08:16 | Chari Walsh | 2005 | 1:23:23 |
| OK | Steve Lee | 2003 | 1:38:22 | None | | |
| OR | Bill Raitter | 2004 | 1:06:56 | Sarah Raitter | 2004 | 1:27:37 |
| PA | Peter Heesen | 1990 | 1:07:24 | Patricia Shiffert | 1987 | 1:24:21 |
| RI | Sean Livingston | 2005 | 1:07:13 | Kim Marie Goff | 1992 | 1:24:03 |
| SC | John Glasscock | 1988 | 1:46:28 | Kathy Kanes | 1995 | 1:19:46 |

| | Men | | | | Women | | |
|---|---|---|---|---|---|---|---|
| SD | None | | | | None | | |
| TN | John Cobb | 1994 | 1:18:06 | | Flora Cobb | 1994 | 1:46:17 |
| TX | Rich Yanacek | 1998 | 1:18:56 | | None | | |
| UT | Karl Meltzer Jr. | 1994 | 1:08:45 | | None | | |
| VA | Michael Wardian | 2004 | 1:08:46 | | Barbara Remmers | 2004 | 1:46:34 |
| VT | Eric Morse | 1999 | 1:01:09 | | Martha Rockwell | 1979 | 1:19:14 |
| WA | Henry Wigglesworth | 2005 | 1:15:07 | | Renee Riedel | 1996 | 1:29:59 |
| WI | Don Smith | 1999 | 1:37:19 | | None | | |
| WV | Eric O'Brien | 1990 | 1:52:38 | | Karen Fuegi | 1986 | 1:59:46 |
| WY | Erich Wilbrecht | 1990 | 1:06:26 | | Jo Gathercole | 1991 | 1:24:23 |

| | Men | | | | Women | | |
|---|---|---|---|---|---|---|---|
| Country | Name | Year | Time | | Country | Name | Year | Time |
| BMU | Jeremy Ball | 1993 | 1:19:30 | | BMU | None | | |
| CAN | Joel St-Louis | 1997 | 1:09:37 | | CAN | Jacqueline Gareau | 1989 | 1:13:13 |
| COL | Domingo Tibaduiza | 1987 | 1:02:52 | | COL | None | | |
| CZE | None | | | | CZE | Anna Pichrtova | 2005 | 1:10:26 |
| DEU | Jan Pruszak | 2003 | 1:22:22 | | DEU | None | | |
| FRA | Thierry Icart | 1998 | 1:04:40 | | FRA | None | | |
| GBR | Gerhard Huber | 2003 | 1:57:46 | | GBR | None | | |
| KEN | Daniel Kihara | 1996 | 0:58:21 | | KEN | Alice Muriithi | 2000 | 1:17:26 |
| NZL | Jonathan Wyatt | 2004 | 0:56:41 | | NZL | Melissa Moon | 2005 | 1:10:11 |
| POL | Tomasz Gnabel | 1992 | 1:06:02 | | POL | None | | |
| PRI | German Fernandez | 2001 | 1:28:36 | | PRI | None | | |
| SCO | Ian Parlin | 2004 | 1:37:59 | | SCO | None | | |
| SWE | Brian Reinhold | 1990 | 1:05:36 | | SWE | None | | |
| TUN | Neji Makhlouf | 1995 | 1:02:35 | | TUN | None | | |

Rudy Fahl #61 (the oldest finisher at age 88), with Fred III, Fred IV, and Christopher Ross (the youngest finisher at age 8). Circa 1986

## Single Age Records

Note: Bolded names are five year age group records.  Course records are underlined.

| Age | Women Name | Time | Year | Age | Men Name | Time | Year |
|---|---|---|---|---|---|---|---|
| | | | | 8 | Christopher Ross | 2:32:18 | 1992 |
| | | | | 9 | Christopher Ross | 2:18:18 | 1993 |
| | | | | 10 | Brian Cooper | 1:52:10 | 1990 |
| | | | | 11 | Peter Broomhall | 1:30:16 | 1990 |
| 12 | Jennifer Paradis | 2:13:10 | 2004 | 12 | Peter Broomhall | 1:39:12 | 1991 |
| 13 | Jennifer Paradis | 2:21:13 | 2005 | 13 | Daniel Kerwin Jr. | 1:34:17 | 1985 |
| 14 | Elizabeth Boucher | 1:50:02 | 2001 | 14 | Seth Williams | 1:18:33 | 1992 |
| 15 | Morgan Smyth | 1:56:25 | 2001 | 15 | Karl Meltzer | 1:19:40 | 1983 |
| 16 | Leslie Thompson | 1:29:57 | 1980 | 16 | Karl Meltzer | 1:12:29 | 1984 |
| 17 | Gretchen Walthers | 1:32:47 | 1988 | 17 | Seth Williams | 1:11:10 | 1995 |
| **18** | **Evelyn Dong** | **1:26:51** | **2003** | **18** | **Sean Livingston** | **1:09:14** | **1987** |
| 19 | Leslie Thompson | 1:33:18 | 1983 | 19 | Bob Hodge | 1:10:19 | 1975 |
| 20 | Leslie Thompson | 1:26:49 | 1984 | 20 | Bob Hodge | 1:05:31 | 1976 |
| 21 | Anna Sonnerup | 1:22:19 | 1983 | 21 | Pete Pfitzinger | 1:04:12 | 1979 |
| 22 | Cathy Hodgdon | 1:22:57 | 1981 | 22 | Bob Hodge | 1:04:13 | 1978 |
| **23** | **Cathy Hodgdon** | **1:22:41** | **1982** | 23 | Bob Hodge | 1:02:08 | 1979 |
| 24 | Naoke Ishibe | 1:27:22 | 1993 | **24** | **Dave Dunham** | **1:00:50** | **1988** |
| 25 | Chris Maisto | 1:14:45 | 1985 | 25 | Dave Dunham | 1:02:59 | 1989 |
| 26 | Alice Muriithi | 1:17:26 | 2000 | 26 | Eric Blake | 1:01:07 | 2005 |
| 27 | Anna Pichrtova | 1:13:48 | 2001 | 27 | Joseph Kibor | 1:00:04 | 2000 |
| 28 | Pam Moore | 1:20:22 | 1992 | **28** | **Daniel Kihara** | **0:58:21** | **1996** |
| **29** | **Cathy O'Brien** | **1:12:24** | **1997** | 29 | Dave Dunham | 1:00:44 | 1993 |
| 30 | Anna Pichrtova | 1:12:50 | 2003 | 30 | Paul Low | 1:03:12 | 2004 |
| 31 | J'ne Day-Lucore | 1:11:45 | 1992 | <u>31</u> | <u>Jonathan Wyatt</u> | <u>0:56:41</u> | <u>2004</u> |
| 32 | Anna Pichrtova | 1:10:26 | 2005 | 32 | Daniel Kihara | 0:59:24 | 2000 |
| <u>**33**</u> | <u>**Magdalena Thorsell**</u> | <u>**1:10:09**</u> | <u>**1998**</u> | 33 | Daniel Kihara | 1:00:06 | 2001 |
| 34 | Peg Donovan | 1:13:26 | 1989 | 34 | Matt Carpenter | 0:59:16 | 1999 |
| **35** | **Melissa Moon** | **1:10:11** | **2005** | **35** | **Dave Dunham** | **1:00:37** | **1999** |
| 36 | Jacqueline Gareau | 1:13:13 | 1989 | 36 | Dave Dunham | 1:02:48 | 2000 |
| 37 | Julie Peterson | 1:20:07 | 1997 | 37 | Domingo Tibaduiza | 1:02:52 | 1987 |
| 38 | Cathy Pearce | 1:20:02 | 2001 | 38 | Simon Gutierrez | 1:04:17 | 2004 |
| 39 | Julie Peterson | 1:16:36 | 1999 | 39 | Simon Gutierrez | 1:00:54 | 2005 |
| **40** | **Joan Benoit-Samuelson** | **1:16:03** | **1997** | **40** | **Matt Carpenter** | **1:02:12** | **2005** |
| 41 | Jacqueline Gareau | 1:16:15 | 1994 | 41 | Chuck Smead | 1:05:20 | 1993 |
| 42 | Cathy Pearce | 1:20:15 | 2005 | 42 | Craig Fram | 1:04:29 | 2001 |
| 43 | Jacqueline Gareau | 1:17:14 | 1996 | 43 | Keith Woodward | 1:10:03 | 1994 |
| 44 | Joan Samuelson | 1:16:47 | 2001 | 44 | Craig Fram | 1:03:27 | 2003 |
| 45 | Kari Distefano | 1:23:05 | 2004 | **45** | **Guy Stearns** | **1:10:29** | **2004** |
| 46 | Dorothy Helling | 1:28:42 | 1996 | 46 | Len Hall | 1:11:40 | 1999 |
| **47** | **Jacqueline Gareau** | **1:18:43** | **2000** | 47 | Sumner Brown | 1:12:37 | 1991 |

| Age | Name | Time | Year | Age | Name | Time | Year |
| --- | --- | --- | --- | --- | --- | --- | --- |
| 48 | Rebecca Stockdale-Wooley | 1:23:54 | 1999 | 48 | Brad Lebo | 1:14:43 | 2005 |
| 49 | Rebecca Stockdale-Wooley | 1:29:37 | 2000 | 49 | Sumner Brown | 1:11:54 | 1993 |
| 50 | Rebecca Stockdale-Wooley | 1:30:27 | 2001 | **50** | **Sumner Brown** | **1:12:37** | **1994** |
| 51 | Missy Foote | 1:40:39 | 2004 | 51 | Sumner Brown | 1:13:56 | 1995 |
| **52** | **Jacqueline Gareau** | **1:27:08** | **2005** | 52 | Keith Woodward | 1:15:08 | 2003 |
| 53 | Rebecca Stockdale-Wooley | 1:31:18 | 2004 | 53 | Keith Woodward | 1:17:17 | 2004 |
| 54 | Rebecca Stockdale-Wooley | 1:33:13 | 2005 | 54 | Sumner Brown | 1:17:29 | 1998 |
| 55 | Carrie Parsi | 1:43:14 | 1994 | **55** | **Sumner Brown** | **1:17:59** | **1999** |
| 56 | Carrie Parsi | 1:42:33 | 1995 | 56 | Sumner Brown | 1:18:33 | 2000 |
| **57** | **Carrie Parsi** | **1:40:43** | **1996** | 57 | Robert Shelton | 1:27:58 | 1987 |
| 58 | Carrie Parsi | 1:45:22 | 1997 | 58 | Robert Shelton | 1:27:15 | 1988 |
| 59 | Carrie Parsi | 1:48:49 | 1998 | 59 | Sumner Brown | 1:24:07 | 2003 |
| **60** | **Carrie Parsi** | **1:41:16** | **1999** | **60** | **John Pelton** | **1:24:32** | **1999** |
| 61 | Maggie Solomon | 1:51:35 | 1995 | 61 | Jerry Rosa | 1:24:54 | 2005 |
| 62 | Dorothy Bergman | 1:56:41 | 1994 | 62 | John Cederholm | 1:33:50 | 2005 |
| 63 | Dorothy Bergman | 1:54:58 | 1995 | 63 | Donald Ross | 1:31:39 | 1993 |
| 64 | Dorothy Bergman | 2:05:22 | 1996 | 64 | Leon Beverly | 1:36:15 | 1991 |
| **65** | **Barbara Robinson** | **1:46:03** | **1999** | 65 | Gerald Barney | 1:35:56 | 1998 |
| 66 | Carrie Parsi | 1:50:36 | 2005 | **66** | **Gerald Barney** | **1:34:59** | **1999** |
| 67 | Hildy Fosse | 2:12:37 | 1996 | 67 | Robert Hall | 1:43:14 | 1996 |
| 68 | Hildy Fosse | 2:16:38 | 1997 | 68 | Don Ross | 1:44:48 | 1998 |
| 69 | Barbara Robinson | 2:01:43 | 2003 | 69 | Don Ross | 1:41:58 | 1999 |
| **70** | **Barbara Robinson** | **2:00:42** | **2004** | 70 | Carlton Mendell | 1:54:42 | 1992 |
| 71 | Barbara Robinson | 2:01:34 | 2005 | **71** | **Leon Beverly** | **1:53:26** | **1998** |
| 72 | Nancy Stokes | 2:21:42 | 1999 | 72 | Geoffrey Etherington | 1:55:02 | 2001 |
| 73 | Frances Kellogg | 2:36:42 | 1993 | 73 | Don Ross | 1:56:01 | 2003 |
| 74 | Hildy Fosse | 2:22:27 | 2003 | 74 | Robert Hall | 1:56:46 | 2003 |
| **75** | **Hildy Fosse** | **2:24:43** | **2004** | **75** | **Howard Kellogg** | **2:01:51** | **1991** |
| 76 | Louise Rossetti | 2:33:22 | 1998 | 76 | Carlton Mendell | 2:01:52 | 1998 |
| 77 | Louise Rossetti | 2:38:13 | 1999 | 77 | Carlton Mendell | 2:03:12 | 1999 |
| 78 | Louise Rossetti | 2:54:12 | 2000 | 78 | Carlton Mendell | 2:15:31 | 2000 |
| 79 | Louise Rossetti | 3:05:50 | 2001 | 79 | Howard Kellogg | 2:27:17 | 1995 |
| 80 | | | | **80** | **Phil Campbell** | **2:19:48** | **1998** |
| **81** | **Louise Rossetti** | **2:48:52** | **2003** | 81 | Carlton Mendell | 2:31:31 | 2003 |
| 82 | Louise Rossetti | 3:00:52 | 2004 | 82 | Carlton Mendell | 2:47:58 | 2004 |
| | | | | 83 | Carlton Mendell | 2:49:19 | 2005 |
| | | | | 85 | George Etzweiler | 2:33:20 | 2005 |
| | | | | 86 | Rudy Fahl | 3:13:01 | 1984 |
| | | | | 87 | Rudy Fahl | 3:09:51 | 1985 |
| | | | | 88 | Rudy Fahl | 3:18:12 | 1986 |

| Rank | Name | Amount won | Number of times winning money |
|------|------|-----------|-------------------------------|
| 1 | Craig Fram | $9,800.00 | 6 |
| 2 | Dave Dunham | $7,200.00 | 16 |
| 3 | Jonathan Wyatt | $6,000.00 | 1 |
| 4 | Matt Carpenter | $5,650.00 | 5 |
| 5 | Daniel Kihara | $4,600.00 | 4 |
| 6 | Jacqueline Gareau | $4,350.00 | 6 |
| 7 | Anna Pichrtova | $4,350.00 | 5 |
| 8 | Derek Froude | $3,800.00 | 3 |
| 9 | Eric Morse | $3,550.00 | 10 |
| 10 | Simon Gutierrez | $3,300.00 | 6 |
| 11 | J'Ne Day-Lucore | $3,200.00 | 5 |
| 12 | Julie Peterson | $2,675.00 | 7 |
| 13 | Joan Benoit-Samuelson | $2,000.00 | 2 |
| 14 | Magdellena Thorsell | $1,750.00 | 1 |
| 15 | Sumner Brown | $1,620.00 | 13 |
| 16 | Melissa Moon | $1,500.00 | 1 |
| 17 | Chris Maisto | $1,483.33 | 4 |
| 18 | Peg Donovan | $1,433.33 | 5 |
| 19 | Bob Hodge | $1,400.00 | 6 |
| 20 | Keith Woodward | $1,320.00 | 11 |
| 21 | Paul Low | $1,300.00 | 3 |
| 22 | Cathy Pearce | $1,300.00 | 3 |
| 23 | Barbara Remmers | $1,050.00 | 2 |
| 24 | Alice Muriithi | $950.00 | 2 |
| 25 | Cathy O'Brien | $950.00 | 2 |
| 26 | Rebecca Stockdale-Woolley | $916.66 | 5 |
| 27 | Eric Blake | $900.00 | 2 |
| 28 | Mike Casner | $900.00 | 7 |
| 29 | Suzy West | $850.00 | 4 |
| 30 | Pam Moore | $800.00 | 2 |
| 31 | Carrie Parsi | $800.00 | 7 |
| 32 | Martha Rockwell | $770.00 | 4 |
| 33 | Sean Hanley | $750.00 | 1 |
| 34 | Dan Verrington | $750.00 | 6 |
| 35 | Alayne Adams | $700.00 | 2 |
| 36 | Nikki Kimball | $700.00 | 2 |
| 37 | Neji Makhlouf | $700.00 | 2 |
| 38 | Gideon Mutisaya | $700.00 | 1 |
| 39 | Sandra Natal | $700.00 | 2 |
| 40 | Chuck Smead | $675.00 | 3 |
| 41 | Lynn Brown | $600.00 | 1 |
| 42 | Erica Larson | $600.00 | 1 |

| 43 | Tom Borschell | $550.00 | 2 |
| 44 | Julie White | $550.00 | 2 |
| 45 | Louis Dunlap | $508.33 | 4 |
| 46 | Janine Aiello | $500.00 | 1 |
| 47 | Tom Carroll | $500.00 | 3 |
| 48 | Liz Kellogg | $500.00 | 3 |
| 49 | Joseph Kibor | $500.00 | 1 |
| 50 | Sue LaChance | $500.00 | 3 |

## Most top ten finishes

| No. | Name | Best Place | Best Time |
| --- | --- | --- | --- |
| 15 | Dave Dunham | 1 | 1:00:37 |
| 15 | Keith Woodward | 1 | 1:03:06 |
| 14 | Mike Casner | 4 | 1:05:42 |
| 13 | Bob Hodge | 1 | 1:01:14 |
| 12 | Eric Morse | 2 | 1:01:09 |
| 9 | Matthew Cull | 2 | 1:03:41 |
| 7 | Daniel Verrington | 4 | 1:05:43 |
| 7 | Catherine Lifschultz | 4 | 1:21:03 |
| 7 | Julie Peterson | 2 | 1:14:19 |
| 7 | Donna Smyers | 5 | 1:22:37 |
| 6 | Richard Bolt | 4 | 1:06:00 |
| 6 | Gary Crossan | 1 | 1:01:13 |
| 6 | Craig Fram | 1 | 1:03:20 |
| 6 | Simon Gutierrez | 1 | 1:00:54 |
| 6 | Kerry Arsenault | 5 | 1:25:32 |
| 6 | J'Ne Day-Lucore | 1 | 1:11:45 |
| 6 | Jacqueline Gareau | 1 | 1:13:13 |
| 6 | Suzy West | 4 | 1:20:18 |
| 5 | Mark Berman | 2 | 1:03:49 |
| 5 | Matt Carpenter | 1 | 0:59:16 |
| 5 | John Cederholm | 1 | 1:08:26 |
| 5 | Roland Cormier | 1 | 1:09:16 |
| 5 | Tom Derderian | 2 | 1:07:52 |
| 5 | Tom Dowling | 2 | 1:07:10 |
| 5 | Sean Hanley | 4 | 1:07:05 |
| 5 | Daniel Kihara | 1 | 0:58:21 |
| 5 | Brian Reinhold | 3 | 1:05:12 |
| 5 | J Smith | 2 | 1:05:46 |
| 5 | Ralph Thomas | 2 | 1:09:36 |
| 5 | Peg Donovan | 1 | 1:13:26 |
| 5 | Nikki  Kimball | 2 | 1:17:34 |
| 5 | Anna Pichrtova | 1 | 1:10:26 |

## Most sub-1:30 Finishes (women)

| No. | Name | Best time | Best Place |
| --- | --- | --- | --- |
| 11 | Catherine Lifschultz | 1:21:03 | 4 |
| 10 | Donna Smyers | 1:22:37 | 5 |
| 8 | Julie Peterson | 1:14:19 | 2 |
| 7 | Kerry Arsenault | 1:25:32 | 5 |
| 6 | J'ne Day-Lucore | 1:11:45 | 1 |
| 6 | Jacqueline Gareau | 1:13:13 | 1 |
| 6 | Maureen Sullivan | 1:22:21 | 3 |
| 6 | Suzy West | 1:20:18 | 4 |
| 5 | Peg Donovan | 1:13:26 | 1 |
| 5 | Jacqueline Shakar | 1:26:40 | 10 |
| 5 | Gail Turner | 1:26:50 | 6 |

## Most sub-1:10 Finishes (men)

| No. | Name | Best time | Best Place |
| --- | --- | --- | --- |
| 16 | Keith Woodward | 1:03:07 | 1 |
| 14 | Mike Casner | 1:05:48 | 4 |
| 14 | Dave Dunham | 1:00:37 | 1 |
| 13 | Bob Hodge | 1:01:14 | 1 |
| 11 | Eric Morse | 1:01:09 | 2 |
| 10 | Daniel Verrington | 1:05:43 | 4 |
| 8 | Matthew Cull | 1:03:41 | 2 |
| 8 | Stephen Peterson | 1:08:01 | 7 |
| 6 | Gary Crossan | 1:01:13 | 1 |
| 5 | Matt Carpenter | 0:59:16 | 1 |
| 5 | John Cederholm | 1:08:26 | 1 |
| 5 | Craig Fram | 1:03:20 | 1 |
| 5 | Simon Gutierrez | 1:00:54 | 1 |
| 5 | Brian Reinhold | 1:05:12 | 4 |
| 5 | J Smith | 1:05:46 | 2 |
| 5 | Joseph Stanley Jr. | 1:05:33 | 4 |

Streak runners are a rare breed of athlete who keep coming back to the mountain for more. I've listed below the top confirmed "streakers".

| Current Streak | Total Years | Name | From | To | Best time | Best Place | Other Years Run |
|---|---|---|---|---|---|---|---|
| 28 | 29 | Frederick Ross | 1978 | 2005 | 1:23:42 | 63 | 1976 |
| 25 | 25 | Ronald Johnston | 1981 | 2005 | 1:18:34 | 54 | |
| 24 | 26 | Dianne Menard | 1982 | 2005 | 1:34:31 | 210 | 1979, 1980 ... |
| 24 | 24 | William Morse | 1982 | 2005 | 1:18:36 | 44 | |
| 24 | 24 | Everett McBride | 1982 | 2005 | 1:22:34 | 95 | |
| 24 | 24 | Carlton Mendell | 1982 | 2005 | 1:36:19 | 198 | Started streak at age 60! |
| 24 | 24 | Ronald Paquette | 1982 | 2005 | 1:32:54 | 159 | |
| 23 | 23 | Robert Gillis | 1983 | 2005 | 1:22:27 | 75 | |
| 23 | 23 | Curt Hirsch | 1983 | 2005 | 1:15:55 | 33 | |
| 23 | 23 | Dean Rasmussen | 1983 | 2005 | 1:17:29 | 40 | |
| 23 | 23 | Chris Ellis | 1983 | 2005 | 1:24:44 | 135 | |
| 23 | 23 | Ronald Paquette | 1983 | 2005 | 1:30:30 | 159 | |
| 23 | 23 | Lee Grimes | 1983 | 2005 | 1:46:16 | 451 | |
| 22 | 27 | Gaetan Breton | 1984 | 2005 | 1:13:29 | 11 | 1973,74,75,76,77 |
| 22 | 22 | Steve Titcomb | 1984 | 2005 | 1:26:42 | 78 | |
| 22 | 22 | Michael Gillis | 1984 | 2005 | 1:28:24 | 187 | |
| 22 | 22 | David Jefska | 1984 | 2005 | 1:37:47 | 303 | |
| 22 | 22 | Allan Aldrich | 1984 | 2005 | 1:42:11 | 344 | |
| 22 | 22 | Ronn Chaisson | 1984 | 2005 | 1:43:20 | 336 | |
| 22 | 22 | David Roy | 1984 | 2005 | 1:43:42 | 195 | 1977 |
| 22 | 22 | Sumner Rupprecht | 1984 | 2005 | 1:48:20 | 525 | |

## Others of Note:

| Total Years | Current Streak | Name | From | To | Years Missed |
|---|---|---|---|---|---|
| 29 | 19 | Keith Woodward | 1973 | 2005 | 1974, 75, 81, 86 |
| 28 | 14 | James Laprel | 1972 | 2005 | 1974, 75, 77, 79, 90, 91 |
| 26 | 1 | John Cederholm | 1973 | 2005 | 1977, 81, 91, 95 ,96, 99, 2004 |
| 24 | 13 | Len Hall | 1971 | 2005 | 1974-78, 80, 81, 89-92 |
| 23 | 4 | Gerard Tautkus | 1982 | 2004 | 2001 |
| 22 | 18 | Robert Bradlee | 1983 | 2005 | 1987 |
| 22 | - | Bill McNulty | 1970 | 1994 | 1972, 73, 81 |
| 21 | - | Mike Casner | 1979 | 2004 | 1981, 82, 89, 90, 2004 |
| 21 | 21 | Steve Dowling | 1985 | 2005 | None |
| 21 | 21 | Phil Ostroski | 1984 | 2004 | |
| 21 | 3 | Hildy Fosse | 1984 | 2005 | 2002 |
| 20 | 20 | Walter Kuklinski | 1986 | 2005 | None |
| 20 | 7 | Normand Menard | 1985 | 2005 | 1998 |
| 20 | 16 | Peter Pantelis | 1983 | 2005 | 1985, 1989 |
| 20 | 17 | Bob Treadwell | 1975 | 2004 | 1977-84, 86, 87 |
| 19 | - | Diana Avery | 1984 | 2004 | 2002, 2003 |

## Acknowledgements and Resources

Thank you to everyone who helped in creating this book!  I want to especially thank my long-suffering wife Cathy for her patience through the many days and nights I spent researching and typing the book.  Also thank you to everyone who gave me copies of newspapers, results, and personal pictures.

**Proofreading & editorial input:**
Leslie Behan
Kevin Beck
Cathy Dunham
Dan Verrington


**Sources:**
Bob Teschek's race entrant's information packets from 1981 to the 1990's.
Don Drewniak's massive collection of old running magazines.

**Books -**
Not without peril – Nicholas Howe
Into the Mountains – Maggie Stier & Ron McAdow
A history of the Olympic trials – Richard Hymans
Boston Marathon – Tom Derderian

**Magazines -**
New England Runner
Runner's World
Running Wild
Running Times
Running Stats
Boston Runner
Boston Running News
The Runner
The long distance log
Yankee runner
The Hockomock Swamp rat
New England Running

**Newspapers -**
The Manchester Union Leader
The Mountain Ear
The Boston Globe
The Boston Herald
The Derry News
The Haverhill Gazette
The Lawrence Eagle Tribune

<u>Online sources:</u>
Matt Carpenter's skyrunning website – www.skyrunner.com
Ultrarunning online – www.ultrarunning.com

<u>Other written accounts:</u>
North Medford Club newsletter
Greater Lowell Road Runners newsletter
White Mountain Milers newsletter
Mainley running magazine

**Individual Accounts via un-attributed articles or personal interviews –**
Allan Aldrich – Consecutive streak runner.
Rick Bayko – Yankee Runner magazine owner/editor and owner of the Yankee runner store.
Tom Derderian – Writer, top runner.
Paul Donato – Son of former winner Paul Donato.
Bob Fitzgerald – Head honcho at New England Runner Magazine.
Mike Gillis – Streak runner.
Bob Hodge – Seven-time winner, many time finisher.
John Lorway – Account of the 1981 race.
Bill McNulty – "How good a race is"
Bill Morse – Streak runner.
Eric Morse – Sub four-minute miler and top mountain runner.
Steve Peterson – Shoeless finisher in 1991, longtime friend, teammate, and life-partner.
Dean Rasmussen – Streak runner.
Bob Romer – Personal account of the 1990 race.
Fred Ross III – Streak runner.
John Stifler – Mt Washington Road Race press liaison.
Andy Sacket – Mt Washington Road Race Announcer.
Bob Teschek – Mt Washington Road Race Director.
Bill Teschek – Mt Washington Road Race Video.
Steve Vaitones – NEAC/USATF New England Office manager.
Dan Verrington – Shuffler.  Top ten finisher & US mountain team member.  Teammate and training partner.


**Photo Credits**

| Page | Descriptions | Courtesy of |
| --- | --- | --- |
| Cover | The Auto road from Mt. Madison | Kevin Tilton |
| Intro | Location map | Mt Washington Auto Road, www.mountwashington.com |
| Intro | Summit circa 1900 | Hike the Whites, www.hikethewhites.com |
| Intro | Tip Top House 1895 | Hike the Whites, www.hikethewhites.com |
| Intro | Harlen P Amen | Exeter library collection, www.library.exeter.edu |
| Intro | Stanley Locomobile | Mt Washington Auto Road, www.mountwashington.com |
| Intro | Runners at four miles 1972 | Margaret Bergesen |
| 2 | Summit Hotel | Hike the Whites, www.hikethewhites.com |

| Page | Descriptions | Courtesy of |
| --- | --- | --- |
| 5 | Veritcal Mile | Matt Carpenter, www.skyrunner.com |
| 9 | 100th Anniv. Sign | www.climbtotheclouds.com |
| 12 | Kelley and Kelley | Brud Warren |
| 12 | Summit Circa 1962 | www.climbtotheclouds.com |
| 16 | Bayko, Olsen, Kelley, and Kelley | Hockomock Swamp Rat |
| 19 | Mike Gallagher | Castleton State Hall of Fame, www.csc.vsc.edu |
| 23 | Len Hall | Yankee Runner |
| 27 | Keith Woodward | Yankee Runner |
| 29 | Jim Capezzuto | Yankee Runner |
| 31 | Charlotte Lettis | Yankee Runner |
| 33 | Hodge and Mendonca | Marshall Stanton, Yankee Runner |
| 35 | Lisa Powers & SMAC runners | Yankee Runner |
| 40 | SMAC finisher and Hodge | Joann Lequin, Yankee Runner |
| 52 | Team Gloucester | Mike Gillis |
| 59 | Chris Maisto | Granite State Race Services |
| 62 | Peg Donovan | Granite State Race Services |
| 67 | Dave Dunham | Mountain Ear Photo |
| 71 | Dunham and Hodge | Mountain Ear Photo |
| 75 | Ron Johnston | Ron Johnston |
| 85 | Matt Carpenter - 1998 | Granite State Race Services |
| 89 | Gareau & Dunham | Dave Dunham |
| 94 | CMS trio | Granite State Race Services |
| 98 | The "Flag Man" and Mike Casner | Dave Dunham and Granite State Race Serives (Casner) |
| 105 | Magdelena Thorsell - 1998 | Granite State Race Services |
| 106 | Jim Laprel | Dave Dunham |
| 114 | Alice Muriithi | Coolrunning, www.coolrunning.com |
| 115 | Stephen Peterson | Dave Dunham |
| 120 | Craig Fram | Fitzfoto |
| 124 | Morse, Fram, and Gutierrez | Tim Boyd, AP |
| 128 | Anna Pichrtova & S. Peterson | Granite State Race Services |
| 131 | Jonathan Wyatt | Granite State Race Services |
| 137 | Mt Washington Medal | Dave Dunham |
| 149 | Fred Ross IV and Chris Ross | Susan Ross |
| 155 | Louis Rossetti - 2003 | Dave Dunham |
| 155 | Fred Ross III - 1979 | Fred Ross III |
| 156 | Dan Verrington | Dave Dunham |
| 160 | Joshua Ferenc - 2004 | Dave Dunham |
| 163 | Rudy Fahl and the Ross family | Susan Ross |
| 166 | Gary Crossan - 1986 | Granite State Race Services |
| Back Cover | Dave Dunham | Dave Dunham |

Made in the USA
Monee, IL
07 July 2026